Kofi Annan

Also by Stanley Meisler

United Nations: The First Fifty Years

Kofi Annan

A Man of Peace in a World of War

STANLEY MEISLER

John Wiley & Sons, Inc.

This book is printed on acid-free paper. ♾

Copyright © 2007 by Stanley Meisler. All rights reserved

Photo credits: pages 187 top, 190 top, 192, 193 bottom, and 194: private collection of Kofi and Nane Annan; pages 187 bottom, 188, and 189: UN Photo/DPI; page 190 bottom: UN Photo/Milton Grant; pages 191, 195, 196 bottom, and 197 top: UN Photo/Evan Schneider; pages 193 top and 198: UN Photo/Eskinder Debebe; pages 196 top and 197 bottom: UN Photo/Mark Garten

Published by John Wiley & Sons, Inc., Hoboken, New Jersey
Published simultaneously in Canada

Design and composition by Navta Associates, Inc.

For general information about our other products and services, please contact our Customer Care Department within the United States at (800) 762-2974, outside the United States at (317) 572-3993 or fax (317) 572-4002.

Wiley also publishes its books in a variety of electronic formats. Some content that appears in print may not be available in electronic books. For more information about Wiley products, visit our web site at www.wiley.com.

Library of Congress Cataloging-in-Publication Data:

Meisler, Stanley.
    Kofi Annan : a man of peace in a world of war / Stanley Meisler.
       p. cm.
    ISBN-13: 978-0-471-78744-0 (cloth)
    ISBN-10: 0-471-78744-2 (cloth)
    1. Annan, Kofi A. (Kofi Atta) 2. United Nations—Biography. 3. Statesmen—Ghana—Biography. 4. World politics—1989- I. Title.
    D839.7.A56M45 2006
    341.23092—dc22
    [B]
                                                      2006021032

Printed in the United States of America

10 9 8 7 6 5 4 3 2 1

To Elizabeth

CONTENTS

ACKNOWLEDGMENTS

Secretary-General Kofi Annan helped me immensely by passing the word to associates and friends that this project has his blessing and they should not hesitate to talk with me. Over the years, he has always been generous to me with his time. I am indebted to him, both for this book and for helping me understand the UN.

The book could not have been written without the help of Frederick Eckhard, the secretary-general's former spokesman. I have worked with Fred for more than fifteen years. He is one of the world's most unique press officers, for he is completely incapable of spinning. He only knows how to hand out the truth in all its nuances. As spokesman, his only concern was that the press understand the UN and the secretary-general. Fred supported this project from the beginning and helped guide the proposal through bureaucratic thickets until it reached the desk of the secretary-general and received his promise of cooperation. When Eckhard retired, he asked his successor, Stéphane Dujarric, to continue offering me the help of the office of the spokesman.

Dujarric and several members of his team—Catharine Smith, Jane Gaffney, and Maricel Magas-Sniffen—were always helpful.

Maricel, in fact, was invaluable. She searched for facts and figures for me, hunted down photos, and organized appointments with the secretary-general. Dujarric's deputy, Marie Okabe, served as the press officer on my trip to Africa in 2002 and made sure that I was treated as if I were a member of the secretary-general's staff. I also owe much to photographer Eskinder Debebe and librarian Anahit Turabian in the UN photo department for their help in putting together a gallery of photos for this book.

More than three dozen people served as sources of information about events in the life of the secretary-general. They included UN officials, academics, diplomats, journalists, and friends and family of the secretary-general. They communicated with me in person and by telephone, e-mail, and fax. Almost all spoke on the record all the time. In fact, none of the original quotes in the book is anonymous. These source include:

Keek Sugawara Abe, Georges Abi-Saab, Akipataki Akiwumi-Thompson, Kobina Annan, Diego Arria, Francis Bartels, Catherine Bertini, Boutros Boutros-Ghali, Virendra Dayal, Karen de Young, Stephane Dujarric, Fred Eckhard, Maggie Farley, Ahmad Fawzi, Marrack Goulding, David Lanegan, Evelyn Leopold, Susan Linnee, Edward C. Luck, Colum Lynch, Tyler Marshall, Edward Mortimer, Roger K. Mosvick, William L. Nash, Thomas R. Pickering, Julia Preiswerk, Kieran Prendergast, Iqbal Riza, Barbara Roddick, James P. Rubin, Muhamed Sacirbey, William Shawcross, Lamine Sise, Theodore C. Sorensen, James S. Sutterlin, Shashi Tharoor, Brian Urquhart, and Juan Antonio Yañez-Barnuevo.

Of course, many more people have helped me understand the workings of the United Nations. I depended on them while covering the UN for the *Los Angeles Times* during the 1990s. Most are listed in my history *United Nations: The First Fifty Years*.

But I would like to mention two: An old friend, Ángel Viñas, a distinguished Spanish historian, served as the European Union's ambassador while I covered the UN. He helped guide me through some confusing times. Since then, he has published a memoir, which includes a perceptive section about his time at the UN. The book, *Al Servicio de Europa: Innovación y Crisis en la Comisión Europea*, was published by Editorial Complutense in Madrid in 2004.

Anthony Goodman, who served as a Reuters correspondent at the UN for two decades, died in May 2006 during his retirement. Tony, who had an encyclopedic knowledge of UN history, was a continual fount of kindness and information for me.

I was fortunate to be invited to two very useful conferences. Jean E. Krasno, who is editing the official papers of Annan, invited me to a conference of scholars and UN officials discussing "key events and issues of the Annan years." Krasno, who teaches political science at both Yale University and the City College of New York, led the conference, which was held on November 11, 2005, at the Pocantico Conference Center on the old Rockefeller estate in Tarrytown, New York. The Rockefeller Brothers Fund sponsored the meeting.

The secretary-general invited me to a retreat and conference on April 28 and 29, 2006, at the Whitney Conference Center on the Greentree Foundation grounds (the former home of John Hay Whitney) in Manhasset, New York. Scholars, diplomats, UN officials, and journalists took part in these meetings, which attempted to assess Annan's ten years as secretary-general. John Ruggie, professor of international affairs at Harvard University's Kennedy School, chaired the meetings, which were sponsored by the Greentree Foundation.

I am also indebted to my agent, Scott Mendel, whose enthusiasm revived a dormant project. He also suggested the title of this biography. Hana Lane more than lived up to her distinguished reputation as an editor. She used her pencil with great insight and intelligence. John Simko directed the production of the book with painstaking care.

My son and daughter-in-law, Joshua and Elodie, who acted as my agents in Paris, arranged vital interviews for me in France, took part in the delightful session with Kofi Annan's old schoolmaster Francis Bartels, and handled all logistics. Joshua also joined Sam, Gabriel, and Jenaro in solving all my frustrating computer problems. I also had a large family cheering section, including Julie, Hunter, Sarah, Patricia, Sophia, Mike, Ronella, Luke, Jake, Claire, and Michèle.

Authors usually post a paragraph here about a long-suffering wife. But my wife, Elizabeth Fox, handles so much with such good cheer and aplomb that it is hard to think of her as suffering. She manages me, the house, the kids, the extended family, a spectacular cuisine, a myriad of outside activities, and her responsible position at the U.S. Agency for International Development with great ease. This book is dedicated to her with love and awe.

Introduction

In the presence of King Harald V of Norway and two dozen former laureates, UN secretary-general Kofi Annan accepted the Nobel Peace Prize on December 19, 2001, in Oslo's city hall. The Nobel Prize is the world's most prestigious award, and Annan basked in all the adulation. He and his wife, Nane, watched the traditional torchlight parade the next night and then took the floor to dance and open the annual Nobel Prize ball. There was no doubt about Annan's stature then. He strode through the corridors of world capitals with confidence, serenity, and refreshing frankness. One of the world's most popular statesmen, he was looked on as an imposing moral force, and he could stand shoulder to shoulder with others of similar measure, such as Nelson Mandela and Elie Wiesel.

Much changed in the next few years. By 2005, Annan had been battered by the White House. Republicans clamored for his resignation. His real sin, in their eyes, was his defiance on Iraq. But the overblown oil for food scandal, coupled with the mendacity and greed of his son, gave his American enemies enough ammunition to depict him, at the least, as foolishly lax. As Annan's ten-year reign moved toward its close, much of the final stretch turned combative and bitter.

This book is the story of Kofi Annan's rise from schoolboy in Ghana to world statesman and of the joys and despair that marked his decade as leader of the UN. In the most significant act of his tenure, he opposed the American-led and American-inspired invasion of Iraq in 2003. In many ways, he personified the world's confusion and distress over American bullying. But Annan did not cry out and denounce the war in any dramatic way. Instead, he tried, within the confines of UN diplomacy, to slow the march toward war in hopes that time would galvanize worldwide public opinion against it. But President George W. Bush did not intend to let worldwide public opinion deter him. In the end, the UN failed to prevent a disastrous war, and Annan felt the failure like a body blow.

The secretaries-general of the United Nations make up one of the world's most exclusive clubs: There have been only seven in the sixty-one years since the UN was created: Trygve Lie of Norway, Dag Hammarskjöld of Sweden, U Thant of Burma, Kurt Waldheim of Austria, Javier Pérez de Cuéllar of Peru, Boutros Boutros-Ghali of Egypt, and Kofi Annan of Ghana. Annan, who took over leadership of the UN in 1997, is widely regarded as a secretary-general in the mold of Hammarskjöld, the most renowned of his predecessors. Annan was elected when the United Nations was reeling from its debacles in Somalia, Bosnia, and Rwanda. The times required a leader of diplomatic skill, openness, and moral strength, and Annan fit these needs in a remarkable way. His ascent depended greatly on American support, but American ambivalence about the UN would later prove his constant challenge and near undoing.

The secretary-general is a full-time manager of the world's crises, but he must manage them without a standing army or police force, and without great financial resources. The total UN budget— including peacekeeping and the work of subsidiary agencies such as UNESCO and UNICEF—comes to $12 billion a year, less than that of the New York City school system. Whenever a crisis demands military peacekeepers, the secretary-general must assemble them by begging for soldiers from a host of governments. Annan has dealt with violent crises throughout his tenure as chief of peacekeeping and as secretary-general, and much of the book focuses on his role in the main crises of the past two decades, including Somalia, Bosnia, Rwanda, East Timor, Kosovo, and, of course, Iraq.

This book is not an authorized biography. The secretary-general did not ask me to write it and has had no say about its contents. He did not read the manuscript before publication. But he did cooperate with the project. He talked with me from time to time and, most important, encouraged his staff and friends to meet with me. But this book is not history as seen through the eyes of the secretary-general and his associates. I have used his and their account of events, along with views from many other sources, to put together what I feel is a fair narrative of what happened.

Many of his friends and associates describe Annan as a private man whom they do not understand completely. "There is a side to Kofi that is difficult to access," says Dr. Julia Preiswerk, an American friend for more than forty years. That, of course, presents problems for a biographer and, even worse, temptations to elaborate and speculate on paltry evidence. This is especially tempting when dealing with a figure at ease in two very different cultures. I have tried hard to avoid such temptations. Instead I have tried to present a frank and illuminating picture of a complex man based on what we know of his acts and words. There is very little psychological speculation in the book.

There is also very little political science theorizing. Annan is not an ideologue or an academic theorist. He is a pragmatic leader who adheres to some important core values. He believes in the charter of the United Nations and in the words, written by American poet Archibald MacLeish, that open its preamble: "We the peoples of the United Nations determined to save succeeding generations from the scourge of war . . ." Annan is not an inveterate pacifist. He recognizes that the UN should intervene by force sometimes to repel aggression or protect people from government abuse. But for the most part he feels it is his sacred duty as secretary-general to work for peace even when powerful forces conspire against it. In doing so, he has an intuitive sense about how far he can go in pressing and persuading different leaders and ambassadors. Sometimes he succeeds, sometimes not. But his actions do not fit into theory.

The secretary-general and I have something in common. We are both products of the great bubble of American interest in Africa in the late 1950s and early 1960s, when African states emerged from colonialism into independence. The Ford Foundation was trying then to expose Africans to America and interest Americans in Africa. After a scout spotted Kofi in Africa, the Ford Foundation paid for him to travel to the United States in 1959 and attend Macalester College in Minnesota. Just three years later, the Ford Foundation awarded me a foreign area training fellowship to take graduate courses in African studies at the University of California in Berkeley and then travel extensively in Africa.

In less than a decade, I was the *Los Angeles Times* correspondent in Nairobi, Kenya, while Kofi was an administrative officer with the UN Economic Commission for Africa in Addis Ababa, Ethiopia. I would travel to Addis Ababa often but never met Kofi. A junior UN officer was not newsworthy enough in those days to attract the attention of a foreign correspondent. That was my loss. We would not meet until the 1990s, when the *Los Angeles Times* assigned me to the UN in New York, and Kofi took over the department of peacekeeping operations there.

In one of our recent meetings, Annan asked me why I was writing this book. I told him that I had already written a history of the first fifty years of the UN and that I felt a study of his career would help me fill in some of the gaps of the past and take me through another ten years of UN history. When I reflected later, I realized that my reply had been incomplete. In fact, I had also become more and more troubled at his buffeting since the invasion of Iraq. Newspapers treated him as if he were now besmirched with scandal. His reticence about his son made it look as if he were hiding the truth. A universally admired statesman seemed to be stumbling. I wanted to get to the bottom of this. And with this book, I hope that I have.

1

Ghana and America

K ofi Atta Annan came of age in an era of optimism in Africa. In 1957, when the nineteen-year-old completed secondary schooling, his native Gold Coast changed its name to Ghana, lowered the Union Jack, and entered history as the first European colony in tropical Africa to attain independence. Many colonies followed swiftly, and the world was treated to a new and swelling host of colorful flags, exotic robes, and handsome, dark leaders. Africa brimmed with good feelings, electric in hope, and they were shared by the new secondary school graduate.

"I think we were all optimistic," Annan recalled a little wistfully more than forty years later. "We were all very hopeful and determined to help build our nations. We were determined to get education, learn a trade, and make a contribution."

So much cynicism and disappointment cloud our view of Africa now that it is not easy to recall the American excitement about Africa half a century ago. Soon after John Kennedy's election as president in 1960, the Kennedy family helped pay for Tom Mboya's airlift of young Kenyans to small colleges in America. Ghana was the first country to receive a contingent of volunteers from the new

Peace Corps, and they descended from their plane in Accra to sing the national anthem "Yen Ara Asaasa Ni" (This Is Our Homeland) in Twi, one of the native languages. American journalists and doctoral candidates, as ignorant of Africa as the *New York Herald*'s Henry M. Stanley when he searched for Dr. Livingstone almost a century before, fanned over the continent in search of its strange flavors and customs.

There were some doubters. In a 1953 cover story anticipating independence for the Gold Coast, *Time* magazine warned that "the educated few who climb from darkness to light . . . are likely to become the dupes of Communism." But by and large, Americans were entranced by the procession of new states and the awakening of what they regarded as the Dark Continent.

The enthusiasm of Americans would mark the life of the young Kofi Annan. He was born with a twin sister on April 8, 1938, in Kumasi, the capital of the ancient, inland kingdom of Ashanti in the Gold Coast. The family included three older sisters and later a younger brother. Although he had spent much of his life in the heartland of the Ashanti people and had a trace of Ashanti descent, his father, Henry Reginald Annan, was actually a Fante nobleman who could trace his lineage to chiefs. Kofi's mother, Victoria, also was Fante. The Fante, a coastal tribe, had sided with the British in the nineteenth-century wars against the Ashanti that ended with the annexation of the Gold Coast as a British colony. Henry was an executive of the United Africa Company, the African subsidiary of the Anglo-Dutch corporation Unilever, and his main responsibility was the purchase of cocoa for export. The Gold Coast was then the largest producer of cocoa in the world and, by African standards, rich because of it. After his retirement, Henry served as chairman of the Ghana International Bank and other government agencies and won election as governor of Ashanti Province.

Henry Reginald and Victoria bore English Christian names, for they were part of the early elite class of Africans educated by Christian missionaries who encouraged them to modernize with British ways. But British rule was beginning to trouble the African elite by this time, and the couple returned to African tradition and the Ghanian language of Akan to name their children. The new boy was called Kofi (Akan for Born on a Friday) and Atta (Akan for Twin). The embrace of African names did not mean any revolutionary break with English and Christian tradition. Henry and Victoria still regarded themselves as strong Christians and took the family to services of the Anglican Church.

Kofi once said he was brought up "atribal in a tribal world." In an old photograph of perhaps fifty members of the extended Annan family, taken when Kofi was perhaps six years old, most of the men wear suits and ties. Perhaps half the women wear European frocks and bonnets while the other half have African head ties and traditional dresses. Kofi himself is sporting a jacket with short pants. The photograph looks more like a portrait of a family in Michigan in the 1940s than a family in Africa.

The elders in the family liked to bombard Kofi with traditional proverbs to guide his life. One of his favorites is "You don't hit a man on the head when you've got your fingers between his teeth." But his father preferred more modern guidance. After dinner, he sometimes held mock trials to judge acts of tomfoolery and naughtiness by the children. He seemed less interested in punishing the children than in encouraging them to explain their behavior with honesty and confidence, without stuttering and shuffling. Kofi often won his father over with a joke.

Kofi's younger brother, Kobina, now the Ghanian ambassador to Morocco, describes his father as "strict, a stickler for time, and stoic." In one searing incident, while Kofi visited his father's office, a junior manager was summoned to discuss some accounts. The young man arrived hurriedly with a cigarette in his hand. Aware that his boss frowned on smoking, he thrust the lit cigarette into his pants pocket. With his pocket burning, he answered Henry Reginald's questions in obvious discomfort. After he left, a shocked Kofi asked his father why he had forced the young man into such an unfortunate position. His father lectured that he had not forced the young man to do anything. He could have extinguished the cigarette in an ashtray or kept on smoking. "Today you saw something you should never do," his father told Kofi. "Don't crawl."

Henry Reginald had no patience for those who failed to show up for events on time. "Those of us who didn't know time got a little heat from him," says Kobina. As a leader of the Freemasons, Henry Reginald once organized a social event at the Kumasi lodge. Five minutes after the scheduled time for the party, he closed the doors, shutting out all latecomers. As governor, Kobina recalls, Henry Reginald called off his cocktail parties if the bulk of the guests failed to show up half an hour after the scheduled time. "Those who voted for you would not like that at all," says Kobina. "But he was not a politician."

"We lived in every part of Ghana when I was growing up," Annan told the City University of New York's UN Intellectual History Project, "because he [his father] was a district manager and he moved from district to district. Sometimes he'd go there for a couple of years, and we'd go to school there. And then, of course, when he became director, we moved . . . to Accra. . . . It was very interesting for me to grow up dealing with and getting to know so many different groups in Ghana. It gave you a sense of being able to relate to everybody and different groups at a young age."

Henry Reginald's political instincts rarely took him to the mainstream of Ghanian politics. After World War II, he joined most of Ghana's intellectuals in a new political party, the United Gold Coast Convention (UGCC), which campaigned for eventual home rule as a self-governing British colony. In 1947, the UGCC invited one of its best-educated compatriots abroad to come home and lead the party as secretary-general. He was Kwame Nkrumah, a graduate of Lincoln University in Pennsylvania. Lincoln, long known as "the black Princeton," was the alma mater as well of poet Langston Hughes, the future U.S. Supreme Court justice Thurgood Marshall, and the future Nigerian president Nnamdi Azikiwe. Nkrumah also received postgraduate degrees from the University of Pennsylvania, the London School of Economics, and the University of London.

Nkrumah soon proved too fiery for elite Africans like Henry Reginald Annan. In turn, the new secretary-general found his educated colleagues too milquetoast for his own taste. The UGCC proclaimed that it wanted self-government "in the shortest possible time." Nkrumah deplored such gradualism and called instead for Home Rule Now! and later for Independence Now! Within two years, he broke with the UGCC to lead a new party, the Convention People's Party (CPP). In the Annan household, Henry Reginald disdained Nkrumah and his "veranda boys"—the poorly educated, idle young men who whipped up enthusiasm and sometimes riots for Nkrumah.

Nkrumah's emotional appeal excited the Gold Coast. His popularity swelled even more when the British jailed him for leading a strike. In 1951, his party won a landslide victory—twenty-nine out of thirty-three seats in the Legislative Assembly—in the first election allowed by the British. Faced with political reality, the British finally relented, released Nkrumah from prison, and allowed him to serve as prime minister of the self-governing colony of the Gold Coast and finally in 1957 as prime minister of the independent nation of Ghana. Kofi Annan mused years later that the history of Ghana might have been far happier if Nkrumah had come to power surrounded by educated elite like Henry Reginald rather than by the veranda boys.

Nkrumah, with his high forehead and gold and blue kente robe draped over one shoulder, soon became a familiar world figure. Though Ghana had a population of less than ten million, Nkrumah, with all his preaching for pan-Africanism, tried to assume the mantle of prospective or, at least, symbolic leader of Africa as a whole. He created a union with Guinea and Mali in hopes that it would act as the embryonic nucleus of a future continental nation. His projects were grand. He even created a Ghana news agency to compete with the Associated Press, Reuters, Agence France Presse, and all the other international channels of news that were controlled by what he regarded as the neoimperialist corporations of Europe and the United States.

Kofi did not have a role in all the excitement of the Nkrumah-led march to independence, for he spent those years in boarding school in the hill area near the town of Cape Coast. The British believed in the need to isolate students from the turmoil of everyday life so that their bodies and minds could be nurtured in a tranquil academic clime. Nowhere was this more evident than in Mfantsipim, the elite secondary school for boys founded by British Methodist missionaries in 1876. Francis Bartels, the Ghanian headmaster, did not encourage his students to take part in all the Nkrumah rallies for independence. Bartels, in fact, detested Nkrumah as a leader "determined to model his political actions on the successes of Hitler." Yet the political transformations did not leave his boys untouched. "To see the changes taking place," Annan told the intellectual history project, "to see the British hand over to the Ghanians, and have a Ghanian prime minister . . . you grew up with a sense that change is possible, all is possible."

Kofi entered Mfantsipim as a fifteen-year-old in 1953. "Kofi was very affable and jovial, full of wit and character," recalls Akipataki Akiwumi-Thompson, a classmate who is now a businessman in Accra. "He was always making us laugh." Upperclassmen had the authority to punish their juniors for infractions such as talking after lights out or showing up at inspection with dirty fingernails. The usual punishment required the offender to write one hundred lines of ten words each. Kofi had a knack for talking his way out of most punishment. "He had his way of not antagonizing the seniors while talking to them," says Akiwumi-Thompson. "By the time he was finished, he could calm them down and persuade them not to punish him. Or if he couldn't, he could talk them into compromise." He might have to write fifty lines instead of a hundred.

The school was run much like a private boarding school in Britain. The boys arose at 5:30 A.M. After a cold shower, they dressed and lined up for inspection, showing the housemaster, an upperclassman, their combed hair, cleaned nails, and neat shirts. They breakfasted on tea, porridge, and toast with marmalade, and then headed into a full day of classes with English, Scottish, and a few

Ghanian teachers, followed by study and sports. Kofi proved an excellent sprinter on the track. After dinner and homework, lights were out at 8:30 P.M. for younger boys, somewhat later for older boys. At the end of the school year, they had to take the same Cambridge examinations required of students in Britain. Like the graduates of Eton and Harrow in England, the alumni of Mfantsipim, still an elite school in Ghana, call themselves "Old Boys."

One of Kofi's noticeable achievements at Mfantsipim was to lead a strike protesting the poor quality of the food in the dining hall. "We kept telling them and they wouldn't do anything, so we arranged it in such a way—about six hundred or seven hundred of us—that on a Sunday nobody ate," Annan told the Intellectual History Project. "Having arranged to make sure they had something to eat first, when we went to the dining room we all refused to eat. The housemaster tried to calm the situation down, but he couldn't. ... The place was in pandemonium."

Bartels, the Ghanaian headmaster, called Kofi to his office the next morning. "Young Annan," he said, "I understand you had something to do with all this strike nonsense. If you have an issue to discuss, come to me and we'll discuss it man to man. You are reasonably intelligent. Given the chance, you may become a useful member of society."

Otherwise Kofi's acts of schoolboy defiance seem minor. Bartels allowed the boys to walk almost twenty miles to a girls' secondary school on Saturdays but refused them permission to bicycle there. He felt that bikes were dangerous on the road. "I did not want them to compete with the mammy wagons," says Bartels, recalling the overladen trucks that thundered on West African roads with people and freight, "and I did not want them to waste their money." Nevertheless, Kofi and a few buddies would rent bicycles and peddle their way to the girls. Bartels never caught them.

Kofi and a few other classmates would sit on the floor in the headmaster's office for weekly lessons in "spoken English." In a preface to the memoirs of Bartels, published in 2003, the secretary-general recalled that the headmaster had once "put a broad sheet of white paper on the wall, with a little black dot in the right-hand corner, and asked, 'Boys, what do you see?'" The boys shouted in unison, "A black dot." Bartels then admonished them, "So not a single one of you saw the broad white sheet of paper. You only saw the black dot. This is the awful thing about human nature. People never see the goodness of things and the broader picture. Don't go through life with that attitude."

In the classrooms, however, Kofi's performance was not stellar. Of course, passing the entrance examination for Mfantsipim put him among the elite of Ghanian students; only two hundred out of three thousand applicants were admitted for Kofi's first year. But he lagged behind many of his classmates. "He was a late developer," Bartels, who is now ninety-five years old and lives in Paris, told me recently. "There is nothing to be ashamed of. My own son was a late developer. It takes a little longer. If you asked me then if Kofi Annan was going to be secretary-general, I would have said, 'Not on your life.' He made so much of so little."

Under the old British colonial system, pupils had to take an examination to pass from the Fifth Form to the Sixth Form in secondary school. The Sixth Form, the final year, prepared students to enter a university for a classical education. Most Mfantsipim Sixth Form pupils moved on to the University College of the Gold Coast at Achimota. But Kofi did not score high enough on the examination. "Although his father was a good friend," says Bartels, "I just could not push him into Form Six." So Kofi left Mftansipim and entered the new Kumasi Institute of Science and Technology, a British-operated technical college. Since technical studies were not as prestigious as classical studies in Ghanian eyes, the technical college had lower standards for entry than the University College.

In his second year at the Kumasi Institute, Kofi was elected vice president of the Ghana national students union. This brought him to a conference of African student leaders in Sierra Leone, where he drew the attention of a representative of the Ford Foundation acting as a kind of talent scout. Reflecting the American excitement about Africa, foundation executives were trying to attract Africans to study in the United States while encouraging future American professors to mount their Ph.D. fieldwork in Africa. Kofi was awarded a scholarship under the Ford Foundation's Foreign Student Leadership Program to study at Macalester College in St. Paul, Minnesota.

Credited for his studies in Ghana, Annan entered Macalester in the fall of 1959 as a junior. Macalester, a small liberal arts college founded in 1874 with the help of the Presbyterian Church, prided itself as a school with international interests. It even flew the flag of the United Nations beneath the American flag on its main staff. The experience at Macalester was defining. The twenty-one-year-old student had never set foot outside Africa before. But the strangeness and pace of college life in America did not overwhelm him. He was a soft-spoken and polite young man but far from shy, and he rushed into a myriad of activities with striking energy and curiosity. He had never been surrounded by so many whites before, but that did not intimidate or bother him in any way. They were as interested in him as he was in them, and he related to his classmates with good-humored ease.

His range of activities was extraordinary. He even tried out for the football team his first day on campus. The coach was impressed by Annan's speed but not his size. Perhaps, the coach mused, he might make a punt returner. Two linemen, including David Lanegran, now a professor of geography and urban studies at Macalester, were ordered to take part in a punting drill with Kofi. "They would punt at Kofi," Lanegran recalls. "We would rush at him. But we were under strict orders not to touch him. We didn't want to scare him. But he was a soccer player, not a football player. He really couldn't catch the ball. His football career lasted about a day." Annan remembers his football failings somewhat differently. "It was okay so long as I kept running and no one caught up with me," he told a reporter for the college magazine, *Macalester Today*, in 1998. "Otherwise, I was like a piece of paper. I weighed 138 pounds. . . . So I gave it up after 15 minutes."

An African acquaintance kidded Kofi at the time about trying to kill himself on his very first day in school. But Kofi countered that his tryout had been motivated by curiosity about the sport, a desire to meet the players, and the rumor that "the boys on the football team get on very well with the girls." The football escapade did not close his athletic career at Macalester. On the track team, he set a school record in the sixty-yard dash that lasted a dozen years, and he was a mainstay of the soccer team throughout his stay.

In theory, Annan knew all about winter, for he had studied European seasons in school textbooks and had to answer questions about winter on the British examinations administered in colonial Africa. But he was not prepared for a Minnesota winter. The softness of snow surprised him. So did the bitterness of cold. He followed the example of his classmates and wore several layers of clothing. But he stubbornly refused to wear the ridiculous and unsightly earmuffs that clasped their heads. But one day the temperature plunged, with wind chill, to thirty-five degrees below zero, and Kofi, walking to classes, felt his ears cringe in terrible pain, so bitter he felt they would snap off. He rushed to a store and bought the largest pair of earmuffs he could find. The lesson, as he liked to tell students at Macalester many years later, was "Never think you know more than the natives do."

Macalester officials knew so little about Ghana and Africa and the British colonial school system that they assigned Kofi, a junior, to a freshman English class. The class had twenty Americans and four foreigners. Three weeks after the semester began, the English teacher subjected his students to a spelling test. He dictated seventy-eight words. According to the notes she jotted down at the time, Keek Sugawara Abe, a Japanese student, got twenty-six wrong. She marveled that one American student did almost as bad—twenty-five wrong. The worst score came from an Iranian student—thirty-two wrong. Kofi scored highest, none or perhaps one wrong. In a few more weeks, the teacher excused Kofi from attending class. Kofi's English was too good, the teacher said, to waste his time on freshman English.

Shortly after Kofi's arrival, Harvey Rice, president of the college, introduced the young Ghanian at a convocation of the students.

Kofi addressed them for a little more than twenty minutes with a speech about Africa. "The story of colonialism in Africa," he said, "is the story of exploitation, bullying, suppression, and brutality." His words sound somewhat naive and dogmatic now, but it was the typical rhetoric of young educated Africans in those days, and young educated Americans loved to hear it.

A tape recording of the speech exists, offering wonderful insights into the demeanor of the young man. His soft voice resembled that of his later years, though he sometimes rushed his words then with youthful eagerness. His accent was much the same—an educated British West African accent with an occasional lilting use of "in'" at the end of a word instead of "ing." He said "understandin'," for example, rather than "understanding." Despite his ringing denunciation of colonialism, his speech was mainly measured and informative as he surveyed the pace of independence in every region of Africa. To close, he could not resist joking about his football tryout.

Kofi had no trouble at his tryout for the debate team. "I was immediately struck," says Roger K. Mosvick, a retired professor of communications who was the coach of the Macalester debate team then, "with his wonderful, powerful, Ghanian, Oxford-like accent." The young student offered a speech about the responsibility of the United States toward the newly developing nations of Africa and the rest of the world. "I was just floored," Mosvick recalls. "It was a very prescient oration for the times. He had a powerful delivery. He was very soft-spoken but certainly knew how to use volume. There was very little I had to do." With Kofi making the same speech, the Macalester team would win the Minnesota state debate competition.

During the summer, Harry W. Morgan, a Macalester adviser, shepherded Kofi and a few other foreign students on a tour of the United States. Morgan had been hired by DeWitt Wallace, a Macalester alumnus and a founder of *Reader's Digest*, to develop international exchange programs at the college. A Nash Ambassador sedan was donated, and Morgan dubbed the project "Ambassadors of Friendship." The foreign students were so curious about America that they spent a night at a Salvation Army home for the poor in Kansas, and they persuaded the sheriff to let them spend a night in the jail of Flagstaff, Arizona.

Since the tour moved through several southern states during the Jim Crow era, Kofi encountered blatant racial slurs and discrimination. One barber refused him service with a curt, "We don't cut niggers' hair." Kofi replied, "I'm not a nigger. I'm from Africa." The barber then cut his hair. When he told a friend, Susan Linnee, about the incident, he seemed bemused, not angry. Like most educated West Africans of his day, especially after independence, Kofi tended to look on the racial problems of the United States more with scholarly curiosity than personal anger. Unlike Kenya and Rhodesia, British West Africa did not attract large numbers of white settlers who took land away from the Africans to make permanent homes. The British came to the Gold Coast only in small numbers and only as administrators. Few stayed very long. In the march to independence, Gold Coast Africans felt they were struggling against the British government and the British administration, not against whites.

Kofi's college friendships extended beyond Macalester. Linnee, a University of Minnesota student in St. Paul's twin city of Minneapolis, was introduced to the young Ghanian by his Swiss roommate, Roy Preiswerk, a friend of her boyfriend (and later husband). Kofi and a friend visited Susan at her family home in the Minneapolis suburbs one evening while her parents were away. A neighbor spied Kofi and phoned police to report a strange black man near the house. The police later informed her father. When the parents, who had not yet met Kofi, realized what had happened, they became very angry at their neighbors over the incident. The parents then invited Kofi and his roommate to a family dinner. When Kofi and the roommate showed up in their jalopy, a pink Studebaker, Susan's parents stepped out onto the porch so all neighbors could see them greet Kofi in the waning daylight.

A lifelong friendship developed between Susan Linnee and Kofi. Linnee, who has retired from the Associated Press after a distinguished career as a foreign correspondent, tried to recall recently what Annan was like in those college days. "He was very much the way he is now," she said. "He was very self-possessed and very self-confident. He was at ease with himself. It was something that made him attractive to everyone. He came from a tradition of trying to bring everyone into your circle, and he wanted to bring everyone into the circle." That placid, confident, open demeanor, so evident in the Macalester era, became his trademark. It is a manner that entrances his admirers today even as it annoys his detractors.

Annan intended to return to Ghana after graduation from Macalester with a B.A. in economics. He spent the summer working in the New York office of Pillsbury, a Minneapolis company (now owned by General Mills) that hoped to build a flour mill in Ghana. As soon as the deal was signed with the Ghanian government, Annan would head home and represent Pillsbury there, keeping to a career line much like that of his father.

The news from Ghana, however, was dispiriting. Nkrumah had scrapped the Ghanian parliamentary system in favor of a presidential state with himself at the head. He began arresting political opponents and jailing them without trial. His government tried to inculcate the youth with both Ghanian nationalism and Nkrumah adulation through its Young Pioneers and its Kwame Nkrumah Training Institute. Lackeys referred to Nkrumah as "Osageyfo" (Victorious Leader) and, with unctuous reverence, "Our President." When the Anglican bishop of Accra decried the adulation as an atheistic attempt to confuse the acts of Nkrumah with that of God, he was deported. Nkrumah would soon declare a one-party state with himself as president for life. His grandiose pan-African schemes depleted reserves, while his failed attempts at rapid industrialization diverted resources and energy from the vital cocoa crop. The lobby of the new Ambassador Hotel in Accra was fraying and crowding with East European officials seeking contracts. The Pillsbury deal fell through—Nkrumah gave the contract to Bulgaria. Kofi Annan would not come home to follow in the footsteps of his father.

2

Through the UN System

When Harvey Rice, the president of Macalester College, introduced Kofi Annan at one of the first convocations of the academic year, he urged students to make an effort to meet the young African. The football player David Lanegran and the Japanese student Keek Sugawara Abe recall with some awe that Dr. Rice told them Kofi was destined for a lifetime of great accomplishment—he would be a world leader someday. "How many times do college presidents get things that right?" asks Lanegran.

Yet Dr. Rice hardly seemed prescient for the next three decades. After joining the United Nations in 1962, Annan would make his way upward through the system—but only in fits and starts, shifting from one UN agency to another, leaving the UN, coming back, unsure whether his career should belong to Africa or not. His specialties were personnel and budgeting. These were vital UN functions, of course, but not the kind that attracted attention or achieved greatness. Reporters and camera crews did not seek him out in a crisis. He did not make speeches, as he did during his Macalester days. His life was bureaucratic, perhaps humdrum, complicated as well by a broken marriage.

Nor was the United Nations an institution of greatness during those three decades. Annan joined the UN's World Health Organization in Geneva a year after a plane crash killed Secretary-General Dag Hammarskjöld while he dealt with the crisis of the Congo. Hammarskjöld, a Swedish mystic poet, was probably the greatest secretary-general of all, a statesman who attracted worldwide attention and honor. But the Cold War hardened during the years after his death, and the Security Council, the most powerful body of the UN, found itself unable to deal with most crises because the two antagonists, the United States and the Soviet Union, were prepared to veto any action proposed by the other. The paralysis of the Security Council led almost all the former colonies of the world, soon a majority of UN members, to use the General Assembly, which has no executive power, to make bombastic speeches and pass toothless resolutions defying Western Europe and the United States. UN agencies such as the World Health Organization and UNICEF (the UN's children's fund) accomplished a great deal of good, but the foolish rhetoric of the General Assembly made the UN a thing of derision to many Americans and West Europeans.

After the Pillsbury summer, Annan followed the lead of Roy Preiswerk, his Swiss roommate in St. Paul, and enrolled at the Institut Universitaire de Hautes Études Internationales (Graduate Institute of International Studies) in Geneva. A grant from the Carnegie Endowment helped pay for Kofi's tuition. The Geneva institute had been founded in 1927 during the heyday of the League of Nations, mainly to turn out international civil servants. Georges Abi-Saab, an Egyptian classmate of Annan's, says the institute in the 1960s was still "a good fishing pond" for UN agencies in Geneva looking for young talent.

Since the surge of African independence had started only a few years before, there were not too many black Africans at the institute. Yet this was hardly a repeat of the Macalester experience. Annan, who studied economics, was far from a novelty at a school where almost every other student was foreign as well. He did not distinguish himself as an academic scholar. But according to Abi-Saab, who became a professor of international law at the institute and a judge on the International War Crimes Tribunal for Yugoslavia, the future secretary-general displayed a "vivid intelligence" during the give-and-take of classroom discussions. "He had the intelligence," Abi-Saab recalls, "to perceive issues, to capture issues easily, to formulate them and articulate them."

Annan first sported the beard that he now wears when he was a student at the institute. It somewhat resembled the beard of Patrice Lumumba, the fiery Congolese leader murdered by Katanga secessionists in 1961. "It was very fashionable at that time for African students to have Lumumba beards," says Abi-Saab. "It showed that they were nationalistic." When Annan addressed students of the institute during its seventy-fifth-anniversary celebrations in 2002, he was introduced by Professor Abi-Saab. "All my other African friends shaved their Lumumba beards," said Abi-Saab, "but Kofi kept his." The professor lightheartedly hailed this as a symbol of Annan holding on to youthful ideals. But Annan, who often attracted attention in his later years as an international civil servant impeccably dressed in fashionable but tasteful suits, surely kept the trimmed beard because it enhanced his distinguished and handsome look.

He did not earn a master's degree at the institute but accepted a job instead with the World Health Organization (WHO), a specialized agency that is part of the UN family yet autonomous. A UN secretary-general has no power to name the head of the agency or boss it around. Annan entered the agency in 1962 at its lowest level as an administrative and budget officer. He told himself that he would remain in the UN system for no more than two years and then go back to Ghana.

Geneva, the heartland of Calvinism, has never been regarded as one of Europe's romantic cities, but it stirred love in Kofi. He met Titilola Alakija, a Nigerian student taking French-language classes in Geneva. Her family was as distinguished as his own, perhaps more so. Her father, Adeyemo Alakija, was a former justice of the Nigerian Supreme Court and the founder of the *Daily Times* newspaper in

Lagos. He had even been knighted by Great Britain. Kofi and Titi were married in May 1965 at Holy Trinity Anglican Church on Rue du Mont Blanc in the center of Geneva. The small stone church, which holds its services in English, is known throughout French-speaking Geneva as the Église Anglaise or English Church. Befitting the African elite of that time, the wedding did not seem very African. Kofi did not show up in kente cloth; Titi did not wear a Nigerian head tie. Instead, Kofi wore white gloves and a formal coat with tails. His bride wore a long white wedding dress, white gloves, and a white mantilla. Roy Preiswerk, who died in 1972, was Kofi's best man.

According to German journalist Friederike Bauer, Titi's friends described her as attractive, warm, and full of life in those days. Roy's American wife, Julia Preiswerk, now a psychoanalyst in Geneva, attended the wedding and met Titi several times afterward. She recalls Titi as easygoing and pleasant and full of laughter and smiles. Yet she had "a sarcastic sense of humor" and, while she often seemed submissive to the wishes of others, she also "had her own ideas and could be tough when she didn't want to do something."

This stubbornness surfaced a few years later when the Annans visited the Preiswerks for Carnival season in Trinidad in 1969. Roy was working in Trinidad then as director of a new institute of graduate studies for the Caribbean. Roy and Julia expected the couple to stay with them. But when the Annans arrived in Trinidad, only Kofi stayed with the Preiswerks. Titi decided to stay with other friends on the island. Kofi, Roy, and Julia attended all the Carnival and calypso events together and would meet up with Titi only when she and her friends were invited to the same party. The arrangement made Julia feel "there was a problem" in the marriage.

A few months after their 1965 wedding, the Annans returned to Africa, but not to either of their homes. Kofi took a post as an administrative officer in the personnel section of the UN Economic Commission for Africa (ECA), based in the Ethiopian capital of Addis Ababa. It was a fashionable time to come to Addis Ababa. Only a year before, thirty-five African leaders, including President Kwame Nkrumah of Ghana, had met in Addis Ababa and signed a charter creating the Organization of African Unity (OAU). For Nkrumah, it was at least a small step toward his hopeless, lifetime goal of realizing a united and powerful Africa. The organization would headquarter in Addis Ababa. The move brought Annan closer to the heart of the UN system, for the Economic Commission for Africa was an outpost of the UN, not an independent and autonomous agency. The move, however, did not bring him as close to his African roots as he expected.

The site of Addis Ababa could make it one of the world's most beautiful cities. Built on a hilly plateau almost eight thousand feet high, its skies twist into eerie blue-black patterns at dusk, much like the skies in El Greco's *View of Toledo*. But the beauty was marred by what Kofi and Titi could see below the skies.

Addis Ababa was one of the world's poorest cities in 1965, and it suffered from a lack of colonialism. When the European powers carved up Africa for themselves in the late nineteenth century, they left Ethiopia alone. Italian troops tried to conquer the mountainous empire but were trounced at the Battle of Adowa in 1896. Using poison gas, Benito Mussolini, the Italian dictator, avenged Adowa and defeated the fiercely independent Ethiopians in 1936 in a prelude to World War II. But Italian rule lasted only five years. British troops drove out the Italians and reinstalled Emperor Haile Selassie in 1941.

No country in Africa could boast as many years of independence as Ethiopia. The lack of colonialism, however, had left Ethiopia by 1965 with shoddy roads, sporadic education, and inadequate health services. Its poverty was far greater than Kofi and Titi had noticed (but never experienced) when they grew up under British colonialism in West Africa.

Foreigners like Kofi and Titi lived in Addis Ababa in substantial stucco homes guarded by corrugated iron fencing to keep out thieves and undesirables. But Addis Ababa, a sprawling, dirty city, was still almost rural, with many residents living in earthen hovels. The unpaved streets, muddy in the rains, were choked with beggars and goats. Ethiopia has a wonderful national dress called the shamma—a toga-like, porous white cloth with colorful and intricate borders.

Most men and women clambered through Addis Ababa in home-spun shammas that were torn and soiled and without borders.

To make matters worse, Ethiopia was ruled by an emperor and court mired in medieval habits. Emperor Haile Selassie, an international hero for standing up in the League of Nations with a speech denouncing Mussolini and his Italian troops in 1936, now presided over a court of whispers and rumors. Hangers-on jockeyed for position so they could whisper in his ear to condemn or beg. His cabinet members were chosen for loyalty, not competence. Young Ethiopians, trained in land reform at the University of Wisconsin, returned to the Ministry of Land Reform during these years only to discover that their minister did not know what land reform was. University of Addis Ababa students ridiculed the emperor's pretensions. He claimed to be a direct descendant of the biblical king Solomon, stemming from Solomon's seduction of the queen of Sheba. "We don't care if he is the great-great-great-great-grand-bastard of King Solomon," students would mutter out of earshot of his secret police.

The UN Economic Commission for Africa has never accomplished much in its main goal of accelerating the economic development of Africa. But it had its best reputation in Annan's earlier years because its executive secretary, Annan's boss, was Robert Gardiner, a distinguished Ghanian economist. Gardiner had attracted worldwide renown as the UN official in charge of Congo operations when UN peacekeepers finally defeated Moise Tshombe in 1964 and squelched the secession of his province of Katanga. Gardiner fit the mold set after the UN's founding by the African American Nobel Peace Prize winner Ralph Bunche—the international civil servant who could do whatever the UN needed in times of crisis and do it with verve and creativity. Gardiner was a wonderful model for a young UN official like Annan.

The Economic Commission occupied one wing of a complex known as Africa Hall. The secretariat of the Organization of African Unity occupied the other. The centerpiece was a huge conference hall where the charter of the OAU had been signed. The OAU held annual summit meetings, mostly at Africa Hall, and Annan observed the sessions often. It was not an edifying experience. Murderous tyrants such as Idi Amin of Uganda and Jean-Bédel Bokassa of the Central African Republic—the shames of Africa—would join their colleagues in passing unanimous resolutions condemning white rule in South Africa, Portuguese Africa, and Rhodesia. Aside from this hypocrisy, OAU resolutions were replete with threats and promises that bore no relation to reality.

"I attended most of the meetings," Annan recalled more than three decades later, "and quite frankly sometimes I was appalled by the posturing and the lack of realism that goes on." Unable to cope with their problems, he said, some African leaders stirred Africa Hall with bombastic speeches that satisfied their emotions but did nothing about the problems.

Annan worked for the ECA in Addis Ababa for seven years until 1972, when he was thirty-four years old. This stretch was broken by a year's training in New York and a year's sabbatical leave to attend the Massachusetts Institute of Technology (MIT) in Cambridge, across the Charles River from Boston. By the end of his ECA career, he was chief of personnel. His daughter, Ama, was born in Lagos, Nigeria, in November 1969. Although Kofi was based in Addis Ababa then, Titi decided to go home to her parents to have the child.

He attended MIT as an Alfred Sloan Fellow, earning an M.S. in management in June 1972. The MIT experience was different from his other university experiences because he felt a loss of confidence soon after he started classes. He was pitted against some of the finest young minds in America, and he felt that he did not measure up. Annan was simply not an academic scholar.

He talked about this twenty-five years later in a revealing commencement address at MIT. "At the outset," he said, "there was competition—rather intense competition—among my cohorts. Each was equally determined to shine and to demonstrate his leadership abilities. . . . Walking along the Charles River one day, in the middle of my first term, I reflected on my predicament. How could I survive, let alone thrive, in this group of overachievers?

"And the answer," he went on, "came to me most emphatically: *not* by playing it according to their rules. 'Follow your own inner compass,' I said to myself, 'listen to your own drummer.' To live is to choose. But to choose well, you must know who you are, what you stand for, where you want to go, and why you want to go there. My anxieties slowly began to dissolve.

"What I took away from MIT, as a result," he said, "was not only the analytical tools but also the intellectual confidence to help me locate my bearings in new situations, to view any challenge as a potential opportunity for renewal and growth, and to be comfortable in seeking the help of colleagues, but not fearing, in the end, to do things my way."

Commencement addresses are always chock full of inspirational pap. With a quarter century of hindsight, Annan may have embellished and altered the meaning of his walk by the Charles River. All we can say for certain is that Annan felt anxious enough at the start of the semester to try to calm himself with a walk on the riverbank. Yet his words tell us a good deal. The message he said he "took away from MIT" is his clearest description on record of the way he has tried to deal with the adversities and problems facing him in his career and personal life. At first meeting, it is possible to underestimate this good-natured, affable, nonscholarly man. But he knows himself, knows where he wants to go, and knows how to go about getting there. He has surprised onlookers often by exceeding their expectations.

The UN transferred Annan back to Geneva as an administrative management officer in August 1972. This second Geneva interlude would last less than two years. The family grew in Geneva with the birth of his son, Kojo, in July 1973. But Titi, Ama, and Kojo remained behind in Geneva when Annan was given his first taste of UN peacekeeping. He was assigned to temporary duty with the UN Emergency Force in Egypt.

After the Yom Kippur War of 1973, UN peacekeepers deployed in the Middle East to supervise the cease-fire between Egyptian and Israelis forces in the Egyptian Sinai Peninsula. When Annan arrived in May 1974, there were almost seven thousand Blue Helmets on duty, made up of Irish, Peruvian, Swedish, Indonesian, Senegalese, and Finnish soldiers. It was the most important UN operation of that period. Annan's role, however, was rather minor. He was the chief personnel officer for the UN civilians working in support of the troops. He worked in the headquarters of the operation in Cairo. When the headquarters moved three months later to Ismailia, a key town on the Suez Canal, Annan moved with it.

When he returned from Ismailia in November 1974, he made an abrupt change of career. He left the United Nations and took the family home to Ghana. At age thirty-six, he accepted the post of managing director of the Ghana Tourist Agency in Accra. His mentor Robert Gardiner, who had already accepted a post with the Ghanian government, had urged him to do the same. "I think I felt it would be good to go back to Ghana and give something back and make a contribution," Annan says. "I wanted to go back and see what I can do to help. It was a dream of all the people of my generation that after your studies you would want to go home and make a contribution if the circumstances permit." He evidently also wanted to be closer to an aging and ailing father, and he wanted Ama and Kojo to spend some time in his homeland. But the move to Ghana seems quixotic now. "He had hoped to stay in Accra for some time," says his friend Susan Linnee. "But it wasn't a mesh."

For one thing, his assignment was nearly impossible to achieve. Ghana could hardly expect to attract many tourists quickly. Like much of West Africa, it had some glorious beaches but without adequate hotels, restaurants, and other facilities to back them up. Its wildlife paled in comparison with the great game parks of East Africa. Accra and Kumasi had vast markets and colorful town life, but neither city was anything like a Florence or a Oaxaca. Alex Haley's autobiographical and fanciful *Roots* had not even been published yet in the United States, so there were no pools of African Americans anxious to search for their ancestral homes in Ghana. Annan had to make something out of very little.

Moreover, he had to do so under a military regime. Ghana had already been shaken by two coups since independence. Nkrumah was overthrown by the military in the first coup in 1966 while he was on a trip to China and North Vietnam. He settled in exile in Guinea and died there six years later. General Ignatius K. Acheampong, chairman of the National Redemption Council, now ruled Ghana. When the first rash of coups broke out in Africa in the 1960s, some optimists predicted the soldiers would rid their countries of corruption and tribalism, but the soldiers soon proved incompetent, ineffectual, and tyrannical. Angry young Africans used to bristle in fury over the large white Mercedes cars favored by corrupt politicians in independent Africa. When the soldiers took over, according to a popular joke rooted in reality, they accomplished only one major change: they rode around in large Mercedes cars painted khaki instead of white.

From his vantage point in Addis Ababa, Annan could hardly have been under any illusions about the nature of military rule. Years later, he would bemoan the proliferation of military coups in Africa. It "did not only disrupt the political process," he said, "it also bred an atmosphere and spirit that anyone can be president. You don't need experience." You just need guns. As secretary-general, he would continually plead with African leaders to ostracize any other leader who came to power through a coup.

The Ghana Tourist Agency was a parastatal body—a commercial company owned by the Ghanian government that, in theory, made business decisions without political interference. "I had been given the impression that since I was going to be working for a parastatal, there would be quite a lot of autonomy and independence," he recalls. "But that didn't turn out to be the case." Annan could not escape the coils of military bureaucracy—a bureaucracy that was not efficient. Most analysts, in fact, believe General Acheampong took control of a damaged economy and made it worse. "It was frustrating," Annan says. "There was constant interference from them. A minister who was a military colonel wanted to get involved in every decision. It came out wrong, or it took ages to get a decision. . . . It was frustrating, because I was perhaps in a hurry. I saw lots of things that could be done with a bit of imagination and creativity and management. And that wouldn't even need big bucks. But you couldn't move the system. You couldn't get cooperation. There was too much red tape and too many roadblocks." Annan gave up and returned to the United Nations two years later.

The UN assigned him to the personnel office of the Secretariat in New York. He worked there for four years as his marriage deteriorated. In fifteen years of marriage, he had moved for work or study from Geneva to Addis Ababa to New York to Addis Ababa to Cambridge to Addis Ababa to Geneva to Cairo to Ismailia to Accra to New York. The packing and moving, complicated by the spells when the family did not join him, created obvious strains. "The biggest problem for me," Titi told German journalist Friederike Bauer, "were the moves. I had enough of them."

At a recent luncheon in his private dining room alongside his office, I asked Annan if he agreed with Titi's conclusion. "It's possible," he said. "When you have a couple, and they have to move from city to city and are moving around a lot, the person who is employed has perhaps an easy entry. I mean when you go there, you have your job, you have your colleagues, you get to know people. But for the spouse and the children, they start afresh so it could be that was part of our separation at a certain point." His reply rationalized her comment but did not make clear whether he really agreed with her.

In 1980, when he was forty-two years old, Annan received a plum assignment, head of personnel for the highly regarded office of the UN High Commissioner for Refugees (UNHCR) in Geneva. The high commissioner was then Poul Harting, a former prime minister of Denmark. But Titi did not move to Geneva with Kofi. The couple had separated. The eleven-year-old Ama accompanied her mother to London, while seven-year-old Kojo remained with his father in Geneva. The plan was for Kofi to care for the child until he was ready to enter a British boarding school.

Annan was a dutiful single parent. He would take time off from work every afternoon so he could pick up Kojo from La Châtaigneraie, a bilingual, French-English school about half an hour from Geneva by car. Once, when he told Kojo that he would be unable to attend a parent-teacher meeting, the boy protested, "But all the other mothers are coming." In 1981, Annan met Nane Lagergren at a friend's party in Geneva. Nane was a Swedish lawyer working for the office of the High Commissioner for Refugees as well. She could not help paying attention to him at the party. Seeing him for the first time, she has said, was like a thunderbolt. Kofi, as Julia Preiswerk puts it, "was very charming and seductive. He was a presence in a room." Kofi was just as attracted to this tall, slim, blond woman. Within a few weeks, he introduced Nane to the Preiswerks as "somebody special."

Nane, too, was a single parent—a thirty-seven-year-old divorced mother of a ten-year-old daughter named Nina. Nane's father, Gunnar Lagergren, was a distinguished Swedish jurist who had helped settle boundary disputes between India and Pakistan. Her mother, Nina von Dardel, was the half-sister of Raoul Wallenberg, the heroic Swedish diplomat who saved the lives of tens of thousands of Hungarian Jews during World War II and then died in the hands of Soviet Union officialdom. Nane never met Wallenberg, but in his last letter to her mother, which arrived shortly after Nane's birth, he wrote, "Kiss the little one for me." Nane told Evelyn Leopold of Reuters in 1997 that Wallenberg had been "a constant presence, an absence, a shadow" throughout her childhood.

Nane, who had studied painting, also had a tenuous link to art history, for the great star-crossed Italian artist Amedeo Modigliani, painted a portrait of her mother's aunt, Thora Klinckowström, in Paris a few months before his death in 1920. Thora, who met Modigliani at the Café Rotonde in Montparnasse, sat in his atelier twice for the portrait but insisted she had never been alone with the painter, a notorious seducer. This portrait of a very young Swedish woman with a jaunty fedora and a quizzical glance is one of Modigliani's finest.

In 1983, Annan was reassigned to New York as director of administrative management services of the UN Secretariat. Kojo was now in boarding school, and Nane followed Annan to New York, giving up her job as a lawyer with the Office of the High Commissioner for Refugees. The couple lived in an apartment on Roosevelt Island in the East River, with a view of the UN complex. After the divorce from Titi was final, Kofi and Nane married in 1984 at the Church Center for the United Nations, across the street from UN headquarters. They reached Manhattan by crossing the river by the Roosevelt Island tramway. Kofi did not wear formal tails this time. He dressed in an elegant blue and white African robe. Nane wore a simple white robe over white slacks.

Kofi and Nane acknowledged one minor cultural problem early in their marriage. "We would organize a dinner," Kofi told Barbara Crossette of the *New York Times* a few years later. "Nane being a Swede—that's a country where if you invite them for eight o'clock, they will get there at five or ten to eight and circle the block, and ring the bell at eight—was used to punctuality. The Ghanian or the African guests would come about thirty minutes to an hour late, and she used to get furious. So I said just don't do soufflés." He went on, "I'm more punctual now and she's more relaxed." In view of the punctuality of his father, the adjustment would not have been very difficult for Kofi.

Nane turned to painting full-time. She studied at the Art Students League and the New York Studio School and rented a studio for herself in Brooklyn. Years later, when Kofi's status as a celebrity aroused curiosity about his wife's paintings, Nane would call herself "the best-known unknown artist in the world." But she stopped painting when he took office as secretary-general because of the demands of her social duties.

The stability of Annan's second marriage was accompanied by his steady rise in the bureaucracy. Javier Pérez de Cuéllar of Peru was secretary-general of the UN at this time. He is probably the least known of the seven secretaries-general who have managed the UN since its founding in 1945. There is a hoary joke among old UN hands that Pérez de Cuéllar "wouldn't make waves if he fell out of a boat." He shunned publicity and liked to practice his diplomacy quietly and far behind the scenes. He would reply to press questions politely in perfect English, Spanish, or French, but so softly that no one was sure what he said. Pérez de Cuéllar is probably the most underestimated secretary-general of all. Once relations between Mikhail Gorbachev of the Soviet Union and Ronald Reagan of the United States thawed, Pérez de Cuéllar sensed the potential power of the Security Council and moved swiftly to use it to end the Iraq-Iran War in 1988.

Most important for Annan, Pérez de Cuéllar also had a keen eye for talent. He was pleased with Annan's efficiency and competence, and he assigned the Ghanian to posts of increasing importance in personnel, budgeting, and management. In 1987, when Annan was forty-nine years old, Pérez de Cuéllar awarded him the coveted rank of assistant secretary-general and put him in charge of Human Resources (as the UN, following the jargon of American corporations, now called its personnel department). The UN system has nine ranks for its civil servants, and Annan had climbed to the second highest. The highest was undersecretary-general, and it was now within reach.

Even as a specialist in administration and management, Annan spoke with a gentle directness that could be disarming. In 1989, Pérez de Cuéllar sent one of his chief aides, Giandomenico Picco, with Annan to the UN's powerful Advisory Committee on Budgetary Questions. Picco wanted the committee to approve funding for a series of offices throughout the world that would collect political information for the secretary-general and transact political business on his behalf. "Well, in other words, ladies and gentlemen," Annan told the committee, "what Mr. Picco is trying to set up are intelligence offices in this area." Picco thought that Annan's frank description had doomed the project. Instead, Picco received more funding than he had expected.

Fellow civil servants looked on Annan as an affable administrator, the kind of professional who treats your problems with suitable

concern and then goes about solving them in a pleasant and efficient manner. This manner may have misled some to think he was
all fluff. In fact, when he was controller, some wags called him "the
remote controller" because they didn't believe he was working very
hard. Fred Eckhard, who joined the UN in the late 1980s and would
later serve as Annan's spokesman, recalls meeting Annan for the
first time in those years. "I was young and arrogant and feeling
rather full of myself," Eckhard says. Annan struck him as "a very
nice, easygoing guy." Then Eckhard said something that bothered
Annan; Eckhard does not remember what it was. "His soft brown
eyes suddenly turned electric," says Eckhard. "Suddenly here was
this force. It was so strong it shut me up directly. I was speechless."
Eckhard realized that a lot of people were wrong; Kofi was not fluff.

Annan's career seemed to be on course. In a few years, he supposed, he would become an undersecretary-general and serve a
future secretary-general or secretaries-general as the UN's top man
for administration and financial management. That might not be
what Macalester president Harvey Rice once predicted, but it would
be quite an achievement; in fact, Annan could hardly hope for
more. But then Saddam Hussein invaded Kuwait.

3

The Grand Illusion of the First Persian Gulf War

The first Persian Gulf War created a grand illusion of power within the UN. That illusion spawned new attitudes toward the UN and greater expectations. The expectations often crashed in disappointment. Yet the UN still seemed to matter more than it had in decades. That feeling fostered a mood of optimism even in a world bursting with crises. The new mood changed Kofi Annan's career and life.

When Saddam Hussein dispatched tens of thousands of troops across the border into Kuwait on August 2, 1990, claiming that his small neighbor was actually "an integral part of the Iraqi Republic," the UN did not stand helplessly by, wringing its hands and crying out in the wind, as it had so often in the past. Instead, the blatant aggression shocked the UN into action. With remarkable cohesion, the Security Council authorized a military force led by the United States to turn back the aggression. In a little more than six months, Saddam Hussein was defeated and his army ousted from Kuwait.

Basking in victory, most UN diplomats and officials suddenly felt that the UN could now do anything as long as the great powers agreed in the Security Council. The UN behaved or seemed to behave during the Persian Gulf War just the way President Franklin Delano Roosevelt had envisioned. The UN had forced an aggressor to relinquish his conquered territory and retreat. The UN had burst out of its paralysis like a superhero. A mood of euphoria swept through the corridors of the UN buildings on First Avenue.

Yves Fortier, the Canadian ambassador on the Security Council, described the Persian Gulf War later as "a classic case" in the way the United Nations was supposed to act in the face of naked aggression. "It was Political Science 101," he said. Yet the case was not as classic as it seemed. While former undersecretary-general Brian Urquhart was right in calling the war "the first exercise in the unanimous collective security that we've been talking about since the days of Woodrow Wilson," it was a collective security manipulated, led, and, in the main, carried out by a single country: the United States.

From the start, President George H. W. Bush was infuriated by the Iraqi aggression and determined to turn it back. He announced that Saddam Hussein was "going to get his ass kicked." He had no faith in UN sanctions but gave them a try for a few months. When sanctions failed to dislodge the Iraqi troops within those months, Bush was ready to unleash his warplanes and troops. Fortunately for the UN, Bush, a former UN ambassador himself, took his case to the Security Council to obtain international authorization for his policy and international participation in the war.

The American diplomatic campaign had three powerful fronts. President Bush cajoled world leaders by phone and in person. Secretary of State James Baker traveled worldwide to make a persuasive case to foreign ministers in their capitals. And Ambassador Thomas R. Pickering, probably the most effective American ambassador ever to serve at the UN, solidified the campaign with deft diplomacy within the Security Council. The other ambassadors marveled at the near-magical negotiating skills of Pickering, a tall, balding career foreign service officer who could allay their objections and concerns by swiftly changing a few words of a U.S. resolution without altering its main intent. The Security Council approved twelve anti-Iraq resolutions during these months, culminating with the one authorizing the war. Only Cuba on three occasions and Yemen on two ever voted against any of them.

The United States enlisted Britain, France, and Saudi Arabia to furnish significant air and ground forces. Smaller units came from two dozen other countries, such as Egypt and Spain. But the major forces were American, and the entire operation was under the command of U.S. general H. Norman Schwarzkopf. The United Nations had authorized the United States to lead a military coalition against Iraq, but the planes and troops did not receive any UN orders. The UN did not issue blue helmets and berets to the soldiers, as it did to troops serving as peacekeepers under UN command. "It was not a United Nations war," Secretary-General Javier Pérez de Cuéllar told the European Parliament in Strasbourg. "General Schwarzkopf was not wearing a blue helmet."

The UN role—apart from Security Council authorization for the war—was minimal and sometimes humiliating. Pérez de Cuéllar made a fruitless attempt a few days before the bombing began on January 17, 1991, to persuade Saddam Hussein to withdraw from Kuwait. The secretary-general flew to Baghdad but had no authority to compromise. Armed with the UN resolutions, he could only plead with Saddam Hussein to give in. But Saddam refused to heed him. After the meeting, Pérez de Cuéllar told reporters, "I don't see any reason for hope."

When there was a flicker of chance that the UN could help avert the invasion, the White House brushed the UN aside. After weeks of bombing, Saddam Hussein seemed to signal that he was ready to give up. Soviet special envoy Yevgeny Primakov worked out a deal with Iraqi foreign minister Tariq Aziz for the Iraqi troops to leave Kuwait City within four days and the rest of Kuwait within twenty-one days. A hopeful Pérez de Cuéllar asked Undersecretary-General Marrack Goulding, the chief of peacekeeping, to sound out several governments about providing troops to monitor the withdrawal. But the White House scorned the Primakov-Aziz deal. Minutes before the Security Council assembled to discuss the deal, the White House issued an ultimatum demanding Saddam Hussein's withdrawal from Kuwait City within two days—half the time worked out by Primakov and Aziz. Saddam Hussein defied the ultimatum. Schwarzkopf then unleashed his ground forces. In less than five days, the Iraqi forces were routed from Kuwait and defeated.

Exulting over the American victory, the White House then turned dismissive of the importance of the UN in the war. Asked by a group of Arab journalists if he would have gone to war even without the UN's blessing, President Bush replied, "I might have said the hell with them [the Iraqis]. It's right and wrong. It's good and evil. He's evil. Our cause is right. And without the United Nations, [I might have] sent a considerable force to help." In fact, Bush, fearful that he could no longer command resounding majorities in the Security Council, ignored the UN after the war and ordered U.S. troops into northern Iraq to provide relief for the Kurds. Even more significant, the United States, Britain, and France on their own imposed no-fly zones in both northern and southern Iraq to prevent Saddam Hussein from airlifting troops to suppress the Kurds in the north and the Shia Muslims in the south.

The UN did play a significant role in one aspect of the crisis that is largely forgotten now—Saddam Hussein's seizure of foreign hostages. The issue takes up only a few pages in the standard histories of the Persian Gulf War, and the UN role is barely mentioned. But the hostages were the subject of many headlines and much television footage during the months leading up to the war and caused great consternation at the time. Kofi Annan was a player in the negotiations.

When the Iraqi troops invaded Kuwait, they began rounding up American, British, and other foreigners as hostages. British citizens were even removed from a British Airways jet that had landed in Kuwait for a stopover. By late October, the Iraqis had placed more than eight hundred American, British, other European, Australian, Japanese, and Kuwaiti men at dams, refineries, steel factories, weapons factories, and other strategic sites throughout Iraq and Kuwait. These hostages, whose sites were shifted every few days, were placed there to deter any possible air bombing. They were "human shields." Thousands of other foreigners, including women and children, were kept under house arrest. The large pool of hostages even included diplomats and UN workers. In all, the UN estimated, Saddam Hussein had detained thirteen thousand hostages.

Secretary-General Pérez de Cuéllar ordered Kofi Annan, as chief of personnel, to join Virendra Dayal, the secretary-general's chief of staff, in a special mission to Baghdad in late September. They were tasked with trying to persuade Iraq to let the nine hundred UN workers and dependents go. It was the first substantive assignment for the fifty-two-year-old Ghanian in his UN career. He would not be pushing folders around a desk or poring over budget figures but would be engaged in the UN's vital role of diplomatic negotiation on an issue of peace and security.

Annan showed no nervousness about the assignment. When an aide in New York, Elisabeth Lindenmayer, mused about the possibility of failure, Annan told her not to talk that way. "We'll make it," he said. Since Dayal, a native of India, had been vacationing in Ireland, Annan carried an extra suitcase of clothes for delivery to him in Baghdad. Dayal would stay a few days and leave, but Kofi would remain in Baghdad.

Worldwide public opinion was repelled by Saddam Hussein's attempt to protect himself behind foreign civilians. He intensified the repulsion with tasteless television shows in which he paraded his hostages, including women and children, calling them "special guests." On one television show, he asked a frightened seven-year-old British boy if had drunk his milk that day. Saddam even wrote an open letter to families praising the hostages for their role in promoting peace.

The Security Council passed four resolutions demanding that Iraq release all these hostages and that "Iraq take no action to jeopardize the safety, security, or health of such nationals." Annan and Dayal were not alone in Baghdad trying to persuade Iraqi authorities to release foreigners. Former British prime minister Edward Heath flew there to negotiate during the next few months. So did Jesse Jackson, Muhammad Ali, German chancellor Willy Brandt,

King Hussein of Jordan, and Palestinian leader Yasir Arafat. Chargé d'affaires Joseph Wilson exerted American pressure, while the White House insisted that the United States would not call off any military action because of the hostages.

The mission of Annan lasted more than two weeks. "I didn't expect to stay that long," he recalled recently. "I had expected to be there for three to five days. Basically, the original idea was to help get the UN staff out, because in the UN system between Iraq and Kuwait we had about nine hundred people—internationals—in the region, and my initial assignment was to go there and try to facilitate their departure before they get into any difficulties. And we managed to get every one of them out."

Dayal and Annan met during the mornings with Foreign Minister Tariq Aziz, the articulate Christian who served as the public face of Iraq throughout its confrontation with the UN for more than a decade. He consulted his superiors, presumably including Saddam, during the afternoons to work out a response to the entreaties of the UN officials. Their main concerns, of course, were the UN personnel, not the "human shields." It was easier for Saddam to let the UN people go. Aziz finally reached an agreement with the pair of UN emissaries. He promised to meet with Pérez de Cuéllar in Amman, Jordan, on September 30 to see if some deal could be worked out to avert war. As a gesture of goodwill, he announced that Dayal and Annan could return home with all the detained UN workers.

Rounding up the UN workers, obtaining exit permits, and busing them to Jordan for airlifts home proved relatively easy. But Annan discovered two stragglers taking refuge in the offices of the UN Economic Commission for the Middle East in Baghdad. They had not yet obtained their exit permits and had no other place to stay because of a sudden government decree that made it illegal for an Iraqi to house a foreigner. Annan entered the offices in the midst of a raging argument. The UN official in charge of the office, an Iraqi, was trying to shoo out the UN staff people for fear their presence would anger the government. Annan halted the ouster. "Where do they go?" he said. "They can't go into private homes. We have to try and get them out." He then remembered that the deputy chief of the office was a former Iraqi minister of agriculture. "You must have some influence if you were once a minister," Annan told the Iraqi. "We need to get these guys permits to leave." In the end, the Iraqis obtained the permits for the UN workers. They were quickly bused to Jordan in time to join the airlift.

By then, Annan also had become troubled by the plight of several hundred thousand foreigners who had been largely ignored—foreign workers from Asia and Africa who were now stranded, mostly in Kuwait. "I had discovered there were two groups of hostages," Annan recalled. "There were Western hostages who had organization and money to leave but were not allowed to leave. Since they were not allowed to leave, everybody accepted they were hostages. But there were about five hundred thousand Asians from Sri Lanka, Philippines, Bangladesh, India, others from Sudan, who were free to go but had neither the money nor the organization to go. They had sort of been overlooked."

In some ways, their plight was worse than that of the Western hostages shown on television. "These are people who were beggared overnight," Annan said. "They were nurses, workers working for the rich Kuwaiti families, and overnight they were beggared. Their employers were gone. The banks were closed. And they couldn't get any money to go anywhere."

Annan attended several meetings of the Western ambassadors in Baghdad who discussed ways of pressuring the Iraqis to release the Western hostages. Unfortunately, the Asian and African ambassadors had not organized in the same way. So he made the rounds of the Indian, Pakistani, Bangladeshi, and other ambassadors to collect estimates of the numbers of their nationals stranded in Iraq and Kuwait. "I got the figures from them," he said. "I think I was the first to give it to the Iraqi Foreign Ministry." Aziz soon agreed to allow the UN to organize airlifts to take the workers from Jordan to their homes.

Annan traveled to Amman in Jordan to meet Pérez de Cuéllar and oversee the start of the airlift of UN staff people. Phoning from

Baghdad had been difficult, and Annan took advantage of the break to phone Nane. "What about Anatolia?" she asked. "What *about* Anatolia?" he replied. "We are supposed to go there on holiday in a few days." "My God," he said, "I forgot completely about it." Asked recently if he was able to return in time to make the trip to Anatolia, in eastern Turkey, he replied, "I didn't go, and I haven't been."

Annan returned to Baghdad to oversee the departure of the foreign workers. But he had not forgotten the Western hostages. He used his free time to visit and collect letters and messages from a good number of hostages held as "human shields" at sites near Baghdad. When he met with Aziz, he pressed him about the Western hostages as well. According to Dayal, Aziz did assure them that Saddam Hussein would release all the other hostages soon. But that sounded more like blather than a meaningful promise. When Kofi's mission finally ended, he phoned the family of every Western hostage he had met. He read messages, promised to mail letters, and described the health of the hostages.

Saddam did free all the hostages, but not right away. He followed the release of the UN workers with the release of a few other hostages. He allowed elderly and ill hostages to go; then he released women and children. But this did not dissipate the worldwide repulsion against him. It took more than two months before Saddam announced in early December that he would accept an American offer to meet with Secretary of State Baker and followed that news with a statement that all hostages were now free to go. In the first test, a group of 325 hostages left Baghdad on December 9 in a plane chartered by Wilson. Many hundreds more followed in the next few days. The White House was enormously relieved by the release of the hostages. Despite their truculent insistence that the hostages would not deter the bombings, U.S. officials had feared that the presence of "human shields" would force the military to skip some bombing targets.

It is not clear why Saddam Hussein finally relented and freed all hostages. We do not know if Annan had any impact on the decision. He was one of many emissaries who came to Baghdad and advised

Iraq to give up the hostages. Saddam probably released all the hostages as a goodwill gesture in advance of the scheduled meeting with Baker—a meeting that never took place. In any case, neither Annan nor the UN has ever claimed any credit for the release of the human shields and the other Western hostages.

The UN, in fact, did not even trumpet the role of Annan and Dayal in the release of the UN staff and the airlift of the Asian and African workers. "We had to get these people out," says Dayal. "The less song and dance, the better. It would have been wrong for us to negotiate and play the publicity game at the same time, and it would have been stupid of us." It would have been unseemly to boast about success with the hostages when the UN was failing at its more important task of persuading Saddam to avert war by leaving Kuwait on his own. Pérez de Cuéllar, moreover, was obsessive about the need for UN diplomats to operate far behind the scenes without the slightest hint of fanfare.

British newspapers gave most of the credit for release of the hostages to the pleas of former prime minister Heath. American diplomat Wilson credited King Hussein and Arafat most of all. Within UN circles, Annan's mission, whether or not it helped the Western hostages, was regarded as successful, and it set the stage for even more important assignments for him. Pérez de Cuéllar did not shower praise on Annan, not even in private. "The staff were happy," Annan said, "but I didn't get too much praise." Pérez de Cuéllar preferred to show his pleasure in other ways. He promoted Annan to controller or chief financial manager of the UN. When he needed an official to head negotiations with Iraq over oil for food, the secretary-general selected Annan.

This first mission to Baghdad was of extraordinary importance to Annan. Summing up his feelings about it recently, he said, "It was exciting. It was interesting. You were doing something to help people directly. It was rewarding." The mission bolstered his self-confidence, gave him a chance to deal in the most vital work of the UN, and allowed him his first experience at intricate and delicate international negotiations.

The UN did not lift sanctions against Iraq after the Persian Gulf War ended. Led by the United States, the Security Council imposed a peace on Iraq that was as harsh as the peace imposed on Germany after World War I. Borrowing an image from Saddam Hussein's rhetoric, ambassadors called the Security Council's resolution that ended the war "the mother of all resolutions." All the sanctions, according to the resolution, would remain in place until Iraq satisfied the UN that it had rid itself of all weapons of mass destruction. In fact, even that would not satisfy the United States. Deputy National Security adviser Robert M. Gates insisted that the United States would never vote to lift sanctions as long as Saddam Hussein ruled Iraq. "Iraqis will pay the price while he remains in power," said Gates. "All possible sanctions will be maintained until he is gone. Any easing of sanctions will be considered only when there is a new government."

But sanctions hurt ordinary Iraqis far more than it hurt Saddam Hussein and his lieutenants. Stories about crucial shortages of food-stuffs and medicines in Iraq troubled the conscience of American officials. Under American leadership, the Security Council passed a resolution six months after the war that would allow Iraq to sell oil under strict UN controls so long as the revenue paid for the imports of food and medicine. The oil payments would go directly into a UN account. Before releasing the funds for imports of food and medicine, the UN would deduct the costs of administering the program and would set aside some money for a fund to compensate Kuwait for its losses during the invasion. These controls would trample on the sovereignty of Iraq, of course, and were therefore tough for Saddam Hussein to take. Five months passed before Iraq even discussed the issue with the UN.

Annan led the UN negotiating team to a meeting with Iraqi officials in Vienna in January 1992. But he failed to persuade the Iraqis to accept the plan. After three days of talks, the Iraqis broke off negotiations, denouncing the UN conditions as "unnecessary and obtrusive." The Iraqis insisted there was no need for oil for food because there was no need for sanctions. After the failure of the first round of talks, Secretary-General Boutros-Ghali appointed another UN official to resume negotiations. But Annan would never escape the snares of the program. Iraq finally accepted the oil for food plan five years later, and the program with its odor of scandal would embitter the last years of his administration as secretary-general.

The early nineties was the best of times for a senior official like Kofi Annan to be noticed and used by the secretary-general. It was an illusion to believe that the Persian Gulf War demonstrated the new power of the United Nations. The war was fought in the name of the UN, but it was wrought and directed by the United States. During the war, Soviet ambassador to the UN Yuri Vorontsov was asked by a reporter at UN headquarters if it bothered him that the Pentagon was making all the decisions for a supposedly UN war. "Who are we to say they should not?" replied Vorontsov.

Yet Vorontsov was optimistic now about the future of the UN. He had served in the 1960s as a junior diplomat with the Soviet mission to the UN. The Security Council was a den of recriminations then. Nothing could get done. Now almost anything could be done as long as it was acceptable to the five permanent members of the Security Council, who had the power of veto—the United States, the Soviet Union, Britain, France, and China. The American-led Persian Gulf War was a poor model, but there were loads of crises throughout the world that could benefit from UN peacekeeping missions. Vorontsov felt fortunate to have this second chance at the UN.

The Security Council, in the words of Madeleine Albright, would soon become "an international 911 number." As Annan put it several years later, "The new consensus in the [Security] Council permitted agreement on operations that had not been possible. The Council was breaking new ground . . . It was thrilling, and we saw possibilities of doing perhaps, as somebody put it, what the organization was expected to do. So we were all excited." The exciting expansion of peacekeeping would use and test the talents of Kofi Annan.

4

In the Footsteps
of Ralph Bunche

M arrack Goulding was appointed undersecretary-general for special political affairs (as the office of peacekeeping operations was known then) in January 1986. That job had long been one of the most romantic, high-profile positions of the United Nations. Only Count Folke Bernadotte, the Swedish mediator assassinated by Jewish extremists in Palestine in 1948; the African American Ralph Bunche, who won the Nobel Peace Prize in 1950; and the British troubleshooter Brian Urquhart, a hero in UN lore for forty years, had held the job before.

The British government selected Goulding for the job. For many years, the secretaries general had tried to maintain good relations with the five permanent members of the Security Council by appointing at least one national from each country to a high post in the UN secretariat. As Urquhart neared retirement, British prime minister Margaret Thatcher asked Secretary-General Javier Pérez de Cuéllar several times to appoint a Briton whenever Urquhart left. Pérez de Cuéllar promised to do so and fulfilled the promise by appointing Goulding, the diplomat proposed by the British.

Goulding, then fifty years old, was a veteran diplomat in the British foreign service. He was the British ambassador to Angola when Pérez de Cuéllar announced his appointment as undersecretary-general. Goulding had served earlier as a member of the British mission to the UN, and he had worked closely with Pérez de Cuéllar in 1982 when the United States and the UN tried in vain to broker a deal between Britain and Argentina that would avert the Falklands War. Goulding also had had a taste of London parliamentary life, serving as private secretary to three ministers of state for foreign and commonwealth affairs during the early 1970s. It would be easy to mistake the distinguished Goulding for a professor, and when he retired from the UN a decade later, he would assume the post of warden of St. Antony's College at Oxford University.

Goulding feared that his appointment as undersecretary-general would be resented by his new colleagues. They would look on him as he put it in his memoirs, as "almost an upstart, inserted by a major power at a young age into a prestigious post which the bureaucracy would have preferred to see occupied by one of its own." In fact, most UN bureaucrats accepted as a fact of life that plum jobs went to favored outsiders. It was obvious from the start, in any case, that Goulding was no slacker. He worked extremely hard for long hours. He also liked to fly out to visit the peacekeeping operations so he could understand their problems firsthand. He was forced to curtail some of the travel later and remain at his desk in New York for longer periods only because Boutros Boutros-Ghali, who took over as secretary-general in 1992, decided to cut costs by eliminating some of the trips by his senior staff. Boutros-Ghali denigrated the trips as "promenades" and said that undersecretaries-general should spend more time running their departments.

Running the department became ever more difficult as peacekeeping expanded. In 1986, the UN had five peacekeeping operations with ten thousand troops. By the beginning of 1993 that had grown to thirteen operations with fifty-five thousand troops. Yet, when the Indian novelist Shashi Tharoor joined the peacekeeping office in 1989, Goulding was running the operation with only six professionals and three military officers to help him. "We were expanding all over the place," says Tharoor. "In 1990, peacekeeping was still manageable. In 1991, we were all under stress." Aside from needing more staff, Goulding decided he needed a deputy as well. "I found that I could not cope alone," says Goulding.

When rumors spread that the job might be created, Kofi decided to try for it. "He was keen on it," says Virendra Dayal, who was Pérez de Cuéllar's chief of staff. The position was far different from any Kofi had held before. The new job, as Dayal put it, meant long hours and broad shoulders—the new deputy would face the possibility of making harmful mistakes and feeling responsible for failure. Pérez de Cuéllar soon knew that Annan was interested. "I think Kofi recommended himself," says Dayal.

But Goulding did not have Kofi Annan in mind. In a meeting with Pérez de Cuéllar, Goulding proposed that the Field Operations Division, a separate unit that provided peacekeeping missions with personnel and logistical support, become part of the peacekeeping office and that its Iranian director, Behrooz Sadry, move to peacekeeping as deputy director. The secretary-general rejected the proposal to combine the offices but agreed that Goulding needed a deputy. Pérez de Cuéllar suggested Kofi Annan for the job instead of Sadry. Annan, as Goulding wrote, had filled several senior posts in administration and management and thus possessed "experience and skills that were sorely needed in my department." So though Annan was not his first choice, Goulding says, "I had absolutely no hesitation about accepting him."

Pérez de Cuéllar, however, was nearing the end of his administration, and the actual appointment of Annan was made by the new secretary-general, Boutros-Ghali, in February 1992. When Annan came aboard, Goulding regarded him as "a long-desired reinforcement." Most outsiders assumed that Annan would serve solely as manager of the office, freeing Goulding for policymaking and, whenever Boutros-Ghali acquiesced, for travel in the field. But there were too many missions now for Goulding to lay his hands on all of

them. So he decided to divide policymaking and mission super-
vision with Annan, giving his deputy responsibility for peacekeeping operations in the Middle East and most of Africa.

The division of the world led to difficulties. As a manager,
Annan believed in delegating authority. He assumed that Goulding
was doing just that. Since Somalia was in his bailiwick, for example,
he assumed he had full authority to do whatever was needed. But
Goulding had other ideas. As chief of peacekeeping, he wanted full
and final authority on all missions.

"There were some difficulties after he became my deputy," said
Goulding. "We agreed that we would split the world. He would do
Africa and the Middle East and I would do Asia, Europe, and Latin
America. He assumed that he had full authority in his regions and
that there was no need to consult me. But Boutros-Ghali expected
heads of department in the Secretariat to be fully informed about
all the work of their departments and it was me, not Kofi, whom he
consulted. And this meant that Kofi had to keep me fully informed
about Africa and the Middle East. He had thought he had full
authority in his regions. I thought I had full authority throughout
the department. He was not comfortable with that. I tried to remain
on friendly terms with him but I felt that he wanted to create a fief-
dom of his own. That was when things began to deteriorate."

But Annan insists there was no tension between the two. "No, I
didn't have problems working with Goulding because I'm not one
of those who has problems working with colleagues or with other
people," he told me recently. "We had a division of work, and it
worked quite well. Our approaches may have been different, but we
worked well together." Kofi, however, often tries to see events in the
best light, and there is little doubt that Goulding resented what he
regarded as overreaching by his deputy.

There were problems in planning for Somalia, and these
reflected the difference in approach of the two. Somalia was in turmoil then, with two warlords fighting for control of the capital,
Mogadishu. A small group of UN peacekeepers—fewer than five
hundred—tried to patrol a supposed cease-fire line that the two

heavily armed militias constantly violated while attacking each other. The ineffectual Blue Helmets could not stop them.

Goulding had originally opposed sending any Blue Helmets there because the mission in Somalia differed so much from the traditional role of peacekeepers. UN peacekeepers would normally enter an area only after the belligerents had reached some form of peace agreement. Peacekeepers would patrol cease-fire lines and act as a neutral buffer between both sides. They would not use weapons except in self-defense. The UN had strayed from this model in the early 1960s, when Blue Helmets quashed the rebellious province of Katanga in the Congo. Historians, however, looked on that experience as disastrous. Goulding agreed with them. Peacekeepers, in his view, could have no real role in Somalia because there was no peace to keep.

But Annan felt differently. Caught in the upbeat UN mood after the Persian Gulf War, Annan believed it was worth bending the rules to save many African lives. The UN could not ignore such an impending disaster. Goulding gave in when his boss, Boutros-Ghali, joined his deputy in pressuring for some kind of mission to Somalia. "I found myself confronting a steamroller that would not be stopped," Goulding wrote a few years later. American ambassador Thomas R. Pickering and other members of the Security Council had the same misgivings as Goulding. "All of us recognized we were taking a big risk," says Pickering. "We all had doubts. But we were working in an atmosphere of euphoria and that tended to hide some of the issues." So the Security Council approved the dispatch of a small number of peacekeepers. But the limited UN operation did not accomplish much.

The chaos caused widespread starvation, and relief organizations had to dodge armed raiders to bring food to the hungry. Distribution was dangerous and difficult. Food could get through only if the relief organizations paid handsome sums of money to armed protectors. The raiders and protectors were often the same. A UN report called Somalia "a human disaster of appalling magnitude" and "a nightmare of bloodshed and brutality." Boutros-Ghali accused the Security Council, which was preoccupied with events in

Croatia and Bosnia, of "fighting a rich man's war in Yugoslavia while not lifting a finger to save Somalia from disintegration." Images of emaciated black children with skull-like faces filled American television screens. Officials of the U.S. Agency for International Development added their cries of distress.

As a kind of last hurrah, President George H. W. Bush, who had been defeated for reelection by Bill Clinton in the November 1992 election, ordered American Marines into Somalia to save the starving. He did so under the authority of a Security Council resolution of December 3 that called on governments to dispatch troops "to establish a secure environment for humanitarian relief operations in Somalia as soon as possible." Those words would provoke a bitter battle between Boutros-Ghali and the United States for several months.

Boutros-Ghali expected the troops from the United States and its allies to do far more than deliver food. Washington, on the other hand, wanted to get out as soon as possible. In a speech announcing his dispatch of troops, President Bush said, "Our mission has a limited objective, to open the supply routes, to get the food moving, and to prepare the way for a UN peacekeeping force to keep it moving. . . . We will not stay one day longer than is absolutely necessary." Washington insisted that the UN assemble a peacekeeping force swiftly to replace the troops of the United States and its allies. But Boutros-Ghali protested that the UN could not take over until the American-led forces had created the "inescapable condition" of "a secure environment." This could be done, according to the secretary-general, only if the American-led forces disarmed the warlords. If the United States was unable to create a secure environment, the UN could not be expected to do so.

But Boutros-Ghali's pleas were dismissed. Assistant Secretary of State John Bolton (who would be named UN ambassador by President George W. Bush in a contemptuous appointment more than a decade later) accused Boutros-Ghali of trying to move the goal posts after the game had started. The United States contended that it never had any intent to disarm anyone; the marines had landed in

Somalia to make sure that the food was delivered. The Somalis were encouraged to turn in their heavy weapons, but the most dangerous warlord, Muhammad Farah Aideed, refused to do so. The American troops disarmed any Somalis who tried to interfere with food distribution. But the marines did not attempt to confiscate any heavy weapons that had been set aside or hidden. Logic was on the side of Boutros-Ghali, but he had no power to make the United States do what it did not want to do.

The Clinton administration took office in January 1993 but did not reverse the Bush administration's position. The Pentagon applied continual pressure for the UN to take over so that the American troops could come home. As the official responsible for Somalia, Kofi Annan worked with the Pentagon during this period. Despite Washington's insistence, Annan refused to believe that the Americans would forgo disarmament altogether. With his innate optimism and almost naive trust in the goodwill of Americans, Annan hoped that the Americans could be persuaded to engage in "more aggressive" disarmament once the troops reached full strength. Yet, even in January, when there were 25,400 U.S. marines and 12,900 troops from other countries in Somalia, the force did no more disarmament than was necessary to let the food through. Boutros-Ghaili shared Annan's optimism and delayed forming a UN force as much as possible, hoping for an American change of heart. But there was no change of heart.

Goulding was now even more opposed to sending Blue Helmets into Somalia on a peace enforcement mission. U.S. military officers who dealt with the UN on Somalia found Goulding rigid on the issue, but Kofi Annan, one officer told me, "is more flexible than Goulding about a new role for the peacekeepers." Perhaps that was a matter of style more than substance. Goulding told James Traub of the *New York Times* a few years later that Annan never expressed his doubts about policy "nearly as vociferously" as Goulding. "It wouldn't come naturally to him to express strongly dissenting views about what the Security Council wanted to do," Goulding said.

In any case, Secretary-General Boutros-Ghali could not delay forever. He had to follow the dictates of the Security Council and dispatch a peacekeeping mission to Somalia. Madeleine Albright, the new UN ambassador, was under pressure from the Clinton administration's National Security Council in Washington to make sure this happened. "The NSC was relentless, calling me nearly every day to ask, 'What's taking so long?'" she wrote in her memoirs. "New on the job and eager to earn my place as a full member of our foreign policy team, I told the secretary-general he had no choice, U.S. troops would leave whether the UN was prepared to take their place or not." Boutros-Ghali gave in but told Albright in a confidential letter that he was "uneasy" over the gap between the strength of the departing American-led task force and his own weak peacekeepers. "You would agree with me," he wrote, "that this transfer is taking place under less than ideal circumstances." Boutros-Ghali still did not act fast enough for Washington. The American mission left before the first UN troops arrived in May 1993.

Despite the addition of Annan as deputy, the peacekeeping office still operated in an atmosphere of chaos. "Goulding was a brilliant, highly competent workaholic," says Tharoor. "He was hands on. Everyone reported to Goulding, not to the deputy. Goulding wouldn't sign a cable unless he checked every comma and improved the drafting. This went on for a year, and it was crazy. Goulding was working every night until 11:00 P.M. He was beginning to collapse under this."

In mid-February 1993, Boutros-Ghali called Goulding and Annan separately to his offices on the thirty-eighth floor. Boutros-Ghali was good-humored but blunt. "You are always telling me, Goulding," he said, "that we can't do this and we can't do that because that's not the way we do peacekeeping in the United Nations." Goulding was a traditionalist, always insisting that the UN could mount a peacekeeping mission only when conditions were right for it. Boutros-Ghali, on the other hand, wanted the Security Council to dispatch peacekeepers more easily. He looked on Goulding's rigid conditions as details that could be ironed out later.

Boutros-Ghali told Goulding that it would be best for him to switch back to the department of political affairs. He would now be undersecretary-general of political affairs. He would be charged with "preventive diplomacy"—the arduous and amorphous art of preventing war before it got started—and with analyses of the political situation in countries where peacekeepers operated. His deputy, Kofi Annan, would step up now and take over as chief of peacekeeping. One reason for the change, Boutros-Ghali wrote later in a memoir, "was to strengthen Africa's presence in the higher echelons of the United Nations." Goulding did not want to give up peacekeeping, but he knew it was pointless to argue. Boutros-Ghali was a stubborn secretary-general.

Annan said he had not heard about the change at all until he walked into the secretary-general's office. "I had not expected the changes that took place," he said. "So it was a surprise when the secretary-general asked me to take that on."

When Goulding returned to his own office, he was shaken. His eyes were red-rimmed. "I've been fired," he told Tharoor. When Tharoor pointed out that Boutros-Ghali had assigned him to a major position at the UN, Goulding replied that peacekeeping was "the job I really wanted to do."

There has long been speculation at the UN that the Pentagon pressured Boutros-Ghali into making the change. But Goulding does not believe this is true. "I did not see an American hand in pushing Kofi Annan into the top job at the department of peacekeeping operations," he says. But there is no doubt the Americans were pleased with the result. Goulding believes they looked on Annan as "a malleable kind of guy." "They recognized," Goulding says, "that he would be amenable to American ideas of peacekeeping."

When the fifty-four-year-old Annan returned to the peacekeeping office, Tharoor asked him if the promotion also meant he had been elevated to the rank of undersecretary-general. Annan nodded. It had taken him more than thirty years, but he had climbed from P-1, the lowest rank in the UN civil service, to the highest.

Moreover, his new post had the highest of profiles. He would now deal with worldwide peace and security every day—the issues for which the UN was created by visionaries at the end of World War II. No one else from the Third World had ever held the post. The others were all European or American. He would walk now in the footsteps of that great black hero Ralph Bunche.

Although Washington was, indeed, pleased with the promotion, it was less well received within the peacekeeping office. "There's no way Kofi Annan can cope," said one official there. "Goulding is peacekeeping."

5

Peacekeeping

As undersecretary-general in charge of the department of peacekeeping operations, Kofi Annan presided over the most spectacular rise in peacekeeping in UN history and over its most spectacular fall. In 1986, when Marrack Goulding joined the UN hierarchy, there were five peacekeeping operations in the field with ten thousand soldiers and police. By 1994, the second year of Annan's tenure as peacekeeping chief, the UN deployed more than seventy-five thousand Blue Helmets and Blue Berets throughout the world. From 1992 to 1996, Annan would supervise peacekeeping operations in Egypt, Kashmir, Lebanon, Cyprus, the Golan Heights, the Iraq-Kuwait border, Angola, El Salvador, Western Sahara, Cambodia, Somalia, Mozambique, Rwanda, Georgia, Liberia, Haiti, the Chad-Libya border, Tajikistan, and Guatemala. The rapid deployments heightened the frustration of his predecessor. "Although pleased at first to be relieved of a burden that had become almost intolerable," Goulding wrote in his memoirs, "I watched with envy as Kofi Annan took charge of peacekeeping and launched six new operations in his first eight months in the job."

But there were striking failures as well during Annan's watch—in Somalia, Rwanda, and Bosnia—and these failures would lead both to a rash of UN-bashing in the United States and to a realization of the limits of UN peacekeeping. The Security Council may have become, as Madeleine Albright put it, an international 911 number, but it never responded with any alacrity. Secretary-General Boutros Boutros-Ghali did not have anything like a French Foreign Legion to send into battle. The United States and the rest of the Big Five felt that a military force would infuse a secretary-general with far more power than the position required or deserved. Instead, Annan, as chief of peacekeeping, had to cajole governments into contributing troops and then had to find weapons and transport for those Third World troops who showed up without equipment. Despite his affable and persuasive charm, Annan did not always succeed.

"If the world wants the United Nations to serve occasionally as a fire brigade," Shashi Tharoor, who was a special assistant to Annan, said during this era, "it will have to do better than the present system, under which the fire breaks out, the aldermen on the Security Council agree it needs to be put out, and the fire chief is then sent out to hire firemen, rent fire trucks, find hoses of the right length, and look for sources of water to put into them."

By all accounts, Annan ran the department of peacekeeping with efficiency, thoughtfulness, and, despite his understated manner, a dash of flair. He had a talent for selecting intelligent, well-informed, and enthusiastic lieutenants and allowing them full rein to speak out and to manage their overseas operations without his meddling and double-checking. He did not follow the lead of Goulding and peruse every comma. His friends like to talk about Annan's inner wholeness and self-confidence. This enabled him to feel no threat when subordinates shined in his presence. In fact, this virtue may have created problems for him in later years when some critics complained that he gave his aides too much leeway and supported them steadfastly even when they no longer merited support.

Fred Eckhard was assigned during these days to brief the press about peacekeeping at the daily news sessions of Joe Sills, the spokesman of Secretary-General Boutros Boutros-Ghali. To ensure that Eckhard knew what he was talking about, Annan allowed him to attend his morning meetings with the directors of the various regional operations. Staff meetings often waste a good deal of bureaucratic time, but Eckhard found these sessions lively, eventful, and substantive.

The special quality of these meetings was underscored in late 1995 when Boutros-Ghali sent Annan to Bosnia for five months and temporarily replaced him as chief of peacekeeping with Ismat Kittani, a Kurd with a long career in both the Iraqi foreign service and the UN Secretariat. "The staff meetings then went down the drain," says Eckhard. "These competitive, bright, eager directors started to snipe at each other or else shut up. They didn't have to show off for Kofi Annan. On the other hand, when Kofi came back, they all snapped back to attention. That was when I got a sense of his natural ability to lead."

Despite a time of general cost cutting at the UN, Annan persuaded the budgeteers that an expansion of peacekeeping overseas demanded an expansion of peacekeeping managers in New York. In one essential and long-needed innovation, he set up a twenty-four-hour crisis center, ensuring that his staff could deal with problems overseas whenever they occurred and that commanders in different time zones in the field did not have to wait hours for replies to their questions. He corrected one long-time foolish problem by taking over the UN's field operations division and tucking it into the department of peacekeeping. Before then, field operations, which supplied the logistics for peacekeeping missions, was an independent division outside the control of the peacekeeping chief. The peacekeeping staff in New York, which once numbered only a dozen, grew to four hundred under Annan.

Although he was quoted in the news from time to time, Annan did not have a high public profile in those days. Boutros-Ghali ran a centralized UN, leaving little room for his top lieutenants to shine. He did not let an undersecretary-general like Annan brief the Security Council on his own. Boutros-Ghali appointed Chinmaya

Gharekhan, a former Indian ambassador to the UN, to serve as his liaison with the Security Council. Almost all information for the council was filtered through Gharekhan or Boutros-Ghali himself. Instead of sending Annan to brief the Security Council on peace-keeping matters, he ordered Annan to brief Gharekhan who would then relay the information to the fifteen ambassadors on the Security Council. That helped explain why Annan was barely noticed when the Somali mission exploded and American politicians were looking for someone to blame.

The UN peacekeeping mission to Somalia—officially known as the UN Operation in Somalia (UNISOM)—was tailor-made to American specifications. This did not bother Boutros-Ghali and Annan, for they never wanted the United States to leave Somalia anyway. They welcomed all the American participation in the UN mission that was offered. Although the mission had been planned during the last days of the Bush administration, it was embraced eagerly by the Clinton administration. Madeleine Albright, the American ambassador to the UN, looked on it as a model for what she called the new administration's policy of "assertive multilateralism." By this she seemed to mean a process in which Americans created and led effective coalitions at the United Nations.

Boutros-Ghali stacked the hierarchy of the mission with American choices. He picked U.S. rear admiral Jonathon T. Howe as his special representative—the civilian in overall command of the mission. Howe, President Bush's deputy National Security adviser, had helped the incoming Clinton administration appointees in the transition at the White House. He impressed Anthony Lake, Clinton's National Security adviser, so much that Lake recommended him for the Somalia job. Boutros-Ghali named Lieutenant General Cevik Bir of Turkey, well known to Americans within NATO, as military commander, with Major General Thomas M. Montgomery of the U.S. Army as deputy commander.

The American troops in the mission—three thousand assigned to logistics and a quick-reaction force of thirteen hundred—reported directly to General Montgomery rather than General Bir.

There were twenty-five thousand troops from other countries, the largest numbers coming from Pakistan, India, Italy, Germany, Morocco, and France. Following normal UN procedure, they reported to General Bir. Later, the United States assigned four hundred rangers and Delta Force commandos to the mission. They did not even report to General Montgomery. Instead, they served under the direct orders of the U.S. Central Command in Tampa, Florida. The UN was often kept in the dark about the activities of these special forces.

The mission deteriorated into a feud between Admiral Howe and the worst of the warlords, Muhammad Farah Aideed. A month after the UN arrived, a battle between Aideed's militia and the UN left twenty-five Pakistani peacekeepers dead. Armed with a new resolution from the Security Council, Howe unleashed a manhunt for Aideed and called for the rangers and Delta Force commandos to help him. He even announced a $25,000 bounty for the capture of Aideed. American ambassador Albright supported the manhunt with enthusiasm. "For Somalia's sake, and ours, we must persevere," she wrote on the op-ed page of the *New York Times*. But as casualties mounted, including the deaths of a few American soldiers, the Clinton administration began to have misgivings.

The misgivings sowed confusion and missteps. In September, Secretary of State Warren Christopher urged Boutros-Ghali to change course. Christopher proposed a cease-fire in Mogadishu, political talks with Aideed's faction, and a scheme for the leaders of Ethiopia and Eritrea to persuade Aideed to go into exile. Boutros-Ghali doubted that the exile scheme could work and repeated his view that "our efforts to restore peace and prosperity in Somalia will not succeed unless we can disarm the clans and factions." He did not order a cease-fire but instructed Admiral Howe to put together an interim Somali government that would include representatives from Aideed's subclan.

Despite Boutros-Ghali's reluctance to end the manhunt for Aideed, Washington soon made it clear in public that the manhunt should be called off. President Clinton urged the UN to focus on "a political strategy" in Somalia. An administration official told reporters that the United States no longer insisted on the capture of Aideed. "We must not personalize the issue," he said. "There is a larger issue than this person. Ultimately, the solution has to be a political solution."

The White House, of course, could have ended the manhunt anytime it wanted, for the main troops assigned to capture Aideed were Americans under American command. But the White House never got the word to Major General William F. Garrison, the commander of the American rangers and commandos in Somalia. Just four days after the change of policy was announced in Washington, General Garrison, who reported directly to the U.S. Central Command in Tampa and not to the UN, sent a fleet of Black Hawk helicopters to sweep down on a building in southern Mogadishu and unload scores of commandos and rangers. They captured twenty-four lieutenants of Aideed, two so high-ranking that General Garrison hoped they would soon supply enough information to find the hiding places of Aideed.

But the mission swiftly fell apart. The images of the events of October 3 and 4 in 1993, played vividly on television screens worldwide, would be reinforced later by Mark Bowden's best-selling book *Black Hawk Down* and the Hollywood movie based on it. Before the Americans could leave the area, hundreds of Aideed's militiamen rushed to the scene and shot down two American helicopters. The other Delta Force commandos and rangers formed a perimeter to protect their fallen comrades, and a battle raged all night until the U.S. quick-reaction force fought its way through and rescued the commandos and rangers. The battle left eighteen Americans dead and eighty-four wounded. More than a thousand Somalis were killed or wounded. The American humiliation was displayed on television with scenes of Somalis dragging an American body through the streets and of a terrified American pilot in the hands of Somali captors.

The reaction from the Clinton administration was shameless. Like frightened children, American officials tried to put all the blame on someone else. Officials acted as if they had no idea that the Americans had been engaged in enforcement. The UN mission in Somalia did not even know that the ill-fated American raid was going to take place, but Clinton aides still pointed their fingers at Boutros-Ghali and the UN. Pentagon spokeswoman Katherine de Laski insisted publicly that the raid was a UN operation. In a televised speech to the nation, President Clinton promised an American withdrawal from Somalia in five months. He announced the deployment of new American troops to help the withdrawal and pledged that these new American troops "will be under American command." This, of course, left the false impression that the troops already there were not under American command. Newspaper editorialists picked up the White House theme and heaped scorn on Boutros-Ghali and the UN for the death of the Americans.

The UN reacted feebly to the Washington onslaught. Boutros-Ghali, a professor and a diplomat for many years, was too old-fashioned and courtly to master the bombast of American public relations. Ahmad Fawzi, the deputy press spokesman, recalls calling on Boutros-Ghali in his office the next morning. "I begged him to let us say the truth about what happened," says Fawzi, "that this was an attack that the UN knew nothing about until it went wrong, that it was being coordinated from Tampa, Florida, by Central Command."

"No, you cannot do that," Boutros-Ghali said.

"Why not?" asked Fawzi. ""Why do we always have to be blamed when things go wrong?"

"Because we are here to serve the member states," Boutros-Ghali replied. "You cannot go out and blame a member state for an operation that goes wrong. I forbid you from doing that."

"I was so dejected," recalls Fawzi. "I went downstairs, and we had to keep quiet."

Boutros-Ghali said nothing publicly for more than a week. Annan, on the other hand, did assign his chief military adviser, General Maurice Baril of Canada, to brief reporters a day after the shocking events in Mogadishu. But Baril was so cautious that he played into the hands of the Washington spinners. Asked under whose orders the raid had been mounted, Baril refused to say, reply-ing only that the rangers and Delta commandos were committed to act "within the overall aim of the mandate of the UN." With that meaningless reply, the UN lost a chance to expose the hypocrisy of Washington.

Boutros-Ghali's first public statement came a week later in an odd way. Instead of holding a news conference, he called a few cor-respondents, including myself, to his office and in somewhat ellipti-cal and diplomatic phrasing told us that he had helped President Clinton by serving as the scapegoat in the Somalia debacle. More-over, he said, serving as a scapegoat was an obligation for the UN and its secretary-general. "I don't want to provoke the member states," he said. "I need the member states . . . I must help the mem-ber states so that they will be able to help me. If the member states need the United Nations to overcome certain internal problems, the United Nations must accept." But, he added quietly and propheti-cally, "it can be dangerous for the United Nations."

Although Kofi Annan was the head of UN peacekeeping, he escaped the vituperation of the critics. It all descended on Boutros-Ghali. Yet the Somalia debacle impacted his career in three ways. First of all, it drove home to him the limits to American participa-tion in peacekeeping and deepened his sense of caution. There was so much American talk about the dangers of "mission creep" and "crossing the Mogadishu line" that Annan knew UN peacekeeping must operate under strict limits from then on.

Second, the outcry over Somalia unleashed a mood of UN-bashing in the United States that would linger and then intensify throughout the rest of Annan's career. Started unfairly by a Democ-ratic president who professed a commitment to the United Nations, the bashing would grow far worse under a Republican who had contempt for the UN.

Finally, the Somalia troubles led to the discovery of Annan by the news correspondents covering the UN. Peacekeeping, which had once seemed routine and even humdrum, was now controversial. Reporters had lots of questions. Boutros-Ghali did not talk with reporters often and, when he did, his replies, while thoughtful and founded on logic and deep knowledge of world affairs, were not altogether clear. But Kofi Annan, when he had the time, replied with clarity, thoughtfulness, and an astounding honesty. He often replied, in fact, even when he knew his words might embarrass the UN or might annoy some government. On those occasions he would smile, hesitate, mull over his thoughts, raise his eyebrows, and then forge ahead with an honesty rare in public life. He did not turn into a media celebrity of any kind. He was quoted only occasionally. He did not hold news conferences. But many correspondents began to realize that he was a remarkable international civil servant.

British author William Shawcross met Annan in 1993 when the peacekeeping chief was visiting the mission in Zagreb, Croatia. "When I first met him," Shawcross wrote to me years later, "... I was astonished by him. He just seemed so completely unlike any official of any organization that I had ever met—so much more dignified, so much more judicious, so much nicer. I just determined to spend as much time as I could following his work." The result, seven years later, was the Shawcross book *Deliver Us from Evil*—surely the most lucid and insightful account of UN peacekeeping yet written.

My own discovery came at a conference on humanitarian aid at Princeton University attended by UN officials, diplomats, relief workers, scholars, and reporters. The conference was held a few weeks after President Clinton's decision to withdraw from Somalia, and I was surprised at Annan's ease, confidence, and frankness as he expressed his disappointment with the United States. Clinton had just sent a letter to thirty heads of state and government asking for troops to replace the departing Americans. With a touch of irony, Annan told the conference, "Other presidents and prime ministers are going to have difficulty explaining to their people that the American president is removing his troops because it is too danger-ous but is encouraging them to send their own troops."

Annan insisted that the American withdrawal would cripple the distribution of humanitarian aid in Somalia and "bring us back to the chaos of before." Some governments had urged the UN to distribute food without the help of military force. But "the reality," Annan said, "is that there are situations when you cannot assist people unless you are prepared to take certain measures." But what could the UN do if its member states would not supply troops? Without military forces to protect them, relief workers would have to talk their way past stubborn Somali warlords. Yet Annan, in the face of the American withdrawal, despaired of the UN having the strength to protect relief convoys in the future.

"The cry 'Bring the boys home' did not come from a weak army," he said. "It came from the strongest army in the world. . . . We are now at a crossroads. I don't have the answers. As long as countries are not prepared to take risks, to take casualties, then we have to negotiate our way through. It's not effective, but we have little choice." He spoke without rancor, but his words were the clearest public repudiation of the American position that came from the UN during the Somali crisis. And it came not from the arrogant and professorial Secretary-General Boutros Boutros-Ghali but from a quiet undersecretary-general whom everyone, including the Americans, liked.

Annan's frankness increased as time went on. Susan Linnee, the AP foreign correspondent who has known Annan since college days in Minnesota, picked up *Le Monde* in Paris almost a year later and was surprised to read a front-page article quoting him. She was even more surprised at the sharpness of his tone. She had always regarded Annan as reserved in public. But Bassir Pour Afsane, the *Le Monde* correspondent, caught him at a moment of disappointment and frustration. He had just met with diplomats from forty-two countries to ask them to send troops to a peacekeeping mission in Rwanda. Only one country, his own Ghana, had agreed. The other African governments, he told Afsane, "probably need their armies to intimidate their own populations." Nothing as true or as undiplomatic had been said openly about Africa in the corridors of the UN for a long time.

Despite the prominence of that article in Paris, Kofi Annan was hardly the voice of the UN. Attention always centered on Boutros

Boutros-Ghali. Asked how Annan attempted to explain the peace-keeping failures in Somalia and Rwanda in those days, Fred Eckhard told an interviewer for the Yale-UN Oral History Project in 2005, "Well, it wasn't for him to explain; it was for Boutros-Ghali and Boutros-Ghali's spokesmen to explain these missions, their failures.

"Boutros-Ghali did not want Kofi Annan to have a high media profile," Eckhard went on. ". . . My sense is that Kofi Annan was basically told to stay at his desk and do his job. To the extent he did deal with the media, he has a very likable trait, that if you ask him a question, he answers that question, maybe not as fully as you would like, but you always sense that he is trying to give you the information that you are asking for. He also as a person, not just with journalists but with everyone, remembers little details about you, the fact that you have two children and maybe even your wife's name and with journalists he would add that personal touch, so that journalists liked him."

In June 1994, the *Los Angeles Times*, at my suggestion, published a lengthy interview of him as part of a regular Sunday series. These articles, each covering seven-eighths of a full page in the editorial section, would feature an important newsmaker, offering a fresh photo portrait, a few paragraphs of introduction, and an extensive transcript of questions and answers. The only other newsmakers with UN affiliations in the series during my years at the UN were Secretary-General Boutros-Ghali and Madeleine Albright, the American ambassador to the UN. The selection of Annan for the series reflected the editors' recognition of the significance of UN peacekeeping.

I joined Annan for the session in his spacious office on the thirty-seventh floor, one floor below that of the secretary-general. The room was decorated with select pieces of African sculpture, mainly from the Ivory Coast and Senegal. He spoke barely above a whisper, but it was worth straining to hear each word, for he covered the problems and status of peacekeeping with significant detail and insight. There was no attempt to posture and spin and make peacekeeping seem more successful than it was. He did not speak in sound bites but in careful, modulated, complex sentences. His manner was calm and self-confident and polite. The interview, I think, was a faithful summary of his views on peacekeeping after less than a couple of years on the job.

"Yes, we are encountering considerable difficulties in finding well-trained and equipped troops for the assignments that the [Security] Council has given us," he said. "This is partly due to perceived dangers the governments see associated with these operations, which are supposed to be peacekeeping but . . . where there's really no peace to keep. . . .

"I think that, as hesitant as everybody is about going in, nobody says don't do anything. And yet, when you turn around and ask, 'How many troops would you give?'—each one is prepared to volunteer the other person's army, the other country's army, and, if necessary, to make some financial contribution. It's a problem that we need to try and resolve quickly."

Asked if American reluctance was hurting peacekeeping, he replied, "I think the role and the attitude of the U.S. always has an effect. It has a leadership role. It is the only superpower now. . . . You saw in Somalia—when the United States went in, lots of other governments followed. In the Gulf, when the U.S. led, lots of others followed. In Somalia, when the U.S. left, they left, too.

"So when the country with that dominant role and position takes a backseat and begins to hold back, it has an impact on the attitude of other nations. But that having been said, nobody would disagree . . . when they [the Americans] say there should be some guidelines for the [Security] Council to determine when they take on a crisis and when they do not—provided it's applied in a flexible and practical manner."

Annan acknowledged that the UN had made a crucial error in Somalia. "I think one of the errors was perhaps the decision to attempt to arrest Aideed," he said. ". . . If you are perceived to be fair, you do not run the danger of being engaged. If you are seen as taking initiatives that could change the military balance on the ground and favor one group or the other, the troops who see themselves as disadvantaged might decide you've taken sides and declare war on you. And this is what happened."

As a result of the Somalia experience, he said, "all of us are going through a certain reality therapy." "I don't think the member states have a stomach for this type of operation," he said. "I think it's going to be a very long time before the UN as an organization takes on a peace enforcement mission and manages it itself. My sense is that if there is going to be another enforcement mission, that it's likely to be the Desert Storm model where the Security Council would authorize a group of member states to take all necessary means to correct or redress a situation."

Annan's comments to me and other correspondents at this time revealed a cautious, practical, thoughtful man. He did not brim with great ideas or grand plans. That was the department of Secretary-General Boutros-Ghali and the ambassadors on the Security Council. Annan's job was to try to implement their policies. In his transparent way, Annan described the problems of carrying out the policies. He was not a man enamored of his own concepts. He was the nuts-and-bolts man who told the public what worked and what did not work. He did not gild or hold back.

Critics would say later that caution and lack of imagination contributed to the UN failures in Rwanda and Bosnia, and they would hold Annan responsible at least in part for failing to prevent massacres in both missions. There is no doubt that the terrible troubles there created the most anguish on Annan's watch as chief of UN peacekeeping.

6

The Stain of Rwanda

There are naysayers who have contempt for Kofi Annan because they believe he has the blood of Rwanda on his hands. Their disdain has not diminished over the years. They opposed his election to a second term as secretary-general and his award of a Nobel Peace Prize, and they continually demanded that he resign.

Nat Hentoff, a columnist who often fights for civil rights causes, called it a "plain fact" in 2001 that "it was Mr. Annan, when he was head of the United Nations peacekeeping office, who could have prevented the slaughter of 800,000 Tutus and their sympathizers in Rwanda in 1994." A group of Rwandan survivors wrote Annan in 1998 that he bore "a heavy responsibility" for the awful massacres. A petition, organized by two Danish researchers, denounced Annan in 2001 for having "gravely failed the victims."

The most telling and subtle criticism has come from Philip Gourevitch, now editor of the *Paris Review*, who has written several articles in the prestigious *New Yorker* that target Annan as a villain in the crisis. Gourevitch faults Annan for failing to raise the alarm when a cable from the UN military commander on the scene warned him of impending genocide of the Tutsis in Rwanda. Gourevitch dismisses the argument that it would not have mattered anyway since the cowardly Security Council led by the United States would not have done anything. "Even if Annan's decision to keep his force commander's warnings to himself did no measurable harm—and that is a big, and unprovable, if—the fact remains that not doing wrong is a far cry from doing the right thing," wrote Gourevitch in a 2003 *New Yorker* article. "[W]hat are we to make of Annan's certainty that it would have been pointless to raise the alarm months earlier? How can he know when he didn't even try?"

There is no doubt that Kofi Annan lives with guilt over Rwanda. As Juan Antonio Yañez-Barnuevo, the Spanish ambassador to the UN, who sat on the Security Council during the Rwanda crisis, put it recently, "The Rwanda experience affected him deeply. That cable should have been brought to the attention of the whole Council—though I am not sure what, if anything, the Council would have done. Whenever he speaks about genocide now, he gets very emotional. He feels the Rwanda experience very strongly, and he feels it with guilt." Yañez-Barnuevo spoke these words with understanding, not contempt.

Annan himself has accepted the finding of an independent commission that his peacekeeping office and the rest of the UN—as well as the governments on the Security Council—failed during the crisis. Thoughts of this failure are continually on his mind. He told an interviewer for the PBS television program *Frontline* in 2004, "It was a very painful and traumatic experience, for me personally, and I think, in some way, for the United Nations. It's not something that you forget. It's an experience that, if you go through, becomes part of you, and part of your whole experience as a human being."

And yet the guilt and blame must be put into perspective. The genocide of Rwanda was not a simple matter of good versus evil. The issues and the history were confusing and complex, and so was the culture of the United Nations that made it so ineffectual in so dire a crisis. There is much blame to go around. Even the Tutsi soldiers who were fighting to save the Tutsi people are not blameless.

Kofi Annan may have some guilt on his hands, but there are players far more culpable than he, including the U.S. government.

Blessed by a land of verdant, cool hills and great beauty, both Rwanda and its neighbor Burundi have been cursed by history. More than four centuries ago, the Tutsi cattle grazers came down from the north and subjugated the far more numerous Hutu farmers of the two countries. A feudal system developed in which the Tutsi lords ruled the Hutu peasants under a Tutsi king or *mwami* in each country. There were sharp physical differences: the Tutsis were tall with thin nostrils and Hamitic-like features, while the Hutus were short with more of what are regarded as Negroid features, such as thick lips and broad nostrils.

By the late twentieth century, some of these characteristics had vanished. Intermarriage had made it harder to distinguish some Tutsis from some Hutus, especially in southern Rwanda. Many Tutsis had left the pastoral countryside to take professional jobs in the towns. But the stereotype persisted in the minds of members of both tribes. Moreover, centuries of tradition had made many Tutsis feel like a privileged, superior people and many Hutus like a subjugated, inferior people. They felt this way despite their numbers—for the Tutsis made up no more than 15 percent of the populations of each country, while the Hutus made up 80 percent or more.

The feudal system remained in place under colonial rule by the Germans and, after World War I, under the administration of the Belgians as a mandate of the League of Nations and a trusteeship of the UN. But things fell apart after independence of the two countries in 1962. Burundi became independent while still under the rule of its Tutsi *mwami*, who was ousted by a cabal of Tutsi army officers within a few years. The monarchy had fallen even before independence in Rwanda in a revolution led by Hutus. Rwanda thus became independent as a republic run by leaders of the majority Hutu tribe while Burundi, after a few years of independence, was a military dictatorship run by the minority Tutsis.

Independence provoked terrible tribal tensions, and both Burundi and Rwanda suffered waves of tribal bloodshed for more than three decades. The turmoil in one country provoked turmoil in its neighbor, and killings of one tribe in one country often begat killings of the other tribe in the other country. Hutus and Tutsis had the right to fear each other. To make matters worse, the massacres were usually not the result of fear-crazed frenzies but of government incitement or command.

Hutu majority power in Rwanda forced two hundred thousand Tutsis into exile in the early 1960s, most settling in Uganda, Burundi, or the Congo. The Hutus, however, still felt some insecurity because they could see the Tutsi military subjugating their brethren next door in Burundi. These fears intensified in 1972.

The horror of genocide erupted in Burundi that year. In a cold-blooded, orderly manner, the Tutsi military killed tens of thousands of Hutus—the estimates range from a hundred thousand to two hundred thousand—within a few weeks. The target was the educated class of Hutus, and the Tutsi killers were motivated by their perceived need to wipe out any Hutu who had the potential to lead his or her people in an uprising against the Tutsi masters. The definition of education and potential leadership was so broad that the Tutsis even tried to round up all Hutus who wore glasses. The genocide was regarded as the great shame of Africa in the 1970s. News of the deaths led to the killings of scores of Tutsis in Rwanda and to a coup in 1973 that brought Major General Juvénal Habyarimana to power. He was joined by a coterie of Hutu Power advocates who did not believe in concessions to the Tutsi minority.

Against this background, the invasion of Rwanda by General Paul Kagame and his Tutsi exiles from Uganda in October 1990 makes little sense. In the mass of books and articles written about the Rwanda genocide of 1994 and the guilt of the UN, the precipitating factor is often overlooked. The Tutsi exile soldiers, many born in Uganda, had helped Yoweri Museveni overthrow the government of Uganda. Once in power, President Museveni rewarded them by encouraging and enabling the invasion of the homeland of their parents.

Howard W. French of the *New York Times* is one of the few journalists to underscore the audacity of the invasion. "Nothing could ever pardon the organizers of the 1994 genocide in Rwanda," French wrote in his book *A Continent for the Taking: The Tragedy and Hope of Africa*, "yet it is no less true a fact that the wild adventurousness of the Tutsi leader Paul Kagame . . . primed a country that had already long been an ethnic powder keg for a sharp escalation in violence and hatred." Tutsis numbered less than a million in Rwanda's population of seven million in 1990. To understand the hazards of the thoughtless Tutsi strike at Rwanda, you have to imagine the consequences if a military force of whites were foolish enough to invade South Africa and attempt to defeat the black majority government and restore white rule. The backlash against whites inside the country might prove ferocious.

The six thousand Tutsi-dominated invaders fought their way to within forty miles of the capital of Kigali before they were stopped by the Rwandan army, augmented by the presidential guard of Zaire (now called the Congo) and paratroopers from France and Belgium. The military standoff led to peace talks in Arusha, Tanzania. President Habyarimana, the Hutu leader, and General Kagame, the Tutsi leader, reached an agreement in 1993 that promised an end to the civil war. The agreement provided the Tutsi-dominated Rwandese Patriotic Front (as Kagame's invaders called themselves) five of twenty-one cabinet posts in a transitional government, eleven of seventy seats in the National Assembly, and half the officer corps of a united army. Elections for a new government were set for 1995.

The agreement called for United Nations peacekeepers to monitor cease-fire lines, supervise a weapons-free area around the capital, and assist humanitarian relief. The Security Council accepted the proposal and approved a mission of 2,458 troops as "a stabilizing presence." The United Nations Assistance Mission in Rwanda (UNAMIR) was a traditional peacekeeping operation without the authority to enforce anything. The peacekeepers were there at the request of both parties because each side wanted a referee to watch what the other side was up to. Since neither side wanted to scare them away, there was little chance, in theory, of danger to the peace-keepers.

From the start, the Arusha agreement was precarious. Hard-line Hutu politicians believed that Habyarimana had given away far too much. They persuaded themselves that they could scuttle the agreement by killing Tutsi civilians. A month after the signing, three hundred Tutsis were murdered in one prefecture. The stance of the Hutu militants hardened in October 1993 when the first Hutu president in the history of Burundi was murdered by the Tutsi-dominated army there. Tens of thousands of Hutus were slain in the aftermath, and two hundred thousand Hutu refugees fled to Rwanda. There has long been suspicion that the Arusha agreement did not satisfy Kagame either, for it fell short of restoring Tutsi rule. Both parties kept delaying implementation of the accords, and the country was bedeviled by sporadic killing.

Kofi Annan appointed Brigadier General Roméo Dallaire of Canada, a forty-six-year-old Québecois who had never served in UN peacekeeping before, as force commander. Dallaire, a brigade commander and the former head of the Royal Military College in Canada, was a friend of Major General Maurice Baril of Canada, who bore the impressive title of military adviser to the UN secretary-general. In fact, he headed military operations within the peacekeeping division and reported to Undersecretary-General Annan, not to Secretary-General Boutros-Ghali. En route to Rwanda on a preliminary fact-finding trip, Dallaire first conferred in New York with Annan, his deputy Iqbal Riza of Pakistan, and Baril. Dallaire liked to call them "the triumvirate."

Dallaire had not met Annan and Iqbal Riza before. In his extraordinary memoir *Shake Hands with the Devil: The Failure of Humanity in Rwanda*, which he wrote with his military assistant Major Brent Beardsley of Canada, Dallaire described the atmosphere of the peacekeeping office in UN headquarters, recording some insightful impressions of Annan and his relationship with Riza. "Annan was gentle, soft-spoken, and decent to the core,"

Dallaire wrote. "I found him to be genuinely, even religiously dedicated to the founding principles of the UN and tireless in his efforts to save the organization from itself in these exceptionally troubled times, where conflict and humanitarian catastrophes, often linked, were breaking out around the world."

Dallaire said the tall, thin, and intense Riza was not "as personable as his boss." Riza "did not suffer fools gladly and at times did not hesitate to make you aware of that fact." But, Dallaire went on, "his occasional intellectual arrogance was offset by his sound common sense and political sophistication."

Dallaire believed that the relationship between Annan and Riza lay at the core of the peacekeeping department, with "Annan very human and concerned, and Riza the cool, calculating master of ceremonies." The Canadian general described Riza as "articulate, businesslike, and direct"—a deputy "who made the place dance to their tune."

By the time he left for Rwanda on a second trip to take command, Dallaire was even more charmed by Annan. "When Kofi Annan shook my hand," Dallaire wrote, "I felt a warmth and genuine caring from him that for a moment overwhelmed me. He was not a political boss sending off one of his generals with platitudes and the expected aplomb. Through the kindest of eyes and the calmest of demeanours, Annan projected a humanism and dedication to the plight of others that I have rarely experienced."

Although Dallaire had a good number of disagreements with Annan and the peacekeeping department later, he did not change his impression of Annan during the more than five hundred pages that tell the story of the mission to Rwanda. One of Dallaire's cables is regarded as a shocking piece of evidence against Annan, but the general did not join the chorus of critics who condemned Annan for failing to prevent genocide.

The cable was sent by Dallaire on January 11, 1994, addressed to General Baril. Titled "Request for Protection for Informant," the cable told a dramatic story. "A very, very important government politician" had put Dallaire in contact with "a top-level trainer" of the armed militia of President Habyarimana's ruling party. (Dallaire had not actually heard the informant in person; he had sent Colonel Luc Marchal, the commander of the UN force's Belgian contingent, to listen to the informant and take notes.) The militia, made up of Hutu extremists, was known as the Interhamwe, which means "those who attack together" in Kinyarwanda, the native language of both Hutus and Tutsis in Rwanda. The unidentified informant told the UN that the Interhamwe had dire plans for the future of Rwanda.

The informant had been ordered to register all Tutsi in Kigali. "He suspects it is for their extermination," Dallaire reported. The Interhamwe had seventeen hundred trained men scattered in groups of forty throughout Kigali. His own personnel (the cable does not say how many they numbered) could kill up to a thousand Tutsis in twenty minutes, the informant said. He had come to the UN because "he disagrees with anti-Tutsi extermination." While he opposes the Tutsi-led Rwandese Patriotic Front, the informant said, he "cannot support killing of innocent persons."

The Interhamwe had other unsavory goals. They wanted to kill Belgian soldiers and thereby provoke Belgium into withdrawing its troops from the UN force. (The more than four hundred well-trained and well-equipped Belgian troops were the backbone of Dallaire's UN force; the other peacekeepers came from Third World nations.) The Interhamwe wanted to assassinate deputies from the opposition parties in the parliament. They also wanted to goad the rebel Tutsi soldiers into a bloody confrontation with Hutu demonstrators, reigniting the civil war.

The informant said he was prepared to show Dallaire the site of a secret Interhamwe cache of 135 weapons. Dallaire told General Baril that he and his peacekeepers intended to seize the weapons in a raid within thirty-six hours. Dallaire was going ahead even though he had "certain reservations on the suddenness of the change of heart of the informant to come clean with this information." The Canadian general went on to acknowledge the "possibility of a trap not fully excluded."

Dallaire did not ask the UN in New York to sound an alarm. He did not even request permission to make the raid on the arms cache. The cable, while keeping Baril informed, only asked Baril if the UN could satisfy the unidentified informant's request for asylum outside Rwanda for himself and his family. But Dallaire did close the cable with what sounded like a battle cry. Using the motto of both his high school and the brigade he had commanded in Canada, he wrote, *"Peux ce que veux. Allons-y."* That can be translated roughly as "If we want to do it, we can. Let's go."

The cable caused a stir in New York. Baril showed it to both Kofi Annan and Iqbal Riza, and they quickly sent a cable to Jacques-Roger Booh Booh in Kigali for his assessment. As the secretary-general's special representative, Booh Booh, a former foreign minister of Cameroun, was the senior UN official in Rwanda. In UN organizational charts, General Dallaire, as force commander, would report to Booh Booh. Judging by Dallaire's memoirs, however, they seemed to work as coequals in Rwanda, with Booh Booh handling political matters while Dallaire supervised the troops. Booh Booh, in any case, cabled New York that he agreed with Dallaire.

The reply from New York, Dallaire wrote in his memoirs, "caught me completely off guard" and "whipped the ground out from under me." The cable, addressed to Booh Booh and Dallaire, was labeled as coming from Annan in New York. The UN peacekeeping department, however, uses the same system as the U.S. Department of State. All its cables are labeled as coming from the secretary of state or, if the secretary is out of Washington, from the deputy secretary. The secretary, however, does not write each of the hundreds of cables that issue forth from the department every day. At the UN during this period all peacekeeping department cables were labeled as coming from Annan. But Annan, unlike his predecessor Goulding, had delegated authority for issuing cables in his name to Riza and others. The cable to Booh Booh and Dallaire was written and signed by Riza as the peacekeeping official supervising the mission in Rwanda. There is no doubt, however, that Annan agreed with the position taken by his deputy. He read the cable several hours after it was sent and could have countermanded his deputy if the cable had upset him. Annan has never tried to deny his own responsibility for the decision in New York, never hiding behind his deputy by pointing to Riza's signature on the cable.

The specter of Somalia hovered over Annan and his aides in the peacekeeping offices of New York. Dallaire's cable arrived just three months after the debacle in Somalia. The UN had been shaken by three Somalia events in swift order—the deaths of the eighteen Americans, the brazen but successful American attempt to brand Boutros-Ghali and the UN as the scapegoats, and the decision by President Bill Clinton to pull out. American politicians denounced the UN mission to Somalia as a notorious example of "mission creep." By that they meant that a mission organized as an exercise in humanitarian assistance had somehow transformed itself into a military expedition out to punish a warlord. That was a distorted and simplistic way of looking at what happened in Somalia, but the danger of "mission creep" became a favored bogeyman for American military officers.

Moreover, Annan knew that the Clinton administration was changing its overall policy toward peacekeeping. President Clinton did not sign his new presidential policy directive on peacekeeping until the outbreak of the mass killing in Rwanda a few months later, but it was an open secret that he would set down stringent conditions for U.S. approval of any new UN peacekeeping mission. These conditions included an "exit strategy"—a concrete plan with a probable date for ending a mission—and consent from the antagonists.

With this in mind, Annan concluded that raising a general alarm about a possible genocide would be self-defeating. The Clinton administration would never approve the dispatch of several thousand more UN troops into Rwanda to prevent a possible outbreak of killing. Instead, it would probably demand that the UN pull out—surely the worst scenario. The Tutsis murdered a hundred thousand to two hundred thousand Hutus in Burundi in 1972 without the UN present. Word of the killings seeped out from missionaries and diplomats only weeks later. By that time, the outside world did not seem to care. If a genocide were attempted in Rwanda, the UN had to be present, at the least to witness.

To prevent "mission creep" and to keep the UN in Rwanda, Annan and his aides decided to stop Dallaire from seizing the cache of weapons. They feared that his military excursion might lead to a bloody confrontation that would alarm the United States and the rest of the Security Council into a Somalia-like withdrawal. The cable informed Dallaire and Booh Booh that their contemplated military action "clearly goes beyond the mandate" of the Security Council resolution setting up the mission. "The overriding consideration," the cable said, "is the need to avoid entering into a course of action that might lead to the use of force and unanticipated repercussions."

But Annan did not ignore the warning about genocide. He tried to deal with it in a different way than that proposed by Dallaire. The cable asked Dallaire and Booh Booh to pass on their information to the ambassadors of the United States, France, and Belgium. This kept two permanent members of the Security Council and the former colonial power of Rwanda in the picture and enlisted their support. In any case, Annan believed these governments already knew the details.

"Let's not kid each other," Annan told a PBS *Frontline* interviewer several years later. "Some [Security] Council members knew more than we did from their own intelligence system and their own embassies on the ground." When Dallaire briefed the diplomats, he wrote, "None of them appeared to be surprised, which led me to conclude that our informant was merely confirming what they already knew."

The cable instructed Dallaire and Booh Booh to request an urgent meeting with President Habyarimana. "You should inform the President that you have received apparently reliable information concerning the activities of the Interhamwe militia which represents a clear threat to the peace process," the cable said. ". . . You should inform him that these activities constitute a clear violation of the Arusha peace agreement and of the Kigali weapons-secure area. You should assume that he is not aware of these activities, but insist that he must ensure that these subversive activities are immediately discontinued. . . .You should advise the President that, if any violence occurs in Kigali, you would have to immediately bring to the attention of the Security Council the information you have received on the activities of the militia, undertake investigations to determine who is responsible, and make appropriate recommendations to the Security Council."

Dallaire and Booh Booh confronted President Habyarimana the next day. Booh Booh reported to Annan that the president "had appeared alarmed by the tone" of their protest but still denied that he knew anything about the reports. He promised to investigate and suggested that the UN officials raise the issue with the leaders of his ruling party as well. The two did so later that day, and Booh Booh cabled Annan that "my assessment of the situation is that the initiative to confront the accused parties with the information was a good one and may force them to decide on alternative ways of jeopardizing the peace process, especially in the Kigali area." American ambassador David Rawson also confronted President Habyarimana. After doing so, Rawson reported to Washington that the Rwandan leader seemed "to get the message."

What was the rationale for sending Dallaire and Booh Booh to President Habyarimana? Annan tried to explain a few years later. "The decision was to ensure that the Rwandan government knows that we have been tipped off and we know what was in planning, and they should not proceed," he told PBS's *Frontline*. The American, French, and Belgian ambassadors were alerted so they could "reinforce that message with the government to make sure that they do not move, that we know what is happening, that they should not make any attempt in that direction."

"Why did we go that route?" Annan went on. "Often, shining light on and telling those planning it at the government level that the international community knows what is being planned—'We are monitoring, we are going to deal with you harshly, and we know what you are up to'—sometimes it is a very good deterrent.

"Quite frankly, we had no other option, because we knew this mood in the [Security] Council. You are not going to get them to say, 'We are going to send in the brigade.' We are not going to rush in to send reinforcements to General Dallaire and his men to stop this. Therefore, one had to use the avenues available to try to put pressure and nip the problem in the bud. It didn't work, and it was really a painful experience for all of us who were involved in this."

An independent commission, appointed by Annan five years later, concluded that the peacekeeping office made a serious error in failing to pass on Dallaire's report to the full Security Council. Only two members—the United States and France—were notified through their ambassadors in Kigali. Yet, in view of the tepid response of the Security Council when the genocide erupted a few months later, it is hard to believe that Dallaire's report would have galvanized the full Security Council into action ahead of time.

In any case, under Boutros-Ghali's system of management, Annan did not meet with the Security Council at its closed-door sessions. That was the exclusive province of Boutros-Ghali and Chinmaya Gharekhan, the former Indian ambassador who was the secretary-general's liaison with the Council. So either Boutros-Ghali or Gharekhan would have had to sound the alarm, not Kofi Annan. Of course, Annan could have persuaded them to do so. While it is fanciful to believe that would have pressured the Clinton administration and other governments to intervene in Rwanda, passing the Dallaire report to the Council might have provided useful information to Spanish ambassador Yañez-Barnuevo, Czech ambassador Karel Kovanda, and New Zealand ambassador Colin Keating—the three members of the Security Council who tried in vain months later to persuade their colleagues to use force to stop the killings in Rwanda.

Annan's hope that President Habyarimana would restrain the militant Hutus evaporated on April 6, 1994, when he and the president of Burundi, also a Hutu, were killed in the crash of their plane as it approached the airport in Kigali. The plane was shot down by rockets, and it is widely assumed that the killers were militant Hutus who believed he was giving away too much to the Tutsis. Rwandan soldiers and the Interhamwe militia, both trained and instructed to kill Tutsis and moderate Hutus, began their systematic slaughter. Egged on by the diatribes of Radio Telévision Libre des Mille Collines (RTLM), the hard-line Hutu Power radio station, other Hutus joined in the killing. It was easy for the radio to exploit Hutu fears of the Tutsis and goad Hutus into revenge against those the station announcers called the *inyenzi* (cockroaches). The call for revenge was intensified by RTLM's false accusation against the Tutsis for shooting down the plane with the two Hutu presidents.

The genocide drove the UN Security Council into some of its darkest and most shameful moments. Council members dithered for months while thousands of Africans died every day. The first crisis occurred when Rwandan soldiers killed Prime Minister Agathe Uwilingiyimana—a moderate Hutu—and the ten Belgian peace-keepers who were guarding her. The deaths of the Belgians prompted Belgium to withdraw all its troops from Rwanda. As a kind of cover for the embarrassing withdrawal, Belgian foreign minister Willy Claes urged the UN to pull out the entire UN mission.

American ambassador Madeleine Albright came to the Council prepared to vote for ending the mission and withdrawing all the peacekeepers. Those were her instructions. But as she listened to other ambassadors, especially Nigerian ambassador Ibrahim A. Gambari, she decided her instructions were a mistake. The UN should not pull out completely. So she rushed to a booth in the UN hallway and phoned Richard A. Clarke, the National Security Council official at the White House in charge of peacekeeping. He repeated the instructions.

"I actually screamed into the phone," she recalled years later. "I said, 'They're unacceptable. I want them changed.' So they told me to chill out and calm down. But ultimately, they did send me instructions that allowed us to do a reinforcement of UNAMIR."

Although Albright and the rest of the Council agreed not to withdraw the peacekeeping force, they voted unanimously on April 21 to reduce it to only 270. But Secretary-General Boutros-Ghali asked the Council a week later to change course. He told the Council that two hundred thousand Rwandans had died in three weeks, and the UN had to do more than act as a neutral observer. But Council members could not agree about what to do. The issue was complicated by General Kagame, who resisted a large-scale intervention. His Tutsi troops had advanced steadily against a Rwandan army more adept at killing civilians than turning back the invaders. Kagame feared that an intervention would halt his advance.

It took more than a month after the genocide started, but the Security Council finally acted. On May 17, the Council authorized a force of fifty-five hundred troops charged with protecting refugees and other civilians and with supporting the distribution of relief supplies. But there was a hitch. At Ambassador Albright's insistence, the resolution included a delay. Dispatch of the bulk of the new force would not start until Secretary-General Boutros-Ghali satisfied the conditions set down in President Clinton's presidential policy directive on peacekeeping. The secretary-general needed to obtain consent from the Rwandan government and from Paul Kagame's Tutsi rebel army, and he needed to set down a strategy that included a probable date for the end of the mission.

Although the delay infuriated some members of the Security Council such as New Zealand ambassador Keating, Albright professed that she was proud of the delay. A few hours after the vote, she told a House Foreign Affairs subcommittee in Washington that "sending a UN force into the maelstrom of Rwanda without a sound plan of operations would be folly." "Emotions can produce wonderful speeches and stirring op-ed pieces," she went on. "But emotions alone cannot produce policies that will achieve what they promise. If we do not keep commitments in line with capabilities, we will only further undermine UN credibility and support."

In the end, the delay did not matter, for Boutros-Ghali and Kofi Annan were never able to persuade enough governments to send troops to Rwanda. Annan convened a meeting with forty-two ambassadors a few days after the resolution was passed. Only one country, his native Ghana, made a firm offer—seven hundred lightly armed soldiers who would need armored cars and other vehicles from the United States or other NATO countries. Bassir Pour Afsane, the tenacious correspondent for *Le Monde*, met Annan and found the usually unflappable undersecretary-general in "an unusual state of agitation."

"If the images of tens of thousands of rotting human bodies, some devoured by animals or floating to the surface of Lake Victoria, do not shake us from our apathy," he told her, "I do not know what can. It is as if we have become totally insensitive, as if we have become indifferent." Annan said that the deployment of a well-equipped and mobile force to Kigali and its surroundings could save thousands of lives immediately. "I do not know if that force would be capable of putting an end to all the fighting," he said, "but if we are able to save a single child's life, that already is not bad." But he was sure far more would be saved. He was confident, he said, that a well-equipped and determined force would intimidate "this band of cowards who cut the throats of women and children."

The ambassadors did not reject Annan's pleas for troops outright. "They assured me that the urgent request of the UN was under study," he said, "but while they study, thousands of people die." "How can I find the fifty-five hundred troops authorized by the Security Council for Rwanda," Annan told the *Le Monde* correspondent, "when there is neither enthusiasm nor political will? . . . No one should have a peaceful conscience in this affair."

By late June, the UN peacekeeping force in Rwanda numbered only 500—less than one tenth of the total authorized by the Security Council a month earlier. France then proposed sending a French force, augmented by Senegalese and other African soldiers, to southwestern Rwanda. The Security Council accepted the offer—although some ambassadors thought it was a cynical move by the French to protect some of their former Hutu allies. The French-led force, dubbed Operation Turquoise, landed in mid-July and included 2,500 French troops, 250 Senegalese, and 100 from other African countries. They managed to prevent further massacres in the southwest and left in late August. By then, Kagame's

Tutsi-dominated Rwandese Patriotic Front controlled all of Rwanda, triggering a mass exodus of several million Hutus into the Congo. Although tens of thousands of Hutus would now die in the Congo, the genocide of Tutsi civilians in Rwanda had finally ended.

Why did so many outside politicians, diplomats, and bureaucrats exhibit so much indifference and ineffectual blathering in the face of so much wanton killing of innocents? That question has gnawed at many people, including Annan, for many years. The independent commission appointed by Annan—comprising former Swedish prime minister Ingvar Carlsson, former South Korean foreign minister Han Sung-Joo, and retired Nigerian lieutenant general Rufus M. Kupolati—concluded "that the failure by the United Nations to prevent, and subsequently, to stop the genocide in Rwanda was a failure by the United Nations system as a whole." By the system as a whole, they meant both the governments that make up the UN and the civil servants who carry out the orders from the governments. In particular, the commission laid "the responsibility for the failings" on "the secretary-general, the Secretariat, the Security Council, UNAMIR, and the broader membership of the United Nations." The conclusion may be correct, but it is unsatisfying, for it seems to assign blame equally, and, of course, blaming everyone has almost the same effect as blaming no one.

In the conclusion of his memoirs, Dallaire was not hesitant about singling out his choice of the main culprits. He cited, of course, "the fanatical far right of the Hutu ethnicity" who "planned, ordered, supervised, and eventually conducted it [the genocide]." But he added a name not often mentioned by others. "The deaths of Rwandans," he wrote, "can also be laid at the door of the military genius Paul Kagame, who did not speed up his campaign when the scale of the genocide became clear and even talked candidly with me at several points about the price his fellow Tutsis might have to pay for the cause." Without much success, Dallaire had continually urged Kagame throughout the crisis to rush troops forward on rescue missions.

Dallaire was just as candid in blaming outsiders. "I truly believe," he wrote, "that the missing piece in the puzzle was the political will from France and the United States to make the Arusha accords work and ultimately move this imploding nation toward democracy and a lasting peace. There is no doubt that those two countries possessed the solution to the Rwandan crisis." He dismissed France's Operation Turquoise, "which moved too late and ended up protecting the *géocidaires* and permanently destabilizing the region." As for the United States, he accused the Clinton administration of working actively against an effective peacekeeping mission, of intervening later only to protect Hutu refugees and killers, and of "leaving the genocide survivors to flounder and suffer."

Compared to the faults of the United States and France, he concluded, "the failings of the UN and Belgium were not in the same league." In short, although he had argued long and hard with the peacekeeping office of Annan about its refusal to allow him to proceed against the Hutu militants, Dallaire understood that the triumvirate, as he liked to call the peacekeeping chiefs, were hamstrung by the Security Council.

Kofi Annan has apologized for the failure of the UN system to prevent and then stop the genocide in Rwanda. Like others, he failed, but he did not fail in a dishonorable way. It is unfair and wrongheaded to brand him with major responsibility for the terrible deaths in Rwanda. The evidence makes that clear. Yet he has been dogged by the accusation, and it has been hard to shake off, mainly because it has been repeated so often by Philip Gourevitch in the prestigious *New Yorker*. There is no doubt that the accusation upsets Annan.

Annan, by then secretary-general, was traveling in Africa in May 1998 when the *New Yorker* published a Gourevitch article quoting from the Annan cable (actually written and signed by Iqbal Riza) that stopped Dallaire from seizing a Hutu cache of arms in Kigali. Annan responded at a news conference in Nairobi, Kenya, countering that "the fundamental failure (to prevent the massacres) was the lack of political will, not the lack of information." The British journalist William Shawcross reported that Annan's voice almost cracked as he insisted that peacekeeping would be easy if information were the only problem. Annan then brought up the ethnic killings in Kosovo and the plight of Hutu refugees in the Congo after the Rwanda genocide. "We would not be having problems in Kosovo because everybody *knows*," he said. "We would not have had a problem in Congo because everybody *knew* we had to separate the troops and refugees. . . . Later everybody *knew* that there were refugees left behind when a million went back to Rwanda. Why didn't that information make us go and save them? The information was there. We have to be logical."

Viru Dayal, the former chief of staff of Secretary-General Pérez de Cuéllar and Kofi Annan's partner on the mission to Baghdad to free the hostages in 1990, tried recently to contemplate the impact of Rwanda on his old friend. "When Kofi was appointed the chief of peacekeeping," Dayal said by telephone from New Delhi, "I wondered how he would be. He was quite emotional in a nice way. His heart would bleed for people. I wondered if his work would now interfere with his peace of mind. I can imagine how Kofi felt about the Rwanda tragedy. It would have seared him."

Yet, no matter how torn he may have been emotionally, Annan acted in a characteristic way. He was serious, conservative, cautious, sensitive to American politics, faithful to UN resolutions, and deeply averse to any dramatic gesture. The crisis also drove home to him the weakness of the UN. The UN has no power of its own, only moral authority. It is completely dependent on the members of the Security Council, especially the United States. The UN can do little if the United States is indifferent, hesitant, or opposed. The UN works best when the United States and the secretary-general are in lockstep. In 1994, they kept far apart while an incredible number of Rwandans were slaughtered.

7

Charade over Bosnia

It might have been funny if so many had not died because of the charade. Throughout most of the bloody Bosnian crisis, the Security Council behaved like Keystone Kops, shouting in indignation, jumping up and down with threats, passing reams of fiery resolutions, and accomplishing little. José-Maria Mendiluce of Spain, the chief of Bosnia humanitarian operations for the UN high commissioner for refugees, once said that his staff looked on their relief work as "an alibi" for politicians at home. Whenever anyone demanded to know what they had done to stop the Bosnian war, European and American politicians, hiding their guilt, could point to the UN humanitarian mission there and insist they had done all they could.

The crisis made the UN look ridiculous and effete, arousing worldwide revulsion at its failure. A good deal of scorn was heaped on Secretary-General Boutros Boutros-Ghali and his hapless representative in Bosnia, Yasushi Akashi of Japan. As chief of peacekeeping, Undersecretary-General Kofi Annan was heavily involved in the scorned mission. In fact, he kept a close eye on Bosnia the way his deputy Iqbal Riza watched over Rwanda. Yet Annan escaped the worldwide scorn, partly because he remained out of the limelight, partly because he struck diplomats as more flexible and more tactful than Boutros-Ghali. A case can be made—and it has been made most forcefully by the American diplomat Richard Holbrooke—that Annan's work on Bosnia eased the way for him to succeed Boutros-Ghali as secretary-general.

The Security Council accomplished little because the United States and its European allies could not agree about what to do until very late in the crisis. In 1992, Bosnia had followed the lead of Slovenia and Croatia in breaking from a Serbian-dominated Yugoslavia. It was a precarious secession. Bosnia was a divided country—40 percent Muslim, 32 percent Serb, and 18 percent Croat—and independence led to civil war. All sides were guilty of atrocities, but the Serbs were more guilty than the others. Aided by the Yugoslav army, the Serbs embarked on their despicable campaign of "ethnic cleansing"—uprooting tens of thousands of Muslims from Serb-dominated areas while killing, raping, maiming, jailing, and torturing many of them.

Neither the United States nor any of its European allies wanted to risk sending troops to halt the Serbs and punish them. Politicians believed their voters would not tolerate the casualties. Instead, the Security Council dispatched UN peacekeeping troops to guard humanitarian convoys, monitor cease-fire lines, and deter any Serb attacks on a handful of Muslim towns that were designated as "safe areas." The Bosnia operation was actually an extension of the peacekeeping mission known as UNPROFOR (UN Protection Force) that had been sent earlier to monitor cease-fire lines between the Serbs and the Croats in Croatia. But the Bosnia extension soon overwhelmed all other UN duties in the former Yugoslavia. By September 1994, there were 22,500 peacekeepers in Bosnia, a third of them French and British, none American.

The Americans—with UN ambassador Madeleine Albright the most vocal advocate—continually urged the UN to authorize NATO to bomb the Serbs. But the British and the French were wary of bombing, for their soldiers were spread throughout Bosnia and might be hurt by the bombing or by the Serbian retaliation that would surely follow. "There is a division of tasks that I don't think is acceptable," said French foreign minister Alain Juppé, "that of having some flying in planes and dropping bombs, and others, especially the French, on the ground."

Public outrage over Bosnian atrocities finally forced the Security Council to give in to the American pressure and authorize NATO bombing when needed to protect the safe areas, the humanitarian convoys, and the peacekeepers. After the vote, Boutros-Ghali called Kofi Annan, Marrack Goulding, and other aides to his office and told them, "Certainly, the resolution has been adopted. But only the United States wants air attacks against the Serbs. You are very quickly going to see the reaction of other countries, especially the French and British who have troops on the ground." According to Hervé Cassan, one of Boutros-Ghali's advisers, the secretary-general was soon bombarded with French and British pleas that he "hold back the Americans and control NATO."

In its resolution, the Security Council set up a cumbersome double-key system—any bombing would have to be approved by both the NATO supreme commander and the UN secretary-general. "I was the one," says Annan, "who negotiated the double-key arrangements with NATO." Without the double key, Britain and France would never have voted in favor of NATO bombing. "Those with troops on the ground," says Annan, "were cautious, didn't want to put their troops at risk, didn't want them to become hostages, and didn't want them to be attacked by the Serbs. . . . We needed to find an arrangement. . . . The dual key would give some protection to the troops on the ground."

The double key put a heavy burden on Boutros-Ghali and his Secretariat. The Americans pressured him to turn the key and allow bombing, while the British and French pressured him not to turn the key. Of course, the Security Council had handed him a series of knotty problems before. Throughout the four years of war, the Security Council had passed more than forty resolutions and issued as many threatening statements. Much of it was bluster, raising false hopes. In carrying out Council policies, Boutros-Ghali always had to weigh a complex combination of factors—his interpretation of the wording of countless resolutions, plus the true mood of the Council, plus the wishes of the UN military commanders, usually French and British, on the scene. The double key gave him the toughest problem and exposed him to the anger of American ambassador Madeleine Albright. Several times he resisted her pleas to turn the key.

The authority to bomb meant that the peacekeepers could become enforcers if the UN wished. But Boutros-Ghali knew that neither the United States nor France nor Britain wanted to be drawn into war against the Serbs. He acted with caution and tried to maintain the fiction that the Bosnia mission was a traditional peacekeeping operation, with the peacekeepers keeping a neutral role. That, of course, was hard to do when the Serbs knew he was armed with the right to bomb them.

Boutros-Ghali passed his key on to Akashi on the scene (although Akashi, a cautious diplomat who had won praise for his management of the large UN mission in Cambodia, surely consulted with his boss before making decisions). For the most part, Akashi simply carried out the wishes of his UN force commanders—mainly French and British generals intent on protecting their troops. But he did veto them once and sometimes delayed his approval to gain time to try to negotiate some kind of temporary cease-fire agreement with the Serbs. At the most, he allowed pinprick bombing. Even armed with the power to invoke NATO bombing, the UN continued to look toothless.

The UN's reluctance to bomb, though it pleased the British and the French, angered Albright. French ambassador Jean-Bernard Merimée was quoted as telling a UN official, "By imposing a double key on any bombing by NATO, the secretary-general has defended the security of the Blue Helmets on the ground and even more the independence of the UN. But he has lost all chance of being reelected."

There is no evidence that Undersecretary-General Kofi Annan, as chief of peacekeeping operations, differed from Boutros-Ghali and Akashi in any major way on Bosnia policy. Annan's office, after all, produced the periodic reports that the secretary-general sent to the Security Council describing the conflict and laying out the alternatives for Council action. These reports, usually written by Kofi's aide Shashi Tharoor, an Indian novelist, were clear, forthright, and often eloquent. They did not reflect any wrangling in the Secretariat. Yet Tharoor believes that Annan, if he were in charge, would have been willing to grant the requests of his generals for bombing authority more often than Boutros-Ghali had been.

Muhamed Sacirbey, the Bosnian ambassador who did a remarkable job rallying American public opinion against the Serbian aggressors, met Annan often during the crisis. Sacirbey recalls that Annan was more willing than Boutros-Ghali to confront Serbian president Slobodan Milosević. "I think Kofi tended to be open-minded and sympathetic," says Sacirbey. "He was more influenced by events on the ground. He certainly was not someone who was rah-rah for us behind closed doors. But there were many other people around Boutros-Ghali whose minds were closed in unreasonable, illogical positions. His was not."

There also were obvious differences between Boutros-Ghali and Annan in mood and tact. It is inconceivable, for example, that Annan, whether in public or in private, would ever have lectured the people of Sarajevo, as Boutros-Ghali did in front of me and other reporters on the eve of the 1993 New Year, that there were at least ten areas in the world in worse shape than Sarajevo.

Diego Arria of Venezuela, who sat on the Security Council during the Bosnian war, discovered Annan at the same Princeton University conference I did. The ambassador was astounded at Kofi's frankness about the peacekeeping mission in Somalia. "I could not believe that I was listening to a UN official," Arria says. "I had never heard a UN official speak this way. I kept wondering, where did he come from?"

Nevertheless, Arria was never treated to that kind of frankness over Bosnia because Boutros-Ghali kept Annan from the Security Council during Arria's stay. The secretary-general controlled the flow of information from the Secretariat to the Council by designating his aide Chinmaya Gharekhan, a former Indian ambassador, as the briefer of the Council. Annan and other top officials briefed Gharekhan who then relayed information to the Council. That prevented the ambassadors from questioning Annan, the official in New York who probably knew most about the turmoil in Bosnia. On one occasion, when Arria became angered over what he regarded as the Bosnia mission's whitewash of a peacekeeper's negligence in failing to prevent the assassination of a top Bosnia official, Boutros-Ghali sent Annan to calm Arria. "Kofi was Kofi," Arria recalls. "He listened. He explained. He said he would do what he could." Since Boutros-Ghali had no intention of changing the ruling in the field, Arria did not make any headway with his complaint. But the mood had changed. Arria felt that he had been heard.

When the issue of safe areas arose, Annan showed a subtle and sure grasp of the politics within the Security Council. Several Muslim towns and villages were isolated deep in Serb-held territory, vulnerable to Serb assault. Their populations swelled with Muslim refugees. Their food and other supplies came in UN humanitarian convoys subjected to Serb harassment, plunder, and delays. To make matters worse, the Muslims sometimes enraged the Serbs by sending guerrillas out of these holds to attack and pillage Serb villages. The UN feared that the Serbs would soon assault the besieged Muslim towns and villages in a fury of massacres. Srebrenica, with its crammed refugee-swollen population in woeful condition, seemed in imminent danger of Serb attack in April 1993.

With the United States and the other permanent members of the Council unable to come up with anything to save Srebrenica, the vacuum was filled by Arria, a former Caracas mayor and newspaper editor, who stepped down UN corridors with a carved cane and brightened meetings with his pastel shirts and elegant ties. Arria persuaded the Council to pass a resolution declaring Srebrenica "a safe area" and authorizing a fact-finding mission to head there immediately. Arria led the mission of ambassadors and other diplomats and reported back that Srebrenica was "an open jail" subject to "slow-motion genocide" by the besieging Serbs.

General Lars Eric Wahlgren of Sweden, the UNPROFOR force commander, deplored the idea of safe areas unless these towns and villages could be demilitarized under agreement between the Muslims and the Serbs. Otherwise, the safe areas would have to be defended by combat troops, not peacekeepers. Peacekeepers had neither the weapons nor the authority to do the job. "One cannot make war and peace at the same time," Wahlgren wrote Annan in a cable.

To turn Srebrenica into a safe area, Wahlgren persuaded the Muslims and the Bosnian Serbs to sign an agreement in which the Serbs promised a cease-fire if the Muslims gave up their weapons to the UN. The Security Council resolution meant very little to the Serbs. The demilitarization agreement seemed the only way to prevent a Serb massacre of the Muslims in Srebrenica.

But the agreement troubled Annan. His reaction reflected his understanding of political realities. He warned Wahlgren that the mood of the Security Council and its resolution was anti-Serb. Council members did not want tough action against the Muslims. The Muslims had given up some arms to the UN, mostly broken weapons or pieces that lacked ammunition. Annan suggested that Walhlgren go no farther. There was no need for "undue zeal" and "house-to-house searches for weapons." In taking weapons from the Muslims, Annan wrote, "UNPROFOR takes on a moral responsibility for the safety of the disarmed that it clearly does not have the military resources to honor beyond a point." Annan's cable was a clear reflection of flexibility and a willingness to depart from traditional UN neutrality when it was obvious that most people in the world wanted the UN to punish the Serbs.

The embrace of the safe-areas idea by the Security Council led to a terrible tragedy. The Council reinforced the status of Srebrenica as a safe area and extended that status to Sarajevo and four other towns. But it failed to provide the military resources to defend the areas. Even though he had campaigned to designate Srebrenica a safe area, Arria abstained rather than vote for the resolution implementing the policy throughout Bosnia. Since there was no definite threat to use UN force to defend these towns, Arria accurately predicted that the safe areas would not be safe.

Although Boutros-Ghali said he would need thirty-four thousand troops to defend the areas, the council authorized only seventy-six hundred. Annan was never able to recruit more than half. Some governments, in fact, even refused to allow him to redeploy soldiers already in Bosnia to the dangerous job of guarding safe areas. Lieutenant General Francis Briquemont of Belgium, commander of the UN peacekeepers in Bosnia, said in 1993 that there was such a gap between Security Council resolutions and reality that he had stopped reading the resolutions.

In July 1995, General Ratko Mladić with perhaps two thousand well-armed Bosnian Serb troops overran Srebrenica in a few days. The UN had only six hundred Dutch soldiers—half infantry, half support—to defend the safe area. The Dutch kept asking UN military headquarters in Sarajevo and Zagreb for air support. But most of the requests were turned down or ignored in a remarkable manifestation of UN military confusion and incompetence. At the height of the Serb attack, the Dutch soldiers expected NATO to bomb the Serbs at 7:00 A.M., only to find that the planes in the air were still awaiting an official request. By the time the renewed Dutch request reached headquarters, the planes had to return to Italy for refueling.

NATO did not bomb until the Serbs had practically taken the town. The targets were meager—two moving Serb vehicles. But the Serbs radioed the Dutch soldiers that if the bombing continued, the Serbs would shell the UN compound with its thousands of refugees and would kill thirty Dutch hostages in Serb hands. The Dutch minister of defense phoned both Akashi and Annan, pleading for a halt in the bombing. Akashi, who had the UN key, felt he had no choice but to comply. The Serbs took Srebrenica without any more UN resistance.

This set the stage for the greatest atrocity in Europe since the end of World War II. General Mladić promised to treat his Muslim prisoners according to the Geneva conventions, but he separated thousands of men and boys over age sixteen and executed them outside Srebrenica. The death toll was more than seven thousand. According to the indictment of Mladić and Bosnian Serb president Radovan Karadžić before the International Tribunal at The Hague, "a truly terrible massacre of the Muslim population appears to have taken place" in "scenes of unimaginable savagery . . . scenes from hell, written on the darkest pages of human history." Neither Mladić nor Karadžić has ever been captured and taken before the tribunal.

Some critics who condemn Kofi Annan for his role in the Rwanda deaths throw in the Srebrenica massacre as another measure of guilt. But I think this is even more fanciful than the first charge. His role in Bosnia was far overshadowed by that of Boutros-Ghali, who liked to micromanage crucial issues. Bosnia was exceedingly difficult to manage. Security Council policies toward Bosnia were hamstrung by the conflict between the United States and Europe. Whenever there was an argument over implementation of a resolution, Secretary-General Boutros-Ghali usually sided with Britain and France, mainly because they had the troops on the ground. It is hard to fault him for that, but his stance infuriated Washington.

Boutros-Ghali harmed his reputation by taking on a military role for which he was not suited: authority to bomb. Although he did turn over his key for bombing to Akashi, his representative on the scene, Akashi—who consulted his boss frequently—was no more suited for military decisions than Boutros-Ghali. The key probably should have been turned over to the UN force commander. Lieutenant General Jean Cot of France, the force commander from June 1993 to March 1994, asked repeatedly for the right to authorize air strikes, but Boutros-Ghali refused to relinquish the key to him. While Akashi usually did what he was asked by the force commander, there were enough delays, hesitation, and, in one case, a veto to demean the UN in worldwide headlines.

Perhaps Boutros-Ghali should have defied the Security Council and proclaimed the UN's inability to defend Srebrenica and the other safe areas with the small number of troops allotted by the Security Council. He could have informed the Security Council and the Bosnian Muslims that there were no safe areas in Bosnia. Defiance would have brought the wrath of the Council down on the secretary-general, but it also might have saved lives. At least it would not have raised false hopes. But, as Boutros-Ghali told me in a recent interview, "That has never been done. The job of the secretary-general is to execute the orders of the Security Council. You cannot say I cannot do it. You are required to execute it."

In fact, both Lieutenant General Bernard Janvier of France, the UN force commander, and Lieutenant General Rupert Smith of Britain, the UN commander in Bosnia, proposed a plan in 1995 that would have changed the whole concept of securing the safe areas. They wanted the UN to pull out most of its peacekeepers from the safe areas, leaving only a few observers and controllers to call in air attacks. Without many peacekeepers vulnerable to seizure by the Serbs, the safe areas, in their view, would have been easier to defend. But according to William Shawcross, the plan infuriated the United States.

"Janvier found himself under fierce and personal attack from Madeleine Albright," Shawcross wrote. "She claimed Janvier wanted to 'dump the safe areas' and insisted that the United States would not allow it. . . . U.S. rhetoric, from Albright and her superiors, condemned the UN to continue its exercise in futility—and condemned those supposed to be under its protection to insecurity, indeed to danger."

The horror of the Srebrenica massacre galvanized outsiders to end the war. Europe and the United States now agreed that the Serbs had to be stopped, by heavy bombing if necessary. This determination was reinforced by the election of Jacques Chirac as president of France; he insisted that the UN's humiliation must end. Other steps made the end of Serb aggression inevitable. The Croats, with American acquiescence, unnerved and weakened the Serbs by launching an offensive that drove them out of most of the land they had occupied in Croatia earlier in that war. France and Britain sent a heavily armed, rapid-reaction force to Bosnia with artillery that could silence Serbian antiaircraft guns. The UN withdrew all its peacekeepers from outlying areas so they could no longer be seized by the Serbs as hostages. The stage was set for a provocation. A few weeks after the fall of Srebrenica, the Serbs foolishly fired a mortar shell into the Markale market in Sarajevo, killing thirty-seven shoppers. It was now time to punish the Serbs.

But NATO still needed the UN to turn its key. Madeleine Albright tried to reach Boutros-Ghali but could not find him. He was flying to a meeting in Barbados. So she called Annan instead. The conversation, according to Annan, followed these lines:

"Where is Boutros?" she asked.

"He's traveling," Annan replied.

"When will he be available?"

"When he arrives."

"How can he be incommunicado for so long?" Her tone made her sound incredulous and exasperated.

"He doesn't have a private plane," Annan said. "He flies commercial."

Albright said she needed a decision as soon as possible. "I spoke to my people [in the former Yugoslavia]," Annan recalls. "I said if this is what is happening we need to turn the key. So I said we must turn the key. And I gave permission to turn the key." The heavy bombing of the Bosnian Serbs began, and, in the view of Richard Holbrooke, then assistant secretary of state, "Annan's gutsy performance in those twenty-four hours was to play a central role in Washington's strong support for him a year later as the successor to Boutros Boutros-Ghali as secretary-General. In a sense Annan won the job on that day."

Other UN officials, such as Akashi, probably would have hesitated to make such a decision without consulting Boutros-Ghali. But Fred Eckhard, Annan's longtime spokesman, was not surprised at Annan's decisiveness. Eckhard, who worked with both Akashi and Annan during the Bosnian crisis, says, "Akashi's focus was on what Boutros-Ghali wanted. Besides, he was much more reticent as a person than Kofi was. Kofi's relations with Americans and NATO officials were warmer. When there was an opportunity to make a decision in Boutros-Ghali's absence, he made a decision, and it pleased the Americans." Annan has never struck others as an ambitious climber. But when opportunities have come his way, he has made the most of them.

With Boutros-Ghali away, Annan then took full charge of the UN's role in the bombing. In fact, he was now the UN's ranking official in a crisis that dominated the news. There was no one to overrule him. He even decided to brief the Security Council personally on the meager bombing reports reaching his office. That was in line with his belief that the Council had been confused and misinformed in the past by Boutros Ghali's system of relaying almost all information to the Council through a single official who had no role in either making or carrying out policy. Kofi Annan was having his first taste of UN power, and members of the Security Council, who would decide his fate more than a year later, had a chance to see him in action.

Before departing on another trip, this time to China, Boutros-Ghali granted Annan authority to make any decisions about bombing if Admiral Leighton Smith, the NATO commander, and the UN's General Janvier failed to agree. When Smith and Janvier could not agree on a suspension of the bombing to allow Janvier to meet with Serb general Mladić, Annan conferred with major political players about what to do. He talked at length with NATO secretary-general Willy Claes but reached no conclusions. Annan then turned to two American officials: Sandy Berger, the Clinton administration's acting National Security adviser, and Strobe Talbott, the deputy secretary of state. Annan and the Americans agreed on a three-day suspension. But the Janvier-Mladić talks did not go well. When Mladić defiantly shouted down Janvier and refused to give in to UN demands, NATO resumed the bombing.

Although Annan talked often with American officials during the bombing, he was hardly an American puppet. He complained to Boutros-Ghali later, for example, that NATO had failed to keep the UN fully informed about the damage inflicted by the bombing. This had embarrassed Annan when questioned by members of the Security Council. Asking Boutros-Ghali to relay his complaint to NATO, Annan wrote in a memo, "We cannot be sleeping partners, taken for granted by NATO." In mid-September the Serbs, after meeting with Holbrooke, gave in to the UN's demands, and the NATO bombing finally stopped.

Meeting for three weeks at Wright-Patterson Air Force Base in Dayton, Ohio, Holbrooke badgered and cajoled President Slobodan Milosević of Serbia, President Franjo Tudjman of Croatia, and President Alija Izetbegović of Bosnia into reaching a peace agreement in late November 1995. Holbrooke's task was eased somewhat by Milosević's ability to force the Bosnian Serbs to accept his compromises. The agreement set up a loose Bosnian union of two parts—a Muslim-Croat federation controlling 51 percent of the country, and a Serb republic controlling 49 percent.

The peace accords did not enhance the UN image—far from it. The reputation of the UN had been so besmirched by critics in Congress and elsewhere that Holbrooke wanted no UN taint on his accords. He even refused at first to allow any UN official into the Dayton conference. He finally relented and allowed Thorvald Stoltenberg of Norway, the UN's chief negotiator in the Bosnian crisis, onto the site but gave him almost nothing to do. The peace agreement provided for NATO to take over all military duties in Bosnia from the UN peacekeepers. The UN was given responsibility for police training and refugee relief, but only because Holbrooke could not find any other agency to do the work. In a series of news conferences, Holbrooke stressed that the coordinator of civilian activities in Bosnia, former Swedish prime minister Carl Bildt, would have no affiliation with the UN. When the peace agreement was officially signed at the Élysée Palace in Paris, Holbrooke found it odd that the French list of speakers included Boutros-Ghali—"a man whose actions had contributed so little to the ending of the war."

Even before the Dayton conference opened, Boutros-Ghali announced that he was removing Akashi as his special representative in the former Yugoslavia and replacing him with Kofi Annan. Ismat Kittani of Iraq, a veteran UN diplomat and civil servant, would take over as undersecretary-general in charge of peacekeeping. "It came as a surprise," Annan says. "I kept hearing rumors. I thought it was only a rumor, you know, but then it turned out. But I accepted the challenge, and it was an interesting assignment."

The changeover provoked a lot of smiles in the corridors of the UN. It was an open secret that Ambassador Madeleine Albright and other American officials disliked Boutros-Ghali so much that they might veto a second term. Annan was a strong possibility as the American choice for a successor. It looked like Boutros-Ghali was shipping a rival as far away as possible. I found Annan and Kittani chatting as they walked along First Avenue near the UN compound and asked them, "Which of you just got a promotion?" Each laughed and pointed to the other.

Boutros-Ghali denies that he was trying to isolate Annan by transferring him to Bosnia. "In fact, it helped him," he says. "While he was in Bosnia, he was preparing his election better." There is no doubt the appointment pleased Washington. "The United States was delighted with his [Akashi's] replacement," Holbrooke writes. "Since the August bombing crisis, Annan was the UN official in which we had the greatest confidence, and his arrival was good news." Albright's spokesman, James P. Rubin, told reporters, "Ambassador Albright has an extremely high opinion of Kofi Annan and believes that his presence in former Yugoslavia will help ensure a smooth cooperation between the United Nations, United States and NATO."

When Boutros-Ghali informed Annan that he was sending him to Bosnia, Annan insisted that the assignment must be temporary. He wanted to return to the job of chief of peacekeeping. Annan sent a memo to the peacekeeping staff in New York and overseas, describing the new assignment as temporary and promising to return to his old job as soon as he could. That made it clear that the reassignment did not amount to a dismissal. Kittani accepted the arrangement and told everyone he was only the acting chief of peacekeeping. While Kofi headquartered in Zagreb, the capital of Croatia, Nane remained behind in New York.

Annan had two assignments. He had to transfer authority from the UN to NATO in Bosnia, and he had to supervise the remaining UN peacekeepers in tense areas of Croatia. By all accounts, he managed both smoothly.

At a ceremony in the Sarajevo airport in December 1995, American admiral Smith of NATO took over military operations from French general Janvier of the UN. Janvier urged NATO to "act quickly and without weakness" because "the peace is still fragile." Smith promised that his troops were coming "on a peaceful mission" and not "as a bunch of cowboys looking for a fight."

Annan's speech was the most impressive—brief, eloquent, meaningful. "The world cannot claim ignorance of what those who live here have endured," he said. "In looking back, we should all recall how we responded to the escalating horrors of the last four years. And, as we do, there are questions which each of us must ask: What did I do? Could I have done more? Did I let my prejudice, or my fear, overwhelm my reasoning? And, above all, how would I react next time?" As secretary-general, he would issue an extraordinary report four years later that tried to answer those questions.

Annan showed no bitterness over the exclusion of the UN from most of the Dayton peace accords. He tried hard to help carry them out. He shared Holbrooke's concern over the orders by Karadžić and other Bosnian Serb leaders that Serbs burn down their homes and leave the Bosnian capital of Sarajevo. This would shatter the most integrated city in Bosnia and reinforce the secessionist ambitions of Karadžić.

Annan urged President Izetbegović to show magnanimity toward the Serbs and encourage them to stay. Izetbegović replied that Serb civilians were welcome to remain in Sarajevo but not soldiers and militiamen. Since most families harbored a warrior, Izetbegović's show of magnanimity did not help.

The British journalist William Shawcross traveled with Kofi Annan a few times during the mission to the former Yugoslavia and became a good friend of the future secretary-general. "The more I traveled with Annan and talked to him in the early nineties," Shawcross wrote in his book *Deliver Us from Evil: Peacekeepers, Warlords, and a World of Endless Conflict*, "the more remarkable he seemed—an international civil servant who had not become a bureaucrat. He dealt with people in a familiar yet persuasive way and managed to retain both dignity and authority. He is not a tall man, but he has an unusual presence that seems to come from an innate sense of calm and politeness. He speaks softly and rarely appears angry or even flustered. He also has a very lively, indeed sometimes even mischievous, sense of fun. He is quite different from anyone else I have met at the United Nations or in most other places."

Shawcross accompanied Annan on a visit to the Serb neighborhood of Grbavica in Sarajevo. The Serbs complained that the Dayton accords were anti-Serb. Annan spoke with calm, frankness, and clarity. "I have to be frank with you," he said. "Dayton was a compromise. But it was signed by the heads of state and it is not negotiable. . . . Don't try to reopen Dayton but work for its implementation. You should let the world hear you—that you want to live in peace."

"I know about your anxieties," he went on, "but try to work with the international community. It's a new period. You should let IFOR [the military acronym for Implementation Force, the name of the NATO mission] into your territory. It will be even-handed."

But the Serbs did not listen. Almost all seventy thousand Serbs left Sarajevo in a few weeks. Apartments burned, and Serbian thugs beat those Serbs who wanted to stay. IFOR did nothing to put out the fires or protect Serbs who remained in Sarajevo. Annan met with Admiral Smith and asked for NATO troops to patrol the streets of the Serb neighborhoods. But Admiral Smith refused. NATO commanders proved just as reluctant to engage their troops in conflict as UN commanders had been.

Annan also met Milosević in Belgrade and asked him to rein in

Karadžić and the other Bosnian Serb leaders. Milosević belittled Karadžić and his cohorts. "They were totally crazy," he told Annan. But he blamed the Muslim-dominated Bosnian government just as much. Annan made no headway on this issue and then asked about Kosovo. Milosević assured him that the tense province of Kosovo was no longer a problem and, in any case, an internal matter.

Major General William Nash, who headquartered in Tuzla and commanded a largely American force, recalls that he and other Americans arrived in Bosnia with an arrogant and disparaging view of the United Nations. A few months later, he says, "I was told this guy from the UN, the head of peacekeeping, wanted to see me." Nash agreed to see him. They talked for almost an hour. "I was impressed," says Nash, "by his centered, calm presence, by his unassuming way, by his interest in what I was doing."

A few weeks later, an aide handed General Nash a political analysis of Bosnia produced by Annan's office. "It was magnificent," says Nash. "It explained political nuances that we didn't know about. I was blown over by the report." Nash eagerly sought more information from the UN. The visit from Annan and the report had made the Americans far less disdainful of the UN.

During his five months in the former Yugoslavia, Annan also visited French and British troops in Sarajevo who had once served as UN peacekeepers and were now reassigned to NATO. More than two hundred UN peacekeepers had died trying to implement the confusing and sometimes contradictory resolutions of the Security Council. Annan told the peacekeepers now under NATO command that despite what politicians, newspapers, and television stations claimed, the UN had done a good job in Bosnia. But, he said, the UN had been forced to do no more than what had been authorized by the resolutions of the Security Council. "Victories always go with governments," he told the troops. "Defeats stay with UN peacekeepers."

Annan returned to New York after five months and resumed his work as chief of peacekeeping. He came back to a UN bristling with rumors about American plans to veto a second term for Boutros-Ghali. Some friends of Kofi were surprised that Boutros allowed him to come back so soon. Canadian ambassador Robert Fowler, meeting Kofi at a dinner, smiled and told him bluntly, "Kofi, I'm glad you're back. But now that you are back, let me tell you, when you left, you said you would be back, but none of us believed it."

8

Supplanting
Boutros-Ghali

A year or so before the end of Boutros Boutros-Ghali's term of office, U.S. ambassador Madeleine Albright dispatched her aide James P. (Jamie) Rubin on what he now calls with a smile "a secret diplomatic mission." Jamie, Albright's spokesman and confidant, was assigned to snoop around at a dinner party to find out if Undersecretary-General Kofi Annan spoke French well enough to avoid a veto by France in any future election for secretary-general. Annan and his wife, Nane, were among the guests at the dinner, hosted by Richard Holbrooke. Jamie sat next to Nane, a soft-spoken, shy woman, and began asking her banal questions about the life of the couple in Geneva. Jamie wanted to know, for example, if she and Kofi read the French newspapers when they lived together in Geneva. At the end, Jamie was satisfied. Kofi spoke French well enough.

The quality of Kofi's French would become an issue in the final balloting, so much so that even Kofi could not help laughing about it. "I now speak English with a French accent," he told his friend William Shawcross. When Annan's assistant Indian novelist Shashi Tharoor heard a news correspondent denigrate Annan for failing to master "the language of Molière," Tharoor, invoking the name of a great nineteenth-century French statesman, retorted, "He may not master the language of Molière, but he does master the language of Talleyrand."

The brouhaha over Annan's mastery of the French language provided a light moment in one of the most bitter and nasty episodes in UN history: the American veto of Boutros-Ghali for a second term as secretary-general. Annan would never have risen to the post of secretary-general if Madeleine Albright had not slapped Boutros-Ghali down. It's hard to regard Kofi Annan as anything more than an accidental secretary-general.

Long before news reporters, diplomats, and bureaucrats started to speculate about Annan's chances, Tharoor tried to broach the subject with his boss. A fire had damaged Annan's Roosevelt Island apartment in 1994, forcing him to live for a few weeks in the Beekman Towers hotel across the street from the UN complex. Tharoor strolled with him there after work one day. While they drank Scotch whisky, Tharoor told him that it was obvious the Americans wanted to get rid of Boutros-Ghali, that they probably would need an African to replace him, and that Kofi was the obvious candidate. Kofi nodded, smiled, but said nothing.

It was difficult for Annan to take such speculation seriously. Several years after he was elected, I asked him when he first felt that he might become secretary-general. "You may not believe this," he replied, "but it was at the very last minute. First of all, it had never happened before. Towards the end of '95, articles appeared that said Boutros may have problems. Names were mentioned. You had people who mentioned my name. I couldn't take it seriously. It had never happened that anybody had come through the Secretariat. The organization had always reached outside to elect a secretary-general. But, as time went on, the speculation became more and more persistent."

The conflict between Boutros-Ghali and Madeleine Albright was personal. Although they both professed in their memoirs to find charm and other admirable qualities in each other, there is no doubt that they disliked each other intensely. Albright, Boutros-Ghali wrote in his memoir, "tended to react to discussions of problems between the United Nations and the United States as though they were criticisms specifically directed at her performance as the American representative to the United Nations. Such sensitivity is not uncommon among unseasoned diplomats." He went on, "We had an apparently warm friendship, but warmth turned to fury the instant problems surfaced."

Boutros-Ghali, Albright wrote in her memoirs, was "hyper status-conscious and seemed to believe that administrative tasks were beneath him. As time passed, he became more and more critical of America, which may have earned points for him elsewhere but made it even harder for me to garner support for the UN on Capitol Hill."

Boutros-Ghali, a Coptic Christian from Egypt who was seventy-three years old at the beginning of 1996, was prickly, stubborn, independent, arrogant, secretive, and professorial. He ran the UN with the instincts of a suspicious politician and the brilliance of a former professor whose mind could absorb data and order it into policy alternatives with breathtaking ease. As a former minister of state for foreign affairs, he knew many world leaders personally and would contact them directly while ignoring their ambassadors in New York. A veteran American diplomat described Boutros-Ghali as "the perpetual outsider, the Court Jew" who has accumulated power by trusting no one. "There is a joke," said an ambassador on the Security Council, "that whenever the secretary-general wants to look for someone he can trust, he stands up on his two feet, walks across the room to the wall, and looks into the mirror."

There were significant policy differences between the United States and Boutros-Ghali. Albright had wanted him to authorize more bombing of the Serbs, for example, while Boutros-Ghali felt constrained by the reluctance of the British and French who, unlike the Americans, had many troops in the peacekeeping mission in Bosnia. On many instances, Albright simply found Boutros-Ghali too independent. She looked on the role of secretary-general as that of an administrative officer who took orders from those who paid his salary—especially the Big Five on the Security Council, even more especially, the United States. Boutros-Ghali, while insisting that he regarded himself as a servant of the Security Council, had a stubborn, independent streak. "The secretary-general is not a lackey to anyone," said a former ambassador on the Security Council. "He is only a lackey to his own ego." Once, when Boutros-Ghali planned a visit to Somalia, Albright urged him not to go. He mulled over her request. Then he read that White House sources had told reporters they did not want him to go. The public disclosure settled the issue for Boutros. He left for Somalia.

In 1993, according to Boutros-Ghali, Albright informed him that the Clinton administration wanted former president Jimmy Carter and the presidents of Ethiopia and Eritrea to head a commission of inquiry into the killing of more than fifty Pakistani peacekeepers by followers of warlord Mohamed Farah Aideed in Somalia. The secretary-general objected that it would be an incredible blunder to have three Christians investigate the killings of Muslims by Muslims. "Don't you have an intelligence service to advise you?" he said. Albright, according to Boutros-Ghali's memoir, "threw her head back, rolled her eyes, made a face, and slapped her thigh with a loud whack, all in one smoothly flowing display of exasperation with me."

Their feuding went on display after the signing of the Dayton accords in late 1995. As a kind of aside to the accords, the Americans wanted UN peacekeepers to police the return of Serb-controlled Eastern Slavonia to the Croatian government. After so many months of insults, this proposal angered Boutros-Ghali. If the UN was too weak and spineless to operate in Bosnia anymore, why should it be deemed strong and resourceful enough to police the equally volatile Eastern Slavonia? He insisted that NATO should do that job as well. But the Clinton administration had enough trouble persuading Congress to accept American troops in Bosnia. So Ambassador Albright tried to persuade Boutros-Ghali not to recommend a NATO operation for Eastern Slavonia.

Albright thought she had succeeded. But when the report reached the Security Council, the secretary-general persisted in recommending a NATO operation, not a UN peacekeeping mission. Albright, feeling betrayed, was furious. She issued a statement accusing Boutros-Ghali of espousing "misguided and counterproductive" ideas. "I believe it is a grave mistake," she said, "for the secretary-general to shy away from legitimate operations, supported by key members of the Security Council, that advance the prospects for peace in the Balkans."

Ambassadors usually do not take issue in public with a secretary-general's report even before it is discussed in the Security Council. After Albright's statement was issued, an angry Boutros-Ghali told the Security Council behind closed doors that he was shocked by its "vulgarity." He was speaking in French, and the word "vulgarity" in French has the connotation of something that is common, tasteless, and crude. Albright replied that his comment was "unacceptable." In the end, of course, the United States prevailed, and the Security Council dispatched a peacekeeping mission to Eastern Slavonia.

Although Boutros-Ghali had come to office promising to serve but one term, it was obvious by 1995 that he wanted to serve another five years. "I believe that only stupid people don't change their mind," he said. Albright was just as determined to stop him. The Czech-born American ambassador had even tried to interest Vaclav Havel, the renowned playwright and essayist who was president of the Czech Republic, in the job. But Havel, who did not speak English or French well enough to communicate with a world public, pleaded his unsuitability. Any American nomination of Havel, in any case, would have angered African governments. Boutros-Ghali had been elected to satisfy an African demand that it was Africa's turn to fill the post of secretary-general. If the United States decided to supplant an African, it might ease feelings if it came up with another African to take his place.

In early 1996, Albright formed a small group of conspirators to help her get rid of Boutros-Ghali. The cabal comprised Jamie Rubin and two members of the National Security Council, Richard A.

Clarke and Michael Sheehan. They dubbed their secret plan "Operation *Orient Express*." The name reflected their mistaken hope that they would soon enlist nation after nation to climb aboard their anti-Boutros express train. Albright had already discussed the matter with Secretary of State Warren Christopher and National Security adviser Anthony Lake. "Both had questions," she wrote later, "but they also had even more complaints about the secretary-general than I had." She also raised the issue with President Clinton on a flight to Bosnia in January, and, she said, he "told me he agreed."

In March, Albright sent a formal memo to Clinton setting down the reasons for the anti-Boutros campaign. "The rationale for opposing BBG is compelling on substantive, legislative and political grounds," she wrote. "He is not committed to, or capable of achieving, our urgent reform goals. Blocking his second term will significantly improve our chances to obtain funds from Congress, to pay our arrearages and sustain our obligations in the future. Finally, the chances of ensuring a domestic consensus that supports UN actions in the future will be greatly improved if he departs from the scene."

She and her team proposed three possible successors: Kofi Annan, Lakhdar Brahimi, and Olara Otunnu. Brahimi, a veteran UN troubleshooter and former Algerian foreign minister, had led the peacekeeping mission in Haiti. But he was handicapped as a North African. Many Africans had felt cheated somewhat when the first African secretary-general turned out to be an Egyptian from North Africa. If they were going to get another chance at the job, they would prefer a black African from south of the Sahara. Otunnu, a former Ugandan foreign minister and president of the International Peace Academy, a private organization that worked closely with the UN, was from sub-Saharan Africa. But he was a political exile who could not get the endorsement of his old political enemy Ugandan president Yoweri Museveni.

Annan was the obvious favorite of Operation *Orient Express*. Albright described him in her memoirs as "my preferred candidate." She wrote, "Annan had been on the front lines of the struggle to make UN peacekeeping more professional and—unlike his bureaucratic brethren—hadn't tried to duck responsibility for failures. . . . [H]e seemed born for leadership. Although not a big man physically, he carried himself in a way that commanded respect. He was soft-spoken, with a lilt in his voice and an engaging manner—a welcome change from the austere Boutros-Ghali."

But Albright and her team decided that they could not promote Annan publicly. "We knew that lobbying on his behalf—or anyone's behalf—would backfire," says Jamie Rubin. As Albright put it, "We knew people were likely to be mad at us and didn't want them taking their anger out on Annan."

In any case, before fretting over a replacement, Operation *Orient Express* had to work out a strategy for preventing a second Boutros-Ghali term. Of course, the United States, as one of the five permanent members, had the ultimate weapon in the Security Council. Albright could veto his candidacy. But the Americans hoped they would not have to reach that conflictive step.

First of all, says Rubin, "We were consumed in trying to convince Boutros to go quietly." Secretary Christopher met with Boutros-Ghali at the secretary-general's residence on Sutton Place in May but failed to persuade Boutros to abandon any plans for a second term. In early June, the Americans offered a compromise. Former secretary of state Cyrus Vance, who knew Boutros-Ghali well, telephoned the secretary-general. "Good news," Vance said. "Christopher has obtained a compromise—one additional year for you." But Boutros-Ghali rejected the extra year. "I don't take baksheesh," he told Vance. Albright wrote that Boutros-Ghali offered to settle for an extension of two and a half years, but Boutros-Ghali insisted in his memoir that he wanted nothing less than a full term. Relations between Boutros-Ghali and Christopher grew so testy that the secretary of state refused the secretary-general's plea that they meet again in person to discuss the issue. Boutros-Ghali sought help elsewhere and, according to his memoir, received a phone call from President Jacques Chirac of France promising that he and President Hosni Mubarak of Egypt would launch a counter-campaign for a second term.

The secretary-general's prospects, however, were weakened when he and his name became an issue in the 1996 American presidential campaign. His odd double-barreled name reflected a twin tribute to his grandfather Boutros Pasha Ghali, an Egyptian prime minister who was assassinated in 1910. In memory of the martyr, the family adopted the first name Boutros (Peter in the Coptic language) as part of the family name. In further honor, the parents of a new grandchild in 1922 decided to give him the first name Boutros as well.

I doubt if the Republicans knew this or even cared about the derivation when they decided to mock his name. Patrick Buchanan, trying to win the Republican nomination, regularly denounced the secretary-general as "Boo Boo Ghali." Invoking the memory of Somalia, Bob Dole, who did win the Republican nomination, promised that he would never let the secretary-general decide where to send American troops. The notion that a UN secretary-general had the power to send American troops anywhere without American approval was, of course, absurd. But Dole's pledge would arouse a good deal of cheering from his followers, especially when he pronounced the secretary-general's name as "Booootros Booootros-Ghali."

Secretary of State Christopher gave up trying to tempt Boutros-Ghali into accepting a one-year extension and called in Steven Erlanger of the *New York Times* on June 19 to leak the news that the United States would deny Boutros-Ghali a second term. "Boutros-Ghali is a distinguished man but an old-fashioned diplomat, and he's not the right man for the times," Christopher said. Under the ground rules set by the State Department, Christopher was identified in the story only as "a senior official." Another official told Erlanger, "[T]he United States has a veto and we're prepared to use it if necessary. Our intention is to see a new secretary-general by the end of the year."

Boutros-Ghali, visiting Germany, countered immediately by announcing for the first time in public that he would seek a second term. "I have the support of the greater number of members of the international community," he said, speaking to Erlanger by telephone from Bonn, "and on the basis of this I will seek a second mandate. I hope that the American administration will change its mind."

American officials told Erlanger that they had no particular candidate in mind as a successor. Erlanger, however, ended his story in the *New York Times* by listing five possible candidates, noting that their names "have been floated." The only African on Erlanger's list was Kofi Annan.

Christopher had failed to let Ambassador Albright know that he was calling Erlanger into his office to leak the news. "I heard about the decision while journeying by car from San Diego to Los Angeles," Albright wrote in her memoirs. "I knew I had to reach my Security Council colleagues in New York, who would be furious about not being consulted. My mobile had started to malfunction, so we found a pay phone in front of a dining establishment called Bubba's Hundred Sandwiches. Feeding in the quarters, I spread the word. As I had anticipated, the other ambassadors weren't happy."

The Boutros-Ghali campaign seemed quixotic at first. The threat of the American veto seemed to make any battle pointless. It was hard to believe that the Clinton administration would back down after splashing its intentions on the front page of the *New York Times*. Yet Boutros came rather close to derailing the U.S. campaign.

The secretary-general continually outmaneuvered the Americans. At the annual economic summit of the seven leading industrial countries, President Chirac of France, Chancellor Helmut Kohl of Germany, and Prime Minister Jean Chrétien of Canada promised him their support. Despite feverish lobbying by the Americans, the Organization of African Unity, meeting in Cameroun for its annual summit, endorsed a second term for Boutros-Ghali. State Department officials called the endorsement lukewarm, but it was an endorsement nevertheless.

The Americans displayed their frustration in July when Jamie Rubin castigated UN officials for campaigning for Boutros-Ghali. Rubin said the Clinton administration was "very concerned that UN officials have seen it to be their business to be promoting the reelection of a particular secretary-general. It is our intention to look into how UN personnel are being used by the secretary-general for this purpose." He did not name anyone but said, "They know who they are." One of his obvious targets was Ahmad Fawzi, an Egyptian who was deputy spokesman for the secretary-general. Fawzi had angered Rubin by reading to reporters past statements of praise by President Clinton for Boutros-Ghali.

The Rubin complaint was kind of petty and mean-spirited—sort of like complaining that American spokesmen on the U.S. government payroll like himself were making comments helpful to Clinton's own reelection campaign. Sylvana Foa, the energetic and sharp-tongued American who was the chief spokesman for Boutros-Ghali, quickly denounced Rubin for "ridiculous charges and a disgraceful campaign of disinformation." "These threats and blatant attempts at intimidating UN staff really smack of the McCarthy era," she said. State Department spokesman Nicholas Burns quickly accused her of using "intemperate and unhelpful language."

In fact, the entire U.S. campaign had an air of meanness. The Americans did not make clear their real complaints against Boutros-Ghali. Albright could not plead for his removal on the grounds that she detested him. Nor could she say that his leadership was so unfairly tarnished by the Clinton administration that the American people could not relate to him. Instead, she made him the scapegoat for everything that had misfired in Somalia and Bosnia and threw in the cant about the dire need by the UN for reforms that he was incapable of implementing. The unseemly campaign upset many other governments.

Albright kept offering inducements to Boutros-Ghali to give up. He could become secretary-general emeritus with, she said, "an office and ceremonial duties." Or the United States could support him for a seat on the International Court of Justice in The Hague. He kept dismissing this as baksheesh.

"The public relations battle was not going well," Albright acknowledged later. "At the UN the embattled secretary-general was playing the role of underdog against a bully who was well behind in paying his dues. The international press was hammering us, and so were critics at home."

The White House members of Operation *Orient Express* found it difficult to keep Clinton from wavering. "We were under enormous pressure to cut a deal, particularly from Chirac and Nelson Mandela, who called the president on many occasions to lobby for Boutros-Ghali," Sheehan told Linda Fasulo, the author of *An Insider's Guide to the UN.* "I never felt more pressure from anything I ever did during five years in the White House. It was hard." To prevent the president from giving in, Clarke wrote, he and Sheehan would often "race to the Oval Office when we were alerted that a head of state was telephoning the president."

Anthony Lake, the National Security adviser, argued for a change in policy. "One day in New York I had a screaming match with Tony Lake as we sat in the den of my residence at the Waldorf," Albright wrote in her memoirs. "Tony said he'd never been sure it was the right decision to oppose Boutros-Ghali and that I was on my own. I countered that we had made the right choice, even though a hard one, and we should switch to another business if we weren't prepared to take some criticism." The argument was so heated that Sheehan, Clarke, and Elaine Shocas, Albright's chief of staff, left the room.

Albright thought that the battle would be easier if it were simply a contest between Boutros-Ghali and Kofi Annan. But she could not put Kofi's name forward for fear of turning everyone against him because of the cloak of American approval. "We were prevented by the logic of our own strategy," she wrote, "from defining the choice in more appealing terms, the charismatic Kofi Annan against the aristocratic Boutros-Ghali."

This was an awkward and stressful time for Kofi. Boutros-Ghali, who knew that Annan had close relations with American officials, assumed he was their choice as his successor. He even told a colleague in early 1996 that Annan had declared himself a candidate. When this was relayed to Kofi, he met privately with Boutros to clarify the matter. The two disagree about what was said. "I told him," Annan recalls, "'Mr. Secretary-General, Boutros, I am not a candidate,' because at that point quite frankly I was not a candidate." In his memoir, Boutros-Ghali recalls hearing something far different. "He had come to my office," Boutros-Ghali writes, "to declare that he would never present himself as a candidate for secretary-general."

That recollection accounts for a bitter tone in some of Boutros-Ghali's words about his successor. "This is normal in political life," Boutros-Ghali told me recently in Paris, "—that you are betrayed by your closest collaborator. You know who is climbing the stairs and is ready to take your job." In any case, Boutros-Ghali and his aides treated Annan like an obvious candidate to supplant Boutros. They kept Kofi away from their meetings. Their antagonism toward him was obvious.

What could Kofi do? There was no doubt in his mind that Madeleine Albright would veto Boutros's bid for a second term. When the questioning became insistent, he told Albright and other inquiring ambassadors that if Boutros were rejected and "the member states wanted me to serve, I would consider it." If Kofi were somehow elected secretary-general, it would be the crowning achievement of his life, far beyond the most extravagant hopes of a Ghanian student who had failed to reach the sixth form at Mfantsipim and had devoted most of his earlier years at the UN to mundane bureaucratic work. The breathtaking enormity of that kind of leap overwhelmed his confidence. There was, in his view, only the slimmest of chances. He told himself he must not take the idea seriously.

Yet he took it seriously enough to know he must prepare himself for the possibility, no matter how slim. Kofi was soft-spoken and kind and never overbearing, but he was not passive. His colleagues did not regard him as a climber consumed by ambition, but he had always accepted and embraced opportunities when they came his way.

The Americans, according to Annan, "were a bit surprised that I didn't take up and go around the world campaigning." But he knew that he could not campaign in any but the most muted ways. An open campaign would be regarded as inappropriate, especially when Africa's candidate was still Boutros-Ghali. Theodore C. Sorensen, who was President John F. Kennedy's closest aide and speechwriter for many years, asked Kofi if he would like to meet to discuss strategy. Kofi agreed. He and his personal assistant Shashi Tharoor met with Sorensen four times at Sorensen's law office, the Ghana mission to the UN, and two restaurants near the UN. Nane came to one meeting. Sorensen's wife, Gillian, a UN official, came to a couple. Fred Eckhard joined the last session. Annan now says he learned more from Sorensen about preparing to take office than he did about campaign strategy.

It was not easy, of course, to discuss strategy for a campaign that must not be a campaign. They talked about the need for Kofi to use every chance to demonstrate his facility in the French language. They agreed that Kofi must ask Ghanian president Jerry Rawlings to send a Ghanian diplomat to New York to manage the campaign once it became open. Kofi and Tharoor asked Sorensen to edit some documents that Annan had written. Sorensen asked Kofi, "What are your skeletons?" Kofi replied, "I haven't any."

Neither Madeleine Albright nor any of her aides took part in these meetings. They were not in contact with Sorensen at all. Sorensen had come up with the idea on his own. Some participants, in fact, wondered at times whether the meetings were superfluous. If the U.S. government supported Kofi, that might be enough to ensure victory. But the meetings boosted Kofi's confidence and made the incredible goal seem closer to his reach.

If the stealth Annan campaign had a stealth campaign manager, it was probably Shashi Tharoor. He talked to ambassadors quietly on Annan's behalf. Ambassador Razali Ismail of Malaysia, the president of the General Assembly, wanted a promise that Annan would not follow Boutros-Ghali's practice of ignoring ambassadors in New York while talking instead to their leaders at home. Tharoor assured him that Annan would never ignore them. At the American mission to the UN, Tharoor dealt with Cameron Hume, a young Foreign Service officer on Albright's staff who had written *The United Nations, Iran, and Iraq*, a well-received, scholarly book on the Security Council. Albright, of course, spoke with Annan directly.

The voting for secretary-general did not begin until after the reelection of President Clinton. By then, Boutros-Ghali, buoyed by so many pledges of support, had persuaded himself that "once elected, Clinton would allow the U.S. assault on me to fade away." That belief was a measure of Boutros-Ghali's naïveté about American politics and his failure to appreciate the tenacity of Madeleine Albright who would soon be named secretary of state. The secretary-general angered Albright by phoning members of Congress, asking for support. The anger intensified when Senator Paul Simon, a Democrat from Illinois, issued a statement ridiculing the campaign against Boutros-Ghali as a blunder. Albright's office then denounced the phone calls of the secretary-general as a "gross interference in domestic politics and the normal functioning of American foreign policy."

Under the UN Charter, the fifteen members of the Security Council nominate a secretary-general, who must then be ratified by the General Assembly, made up of all members of the UN (185 in 1996). The General Assembly has always accepted the nominee of the Security Council. On November 19, 1996, the Security Council met behind closed doors to vote on a resolution by Egypt nominating Boutros-Ghali for a second five-year term. Every member of the Security Council voted in favor of the resolution except Madeleine Albright. She voted no. The 14–1 result was an embarrassment for Albright and the United States. Not even Britain, America's closest ally at the UN, had supported her anti-Boutros crusade. Yet the vote did little for Boutros-Ghali except salve his pride. The United States, Britain, France, Russia, and China have the power of veto in the Security Council. Albright's lone negative vote barred the secretary-general from a second term.

But the battle was not over. Boutros-Ghali did not withdraw his candidacy after the vote, hoping that international pressure would wear down American resistance. Albright acknowledged that she was isolated. "Yes, we had taken a punch," she wrote, "but we were still standing—and had shown that the president's reelection hadn't softened our determination to elect a new secretary-general. If Boutros-Ghali thought we would flinch at the last minute, he was wrong. Moreover, much of the international support he seemed to have was only ankle-deep."

For two weeks, African governments insisted that Boutros-Ghali was their candidate while Albright threatened that the United States would look for a candidate outside Africa if their stubborn support for the secretary-general persisted. "That's not a threat," she said. "It's just a statement of fact." The Africans finally gave in. President Paul Biya of Cameroun, chairman of the Organization of African Unity, wrote a letter to African leaders urging them to nominate additional candidates. "The logjam is broken," Albright said.

Four candidates emerged. The Ivory Coast nominated Foreign Minister Amara Essy, a former president of the UN General Assembly. Niger nominated Hamid Algabid, a former prime minister who was now secretary-general of the Islamic Conference. Mauritania nominated Ahmedou Ould Abdallah, a diplomat who had served as the UN's chief official in Burundi. And Ghana nominated Kofi Annan. Heeding Annan's request, President Rawlings dispatched a senior diplomat and future Ghanian foreign minister, Victor Gbeho, to lobby openly for Kofi.

The fifteen ambassadors of the Security Council met in a small room behind closed doors to consider the four African candidates. Paolo Fulci of Italy, the Council president, likened it to the way the cardinals meet in the Sistine Chapel in Rome to select a new pope. But he pointed out a striking difference—"if you stare at the ceiling, there are no frescoes by Michelangelo to inspire you."

The ambassadors took secret straw polls in which they could set down whether they encouraged or discouraged any of the candidates. In the first round, Kofi had twelve votes of encouragement and two votes of discouragement. Essy had eleven votes of encouragement and four votes of discouragement. The other two were far behind.

In the more complex second round, the five permanent members, who had the power of veto, put their votes down on red slips of paper, while the ten others voted on white slips. The round ended with ten favorable votes for Kofi, but he had one unfavorable vote on a red slip. Essy had seven favorable votes, but he had two unfavorable votes on red slips. The other two candidates also had two unfavorable votes on red slips. It was clear that France was vetoing Annan while the United States and Britain were vetoing anyone except Annan. When the day ended, Fulci, invoking the imagery of the cardinals in the Sistine Chapel, told reporters, "The smoke is black."

For three days, the straw votes followed these lines. France was not vetoing Kofi because he came from British Africa; he spoke French well enough to satisfy that requirement. But the French, annoyed at the United States for its high-handed blocking of Boutros-Ghali, wanted to register their protest by stopping the American choice for a successor.

The third day proved decisive. The French government persuaded Russian foreign minister Yevgeny Primakov to instruct his UN ambassador, Sergei Lavrov, to abstain on the next ballot. That would have stopped Annan's momentum and probably led to the Security Council expanding the pool of candidates to outside Africa. When the Americans heard about the impending Russian abstention, they ordered the U.S. ambassador in Moscow to find Russian president Boris Yeltsin and persuade him to overrule his foreign minister. The ambassador found Yeltsin, and the president agreed to the plea. Primakov was overruled, and the threat ended. France was now completely isolated. On the seventh ballot, even Egypt, which had hoped to revive the candidacy of Boutros-Ghali, voted for Annan. Kofi now had fourteen votes of encouragement and the one red slip from France. "It's fourteen against one again," said an aide to Boutros-Ghali, "but the one is not the same."

France did not want to mimic the role of Madeleine Albright—defying the choice of all fourteen other ambassadors with a veto. Nor did it want to be blamed by Africa in case the Security Council now felt forced to turn to another continent for candidates. Moreover, French diplomats had no personal quarrel with Kofi Annan; they had worked well with him as undersecretary-general in charge of peacekeeping. The French told the Americans they would switch to Annan on one condition: that Annan promise to name a French citizen to succeed himself as head of peacekeeping. Cameron Hume asked Shashi for a pledge from Annan. Tharoor relayed the request to Annan, who agreed. Albright's aide Jamie Rubin calls that promise "the last piece of the puzzle . . . that allowed the French to withdraw their threat of a veto."

On December 13, Essy and the two other candidates from former French Africa withdrew their candidacies. The Indonesian and Botswana ambassadors then proposed that the Council formally elect Annan by acclamation. All waited for the reaction of French ambassador Alain Dejammet. He did not disappoint them; he agreed. "Kofi Annan is an excellent choice," Dejammet told reporters later. "He is African, he speaks French, and he is fully conscious of the place of France both in Africa and in the United Nations." A few hours later, at 6:00 P.M., the Security Council unanimously adopted a resolution recommending the election of Kofi Annan as the seventh secretary-general of the United Nations. At the request of France and Egypt, they also adopted a second resolution, honoring Boutros-Ghali for his service. This, too, was passed unanimously by acclamation.

The election of Annan pleased UN news correspondents as much as it pleased Madeleine Albright and her coconspirators. Boutros-Ghali was not a good communicator, and the press had found the years with him difficult. He liked to talk privately with a handful of favorites and no one else. He hardly held news conferences. His spokesmen could not fill the breach because Boutros-Ghali never let them know what he was thinking or planning.

"I started calling him the sphinx," Josh Friedman, who had been the UN correspondent for *Newsday*, recalled recently. "I never really met him. I covered the UN all that time and I never once met the man or shook his hand. It made it very difficult to do my job."

On the day Annan was elected, Friedman took the elevator up to his office and sat down with the secretary-general-elect to chat for a half hour. "From that moment," said Friedman, "the guy had me. Anyone who could care enough to be human to someone else—there had to be some good qualities. And I think a lot of the press felt like that."

Nane Annan was lunching at a restaurant on Tenth Avenue when she heard the news that Kofi had been elected secretary-general. "I was elated on his behalf," she recalled a few years later. "I had to sit down for ten minutes. I felt I was in the eye of the storm." She knew that she would soon have security guards dog her every walk. So she decided to enjoy a stroll across Manhattan from her restaurant on the West Side to the UN, on the East. A woman noticed her toting a UN bag and asked Nane if she had attended the UN International Women's Conference in Beijing the year before. Nane replied that she had not. A few moments later she felt the urge to do something more dramatic. To explain the UN bag, perhaps she should shout out, "My husband was just elected secretary-general of the United Nations." But she did not.

9

The New Secretary-General

Kofi Annan assumed the role of secretary-general of the United Nations on January 2, 1997. He was the seventh secretary-general of the UN in its fifty-two years, the first black African secretary-general, and the first to rise from the ranks of the UN's Secretariat.

Annan had served as an international civil servant under four of his predecessors: U Thant of Burma, Kurt Waldheim of Austria, Javier Pérez de Cuéllar of Peru, and Boutros-Ghali of Egypt. By now, Annan understood the limitations of a job that provided the aura of a world statesman but no political or military power of his own. His predecessors had wrestled with intractable problems and moods of frustration. Waldheim had sullied the reputation of the office when researchers at the World Jewish Congress came up with revelations about the Nazi associations in his hidden past. Only the second secretary-general, Dag Hammarskjöld of Sweden, an intellectual and mystic poet who died in a plane crash just before Kofi joined the UN system, could truly be regarded as a historic figure of international renown and adulation. But Annan did not dwell on the pitfalls of the job or the difficulty of measuring up to Hammarskjöld. The post was exciting and hallowed enough for the fifty-eight-year-old Kofi Annan, and he came to it with an infectious joy that charmed almost everyone he met or managed.

Marrack Goulding, who remained as an undersecretary-general for half a year before taking the position of warden of St. Antony's College at Oxford University, had misgivings about his successor as chief of peacekeeping moving on to secretary-general. "He is a very kind man who likes everyone to leave his office satisfied," said Goulding recently. "But you just can't do that if you are the secretary-general of the United Nations. I have sometimes felt that he is just too nice for the job."

Yet, Goulding went on, "that made him very different from his predecessor. He could not match Boutros-Ghali's intellectual power. But he was much more polite, much kinder. Kofi seemed to be a breath of fresh air. There was a new spirit at the UN."

The new secretary-general had worked within the UN system for thirty years, and he knew most of the civil servants in New York, some as friends, many by sight. UN workers would be astounded and pleased when Kofi stopped them and asked about their work and then inquired after the health of their families. Sometimes, late at night, when he spied a stressed civil servant working overtime, he would urge him or her to set aside notebooks and go home to the family.

He believed that the UN worked best when its activities were transparent and the rationale for its actions communicated clearly to the press. "He has a very likable trait," Fred Eckhard, his spokesman, told the Yale-UN Oral History Project, "that if you ask him a question, he answers that question, maybe not as fully as you would like, but you always sense that he is trying to give you the information you are asking for. He also as a person, not just with journalists but with everyone, remembers little details about you, the fact that you have two children and maybe even your wife's name, and with journalists he would add that personal touch, so that journalists liked him." The new secretary-general would walk through the front door of the Secretariat building every morning, stop by the cluster of correspondents who waited for him, and reply to their questions.

Unlike Boutros-Ghali, Annan did not make decisions by himself or within a restricted coterie of privileged aides. Instead, the new secretary-general initiated weekly cabinet meetings where the heads of departments would share information and discuss courses of action. Annan listened carefully to all points of view before acting or delegating authority.

His calm and lack of histrionics appealed to outsiders as well. When he visited Washington, Senator Jesse Helms, the North Carolina Republican who chaired the Senate Foreign Relations Committee, told him, "You know, I asked my staff to look into your background and try to find somebody who doesn't like you, and they couldn't find anybody who doesn't like you. Everybody likes you. I like you." Helms and the State Department soon worked out a deal where Congress eventually appropriated most of the billion dollars it had withheld from the UN in the past as punishment.

(Using sports imagery, Albright's spokesman, Jamie Rubin, boasted to me in 1997, "We traded Boutros-Ghali for Kofi Annan and a billion dollars. Wasn't that worth it?" Unfortunately, Republican attempts to slap an antiabortion provision on the appropriation held up the money; the UN did not get the payment of the U.S. arrears until the last year of the Clinton administration.)

Despite the good feelings, Annan knew that he reigned over a battered and weakened UN. The three great crises of Boutros-Ghali's term—Somalia, Rwanda, and Bosnia—had taken a bitter toll. The UN had failed in these crises because of American or European blundering and confusion and cynicism. But the circumstances in each case were too complex to make outsiders understand what had happened. It was easier to blame the UN. UN civil servants always referred to their boss as "the SG." Kofi liked to joke that the initials stood for "Scape Goat."

As chief of peacekeeping, Annan had lived through each of these crises. He knew the enormity they had wrought. They had not only demeaned and humiliated the UN, they also had made the major powers, especially the United States, determined never to embrace similar crises again, at least not through the UN. If the major powers had taken the lessons of the crises to heart and had prepared the UN to handle new crises in new ways, a case could be made that Somalia, Rwanda, and Bosnia had strengthened the UN by preparing it for new ventures. But the lesson learned was far different. The major powers had learned instead to avoid these crises whenever possible.

Moreover, Madeleine Albright's campaign against Boutros-Ghali had harmed the UN as well. Every blow at him shook the UN. The conspirators persuaded themselves that they were railing at Boutros-Ghali to save the UN. But it was hard to make outsiders understand that the condemnation of the leader was not a condemnation of the institution itself.

Kofi also knew that he himself was largely unknown outside the UN. "People were doubtful," he recalls. "Some were doubtful and suspicious. . . . Even though I was running the peacekeeping operation, I wasn't exactly a household name. There was a feeling that anyone who works in a bureaucracy is a bureaucrat, and can this bureaucrat ever rise to the level of the job and deliver or are we going to have an indecisive, scared bureaucrat leading the organization?"

Some suspected that this "indecisive, scared bureaucrat" was a stooge of the United States. After all, he would not be in power if Madeleine and her conspirators had not defied everyone else on the Security Council to unseat Boutros-Ghali. It was obvious that Kofi Annan had been her first choice to replace Boutros. To make matters worse, if he were a stooge, he was a stooge of an American administration that did not want the UN and the secretary-general to do very much. That notion hardly strengthened the UN.

The weakness of the UN was most glaring in Africa. In 1996, fifteen of Africa's fifty-four countries foundered in bloody wars. More than half the world's war deaths took place in Africa. The violence spawned more than eight million refugees. Sadako Ogata of Japan, the UN high commissioner for refugees, and her brave workers did an admirable job of stanching some of the misery. But the UN failed often at preventing or ending war.

The UN failed just as badly in dealing with the aftermath of Rwanda as it had in dealing with the original genocide. A terrible crisis erupted while the Security Council was arguing about the veto of Boutos-Ghali and the election of Annan during the last months of 1996. More than 1.2 million Hutu refugees had gathered in the hovels of UN camps in eastern Zaire. Some were defeated Rwandan soldiers. Many had the blood of Tutsi victims on their hands. But the rest were innocent Hutus who had fled in terror from the advancing army of Paul Kagame. That army was now intent on breaking up those camps and forcing the refugees back into Rwanda.

In mid-November, the Security Council agreed to authorize a Canadian-led force to protect the refugees. But before the troops could be dispatched, Kagame and his Tutsi army launched powerful and bloody assaults on the camps that forced several hundred thousand Hutus back into Rwanda. Then came a strange twist in the drama.

The United States, employing reconnaissance planes, reported that almost all the refugees were back in Rwanda, ending the need for the Canadian troops. The vision of the Americans, however, was blurred by their admiration for Kagame, who did not want the intervention and insisted it was not needed. *New York Times* foreign correspondent Howard W. French believes that Clinton administration guilt over failing to prevent the massacre of the Tutsis in Rwanda deluded the Americans into ignoring the Tutsi butchering of the Hutus in Zaire.

Ogata came up with a far different assessment than the Americans. She and her staff estimated that seven hundred thousand Hutus were still in Zaire, fleeing westward in their misery. But the Security Council and the Canadians listened to the Americans and called off the intervention.

By the time Annan took office, an army led by rebel Laurent Kabila but manned mainly by Kagame's Tutsi soldiers was sweeping through Zaire. Kabila intended to overthrow the Zairean despot

Mobutu Sese Seko, but his Tutsi soldiers massacred thousands of Hutu refugees along the way. Kabila took power in May, and the UN could do no more than send a team of investigators to Zaire (renamed the Congo) to find out if massacres had taken place. But Kabila delayed, harassed, and obstructed the investigators. They accomplished next to nothing, and Annan withdrew them after a year.

But though his institution was weak, Annan discovered that his voice was not. He issued reports and made speeches of remarkable frankness. In April 1997, after a little more than three months on the job, he sent a report to both the Security Council and the General Assembly on conflict in Africa that urged Africans to stop blaming all their ills on colonialism. "Today more than ever," he wrote, "Africa must look at itself." He lamented that the winners of political victory in Africa often assumed a "winner takes all" attitude and refused to share wealth, patronage, and power with anyone outside the tribe of the victors. "In extreme cases," Annan wrote, "rival communities may perceive that their security, perhaps their very survival, can be ensured only through control of State power. Conflict in such cases become virtually inevitable."

Annan was even more blunt two months later, when he addressed the annual summit meeting of the Organization of African Unity (OAU) in Harare, Zimbabwe. Speaking as "a son of Africa," Annan told the heads of state and government, most of them despots, many coming to power in military coups, "Africa can no longer tolerate, and accept as faits accomplis, coups against elected governments and the illegal seizure of power by military cliques, who sometimes act for sectional interests, sometimes simply for their own." He went on, "Where democracy has been usurped, let us do whatever is in our power to restore it to its rightful owners—the people."

After the speech, Salim Ahmed Salim of Tanzania, OAU secretary-general and an old friend, told Kofi, "That was a bold speech. You are the only one who can make this speech and get out of here without being lynched." They both laughed.

In July 1997, Annan made one of his most fateful decisions. He appointed Richard Butler, the Australian ambassador to the UN, as executive chairman of the United Nations Special Commission (UNSCOM), making him the chief inspector hunting and destroying weapons of mass destruction in Iraq. Under the terms of the resolution ending the Persian Gulf War, the Security Council refused to lift the economic sanctions against Iraq until its weapons of mass destruction were eliminated. Rolf Ekeus, a Swedish diplomat, had led the commission since its inception, but he was leaving to take up a new post as the Swedish ambassador to the United States. He proposed that Butler take his place, and Annan agreed.

During the six years of inspections under Ekeus, the Iraqis had lied and cheated, concealed evidence, harassed inspectors, and fulminated nonsense. But Ekeus and his inspectors had managed to eliminate all of Saddam Hussein's programs for weapons of mass destruction. They did so with the help of Saddam's son-in-law Hussein Kamal Hassan, who headed all Iraq's weapons programs before he defected to Jordan in August 1995 and revealed all to Ekeus in secret meetings. By the time Butler took over, the job of eliminating the weapons was largely over. There were sticking points. The Iraqis could not come up with the paperwork that would verify their claims of destroying the last of their chemical and biological agents. But we now know that the Iraqis were finally telling the truth.

But neither Ekeus nor Butler realized this. Although the Iraqis were no longer lying, they still cheated, concealed, harassed, and fulminated, as if they were hiding weapons of mass destruction. It is not clear why. The prevailing theory is that a strutting Saddam was trying to hide his weakness and fool the world into thinking he was a secret power. The American inspector David Kay also suggested that greedy scientists, enriching themselves with funds for phony projects, may have hoodwinked Saddam into thinking he had more than he did. Perhaps more important, both the George H. W. Bush administration and the Clinton administration had pledged never to vote to lift sanctions as long as Saddam remained in power. There was thus never an incentive for the Iraqis to cooperate with the inspectors.

Butler published his book *The Greatest Threat: Iraq, Weapons of Mass Destruction, and the Growing Crisis of Global Security* two years before President George W. Bush ordered the invasion of Iraq in March 2003. In view of what we now know about the lack of Iraqi armament, the book is so wrongheaded and delusional that it can infuse a reader with waves of sadness. Butler's stubborn certainty—which inspired so many false assessments by others— was founded on very little evidence except his distaste for Iraqi posturing and his abhorrence of what struck him as blatant Iraqi lying. Many of his conclusions came from the whispers of American intelligence agents and Iraqi exiles.

Annan had no problem with Butler at first. The Australian told him, "I accept the job because *you* asked me." "I meant this sincerely," Butler writes. "I was very committed to Kofi Annan as secretary-general, and I wanted him to know this. I knew I would need his support in return."

"Richard started well," says Annan. "But after a while I was beginning to get worried in the sense that he was not working with the Council in the way Ekeus and others did. He tended to think that he could do it alone with the United States and United Kingdom. I had to tell him that we had a Council of fifteen, and we need to make sure that you deal with them and that you not only stick to one or two members. Otherwise, you are going to get into trouble and the program is going to get into trouble."

The fifty-five-year-old Butler was an aggressive and undiplomatic diplomat. Scott Ritter, an American inspector, says that Butler "wanted to give the impression that he was the rough-and-tumble rugby player he once had been." Aides of Annan regarded him as a cowboy, a grandstander, and a blowhard who did the bidding of the United States. Butler acknowledges that he was an aggressive chief inspector who spoke directly and clearly. He believes many people appreciated his directness because it helped them understand the complex problems in Iraqi disarmament. And he denies "that I took direction from the United States." There is no doubt, however, that his tough and skeptical treatment of Iraq fit nicely with the approach of Secretary of State Madeleine Albright.

UNSCOM reported to the Security Council, not to the secretary-general, and Butler acted independently of Annan. The secretary-general was technically not Butler's boss. Butler believes that Annan's aides—though not Annan himself—resented this arrangement. "Whatever our disagreements—and they became serious," Butler writes, "Kofi Annan always treated me with courtesy, and in any case he is a far larger man than some of those around him."

Nevertheless, it made no sense to irritate the secretary-general, and there is no doubt that Butler began to irritate Annan. "When he started making his reports," says Annan, "some of their claims he was making were really quite extraordinary. . . . The stakes were so high that you couldn't leave it alone to him and to his judgment. Quite a number of Council members were dubious about his reports. This was the sense that I was getting from some other Council members that he was exaggerating. He was coming up with such huge claims, huge quantities."

We must not make too much of Annan's prescience. He did not realize that Iraq no longer had any weapons of mass destruction. But he was troubled by Butler's exaggeration of the evidence. And he was troubled as well by Butler's bullying. As a Ghanian born under British colonialism, Annan felt the need and the right of Third World countries to command respect. Enough time had passed since the Persian Gulf War for diplomats to treat the sovereignty of Iraq with respect. Annan did not believe Butler handled this part of the job well. Butler, on the other hand, believed that Annan had fallen under the influence of Iraq and of the three members of the Security Council—Russia, France, and China—who, in the view of Butler, parroted the lies of Iraq.

There was continual bickering between Butler and the Iraqis and numerous incidents in which the Iraqis resisted inspections. Butler often dealt with Tariq Aziz, the deputy prime minister who served as chief Iraqi negotiator and the main voice of Iraq to the rest of the world. Aziz had been Kofi Annan's main contact when the future secretary-general negotiated the release of UN hostages in 1990. Butler found Aziz insufferable. In Butler's view, the Iraqi was abusive, threatening, and "utterly without humor." Butler writes in his book, "His attitude at all times was very haughty. 'How dare you ask me that question?' was his continual tone."

In late October 1997, Iraq precipitated a crisis when Aziz informed the Security Council that Iraq would no longer allow Americans on the inspection teams. Annan tried to defuse the tension by sending a team of three negotiators to Baghdad. The move disheartened Butler. It undercut the independence of Butler and UNSCOM. Even more important, the dispatch of envoys made it clear that Annan would be satisfied if some diplomatic solution could be found to the incessant conflict over inspections and sanctions.

"The secretary-general's decision to send the envoys," Butler writes, "was seen by Iraq as further confirmation that Annan was committed to a diplomatic solution to Iraq's recalcitrance, without obliging it to be disarmed. Iraq's new policy of enhanced resistance to and then destruction of UNSCOM was given a boost."

Annan's envoys failed. Butler then removed all inspectors, and the United States threatened military action. The Russians, at the request of the Americans, finally stepped in and pressured the Iraqis to drop their objections to American inspectors. Butler sent his inspectors back to Iraq, and their work resumed—but for less than three months.

A new crisis arose in the new year when Aziz announced that eight palaces and large complexes in Iraq were "presidential sites" used by Saddam Hussein and therefore off-limits to the inspectors. Once again, President Bill Clinton threatened to bomb Iraq, and once again Butler withdrew his inspectors. The crisis led to a flurry of diplomatic delegations to Baghdad. According to the *New York Times*, quoting a paraphrased account of the conversation, President Jacques Chirac of France telephoned President Boris Yeltsin of Russia and said, "You know, Boris, you and I are trying to avoid a war over there. Bill wants to strike. Maybe you and I have a role to play." At first Kofi Annan, while conferring continually with many parties, said he would stay out of the crisis. "With so many cooks," said one of his aides, "he is waiting to see if he can be helpful. He doesn't want to be another cook stirring the soup."

The Americans insisted that nothing short of unconditional inspections would satisfy them. In a CNN-televised public meeting at Ohio State University, Secretary of State Albright, Secretary of Defense William S. Cohen, and National Security adviser Sandy Berger tried to explain why the United States would have to bomb Iraq if the demands were not met. They made a weak case to an inhospitable audience. Protesting hecklers interrupted them twenty times in ninety minutes. The public relations fiasco, however, did not temper the Clinton administration's resolve to bomb, at least not in public.

Kofi Annan finally decided to go to Baghdad to try to end the crisis. "I saw it as a sacred duty of the secretary-general," he told me recently, "to do whatever he can in situations to avoid war and use of conflict." The phrase "sacred duty," which he has used before to explain the trip, was significant, because it reflects a controversial view of the role of a secretary-general first set down by Dag Hammarskjöld. Nowhere in the UN Charter does it say that the secretary-general has a sacred duty to prevent war.

The Charter describes the secretary-general as "the chief administrative officer" of the UN. Critics such as American ambassador John R. Bolton insist that is the limit of a secretary-general's authority. The secretary-general, in their view, is no more than a bureaucrat in the pay of UN members, especially of the United States and the four other permanent members of the Security Council. The Charter, however, also states that "the secretary-general may bring to the attention of the Security Council any matter which in his opinion may threaten the maintenance of international peace and security." That responsibility has spawned an elaborate system in which the secretary-general and his staff issue scores of reports on international crises with recommendations for action. These reports are usually cited in Security Council resolutions that call on the secretary-general to carry out the Council's wishes. This system has made the secretary-general a kind of executive officer as well as administrative officer.

But Hammarskjöld went farther. At his first news conference, in 1953, he was asked how much initiative a secretary-general had in "critical situations involving peace." Hammarskjöld replied that the Charter gave him "a fairly well-developed right of initiative," but, he went on, "I think the right of initiative in a certain sense, informally, of the secretary-general goes far beyond what is described in the Charter, provided that he observes the proper forms, chooses his approaches with tact, and avoids acting in such a way as, so to say, counteract his own purpose."

Hammarskjöld demonstrated this in 1955 when, despite American misgivings, he flew to China to ask Prime Minister Chou En-lai to free fifteen American fliers who had been shot down and jailed as spies. He acted while a good deal of foolish war talk emanated in the United States. As one justification for his action, Hammarskjöld cited the "philosophy" of the Charter. The preamble to the Charter, in the wonderful words written by American poet Archibald MacLeish, states that "we the peoples of the United Nations" are "determined to save succeeding generations from the scourge of war." The secretary-general, elected by all the member governments of the world, is the only UN official in a position to reflect and help carry out that determination. Hammarskjöld and Chou En-lai met four times in sessions that lasted between three and five hours each. The Americans were released several months after the dramatic trip. Hammarskjöld's flight to China made him a romantic hero back home in UN headquarters on First Avenue.

As the crisis intensified in 1998, Annan consulted with many colleagues, diplomats, and representatives of human rights and church groups. It struck him that many people might die soon for a flimsy cause. "Here we had a situation," he says, "where the main reason for the military action was the fact that Saddam was refusing to open his palaces, and I was convinced that it ought to be possible to convince him to open the palaces and have them inspected and avoid destruction and the possibility of putting his people at risk." This kind of thinking exasperated Butler, for he, like the American and British governments, believed that Iraq had no right to negotiate conditions for inspections.

Aziz proposed that Annan come to Baghdad to talk with Saddam Hussein. After consulting with Middle East leaders and President Jacques Chirac of France, Annan asked the ambassadors of all fifteen countries on the Security Council to assemble for an informal meeting in the small conference room next to his office on the thirty-eighth floor of the Secretariat Building. He told them he intended to fly to Baghdad but needed an understanding from the Council on what they wanted him to accomplish.

"I decided to go myself," Annan told the Yale-UN Oral History Project, "because the stakes were extremely high, and the issue had been festering for a while. We were dealing with the issue of peace, the issue of weapons of mass destruction. . . . I was worried that if the bombing went ahead without this effort, it could mean the end of the inspections, and it could also have impact, negative impact, on the humanitarian efforts that we were doing for the Iraqi people."

American ambassador Bill Richardson, who had been appointed by President Clinton to succeed Albright in New York, objected. So did British ambassador John Weston. But Annan was not asking for permission from the members of the Security Council. "I wanted to have a clear understanding of what it is they were looking for, that we were looking for," he said. "Otherwise, I was not asking for rigid instructions or marching orders. I think it was important when you are going to have a discussion with President Saddam Hussein and come back with the proposals that the Council can work with, can accept and move forward, that you have a rough idea or some idea as to what the Council is looking for and what they would accept as a solution to the crisis." He told Secretary of State Albright later that he would go to Baghdad even if the United States objected. He warned her, in fact, that the United States would lose credibility if it stopped the secretary-general from trying to reach a peaceful settlement with Saddam.

On Sunday morning, February 15, Secretary of State Albright flew to New York on a C-20 Air Force plane for a secret meeting with Annan at his official residence on Sutton Place by the East River. Despite their earlier reluctance, she and Sandy Berger had decided to support his trip. "Of course," Annan said later, "she indicated they were not enthusiastic, but they had decided to join the consensus, since others felt the trip would be useful." But she presented Annan with a paper listing "red lines"—the measures that the United States insisted must be included in any agreement with Saddam Hussein. The inspectors must have complete access to all sites. UNSCOM must have "operational control" of all inspections. The Iraqis must cooperate with the inspectors. The resolutions of the Security Council must not be watered down by any understanding between Saddam and Annan. Any agreement must be written and signed; oral promises were not good enough. "The American 'red lines' posed no problems for me," Annan said.

At his last session with members of the Security Council, Annan found himself bombarded with numerous suggestions for the wording of acceptable provisions in an agreement. "When this discussion started to go into the tiniest details of the text, which frankly would never be used in his conversations in Baghdad," said Russian ambassador Sergei Lavrov, "it was maybe one of the only times when I saw him lose his temper but lose his temper in a very dignified way. It never showed in his face. He just got up and said, 'Thank you very much. Dear colleagues, I believe I've got the sense of the house. I'm leaving tomorrow, good luck.'"

British ambassador Weston talked with Annan before he left for Baghdad. There were no written instructions, but Weston offered an oral rundown of the consensus of the Council. This followed Madeleine Albright's "red lines" closely. Fed up by now with all the advice, Annan told Weston politely that he was not flying to Baghdad as the Security Council's messenger; he needed room to negotiate.

President Clinton phoned Annan the next day. "I want a

diplomatic solution as much as you," Clinton told him, "but it must be principled, have integrity." A senior administration official summed up the thrust of Clinton's message: "Kofi, don't jam me. Jam the Iraqis." The president marveled that the whole world was running around trying to satisfy this dictator who had defied UN resolutions. Annan should be putting pressure on Saddam, not on the United States. Saddam should not feel at the end of the talks that he had won a big victory. Annan replied that he understood what the Americans wanted.

Before he left New York, a reporter asked him if he was ruthless enough to deal with Saddam Hussein. "I don't know if what is required to get a solution is ruthlessness," Annan replied.

Annan flew to Paris by the Air France Concorde and conferred with President Chirac. Chirac and his aides described Saddam as reflective and well informed and warned the secretary-general not to underestimate him. Chirac authorized use of a presidential plane, a three-jet-engine Falcon 900, to take Annan and his aides to and from Baghdad.

The secretary-general arrived in Baghdad on Friday night, February 20. The Iraqis wanted to start talks immediately, but Annan insisted he needed a good night's sleep. The meetings began at the Ministry of Foreign Affairs the next morning. Annan had Hans Corel, the chief UN legal counsel, and three close aides, Lakhdar Brahimi, Shashi Tharoor, and Rolf Knuttson, at his side. Tariq Aziz was accompanied by the minister of foreign affairs, the minister of oil, and others. For a good deal of the time, Annan and Aziz conferred alone.

They agreed on the broad outlines of a memorandum of understanding but failed to reach agreement on two issues: whether the palaces and other presidential sites could be inspected more than once, and whether the inspections of these places could be called something else. Tariq Aziz wanted to call them "visits." But Annan said, "Visit is too loose. People might think you are inviting us for tea or something." And Annan insisted the inspectors had to have the right to return to the sites.

Annan listened to a lot of angry talk about the need to respect the sovereignty of Iraq. "They maintain the dignity and sovereignty of Iraq had to be respected," he told the Yale-UN Project, "and that the palaces are places where they also work in, and they cannot have inspectors coming and disrupting their work, demeaning their authority and their leadership."

The secretary-general also listened to the Iraqis rail against the onerous provisions of the resolution that ended the Persian Gulf War and subjected Iraq to continued sanctions and inspections. "You have to accept this resolution," Annan told Aziz and the other Iraqis. "If you want to see light at the end of the tunnel, you have to implement the disarmament provision, the disarmament agreement, and then you will see light at the end of the tunnel, our sanctions being suspended or lifted, because the resolution was clear: disarm and the sanctions will be lifted." But Annan was told that the Iraqis "feel that the resolutions are so complicated, the demands are so many that those who do not want to lift the sanctions will always find an excuse to say they have not complied."

By 2:00 A.M., Annan gave up for the day. Aziz suggested another meeting the next morning, but Annan refused. A session with Saddam was scheduled for midday Sunday, and Annan would try to iron out the last contentious issues with the Iraqi president.

While her husband negotiated in Baghdad, Nane visited St. Patrick's Cathedral on Fifth Avenue in New York to pray for the success of the mission. "He is a person who does not contemplate failure," she told James Bone of the *Times* of London. "I am a bit more superstitious. In this case, it was so important that I just wanted to be part of the wall of support that would carry him. Part of that was going back to the cathedral and just sitting praying for him."

On Sunday, February 22, Annan and his aides were driven to Saddam Hussein's nearby presidential palace on the bank of the Tigris River. Annan was pleased that the Iraqi leader met them in a business suit, not in his usual military uniform. After a while, the UN and Iraqi aides left the room, and the secretary-general and the Iraqi president were alone. But Saddam soon excused himself. He told Annan he had to pray. "That was the first time that I have been in a meeting when someone has left me to go and pray," Annan recalled. When Saddam returned, he offered the secretary-general a cigar, and the two smoked and chatted.

Annan tried to appeal to the Iraqi dictator's ego. "You're a builder," the secretary-general said. "You built modern Iraq. It was destroyed once. You've rebuilt it. Do you want to destroy it again? . . . If we can work out an agreement that will prevent military action and you would undertake to comply, it will save the day."

The secretary-general also tried to warn Saddam of the consequences of failure. "This time, let me tell you, you'll be hit and hit very hard," Annan said. "All the reconstruction you've done will be gone and you'll have to start again. Think of the suffering of your people."

The session lasted for three hours, and Annan found it exhausting. He told his friend William Shawcross later, "I had to really draw on all my inner resources—creativity and stamina and almost a spiritual courage—to really engage him in this. So at the end it was very draining."

Shawcross asked him what it was like to deal with a bloody tyrant like Saddam Hussein. "Saddam is very calm and polite," Annan replied. "You wouldn't think he was capable of what he has done. . . . He looks like somebody's uncle. But if you mistake his calmness, soft-spokenness for weakness, you're in trouble." Nane's uncle Raoul Wallenberg had once said, "To do good one sometimes has to deal with the devil," Annan recalled and went on, "What I find is that even with these evil ones, one can touch them, can reach them somehow. . . . In the end, the only means I have is reason and persuasion. I cannot call on an air force or an army."

Throughout the session, Saddam took copious notes on a yellow pad. Toward the end, he and the secretary-general could agree on the sticking points of the proposed memorandum of understanding. Instead of inspections or visits, the memorandum would call for "entries" to the presidential sites. There would be "initial and subsequent entries"—in short, more than one. Annan agreed that diplomats would accompany the inspectors. Saddam, trying to underscore the delicacy of these inspections, wanted the inspectors accompanied by ambassadors. Annan accepted only "senior diplomats." Finally, the aides were called back into the room, and Annan announced, "We have an agreement. We have a text." He and Saddam drank orange juice, shook hands, and ended the meeting.

The secretary-general messaged members of the Security Council that an agreement had been reached but said he would not release the full text until it was reviewed by lawyers for both sides and signed by himself and Tariq Aziz. He feared that the Americans and others might badger him for changes if they had a copy before the final signing.

This did not satisfy Secretary of State Albright. She phoned in the early morning and demanded that the staff wake Kofi. He had been fast asleep. "And in Iraq—I was with him—Madeleine Albright was on the phone with him at four o'clock screaming at him, screaming at him," Fred Eckhard told the Yale-UN Oral History Project. She wanted a copy of a draft of the agreement. She and her staff were being asked questions in Washington they could not answer. She also wanted to make sure he had made an agreement the Americans could live with. Annan told her, he recalls, "that we were in the middle of negotiations and the document will change and when I have a document I will send it and I will send it to her and the other fourteen members of the Council at the same time." After the call ended, the annoyed secretary-general told a member of his staff that Madeleine sometimes abuses friendship.

A rumor spread, in fact, that he had hung up on the secretary of state. But when asked about this a few years later, he told Lynne Duke of the *Washington Post*, "I don't go around hanging up on people. That is not my style."

The memorandum of understanding was signed by the secretary-general and Tariq Aziz on Monday, February 23, averting an American bombing of Iraq. Annan flew back to Paris and New York. Nane met him at the airport in New York. When he entered the Secretariat Building with Nane at his side, hundreds of UN workers greeted him with cheers and applause. It was a hero's welcome much like that of Dag Hammarskjöld more than forty years before.

Annan presented the memorandum of understanding to the Security Council in a closed meeting. In the memorandum, Iraq promised to accept all relevant UN resolutions and cooperate with the UN inspectors. In turn, the UN promised that its inspectors would respect the national security, sovereignty, and dignity of Iraq. Butler and UNSCOM would continue to have the right to call for inspections of presidential sites, but these "entries" would be carried out by special inspection teams that included senior diplomats. "Whether the threat to international peace and security has been averted for all time," Annan told the Council, "is now in the hands of the Iraqi delegation."

Butler and his inspectors were upset by the memorandum and, perhaps more important, by the secretary-general's role in the crisis. They felt that Annan was treating them and the Iraqis as if he were mediating between equal antagonists. In their view, they and Iraq were not equal—UNSCOM had been created by the Security Council as a superior force to do away with Iraq's deceits and its weapons of mass destruction. Charles Duelfer, Butler's American deputy, says he was shaken at the Security Council meeting when he heard Annan refer to the inspectors as "cowboys." In his memoir, Butler wrote "I had no illusion about what had happened—UNSCOM's mandate had, at least in part, been bargained away in Baghdad." Nevertheless, Butler, after Annan assured him his power had not diminished, decided to support the agreement in public.

The United States was wary. American ambassador Bill Richardson called the agreement a step in the right direction but insisted it needed some clarification. "We believe very strongly that it needs to be tested soon," he told the press. Some Republicans were far more skeptical. Senate Republican leader Trent Lott of Mississippi accused Annan of appeasing Saddam Hussein. "Kofi Annan really sold us down the drain," said Representative Gerald Solomon of

New York. Nevertheless, the United States joined the fourteen other members of the Security Council in approving the agreement and congratulating Annan for his mission.

After meeting with the Security Council, an exhausted Annan met with the press. He was asked if he felt he could trust the Iraqi president. "Can I trust Saddam Hussein?" he replied. "I think I can do business with him. I think he was serious when he took the engagement. I think he realizes what it means for his people." When Madeleine Albright, who had called Saddam "the most evil man since Hitler," heard the remark about doing business with Saddam, she "cringed."

Annan's triumph did not last very long. The memorandum of understanding did not ease relations between Butler, still the chief inspector, and Deputy Prime Minister Tariq Aziz. At a bitter confrontation between the two in Baghdad six months later, Aziz demanded that Butler declare Iraq free of weapons of mass destruction. Butler refused. Lifting a cup and spoon, an angry Aziz spoke in a voice laced with contempt. "You need to verify, verify, and verify whatever we tell you," said Aziz as he began to mock his antagonist. "This is a cup of tea. Yes, it looks like a cup of tea, but we are going to verify it. This is a spoon. Yes, it looks like a spoon, but we are going to verify it." Aziz insisted that Iraq "has no proscribed weapons," but Butler looked on this as "the blackest lie."

By the end of October 1998, Iraq announced that it would no longer allow any UN inspections or monitoring of its military activities. The United States and Britain prepared to bomb Iraq. Annan wrote a letter to Saddam Hussein urging Iraq to change course. With American and British planes already en route to Iraq, Tariq Aziz announced that the government had reversed itself and would now allow inspections. The United States and Britain called off the air strikes.

The truce lasted only a few weeks. When the Iraqis began to frustrate inspections once again, Butler ordered all his inspectors to leave Iraq. The memorandum of understanding negotiated by Kofi Annan and Saddam Hussein was dead. On an official visit to

North Africa, the secretary-general, talking with his friend the British journalist Shawcross, said, "Not only has he torn it up, but even people sympathetic to him in the Security Council are fed up with him." Shawcross asked Annan about the remark that had made Madeleine Albright cringe. Did not the latest events prove that you cannot do business with Saddam Hussein? "It proves you cannot take his word," Annan replied. "I used that phrase in that I got him to change his mind. I did not mean that he was a man of honor. You cannot rely on him."

The secretary-general still hoped that the Americans would not bomb Iraq. He feared that would punish the people of Iraq far more than Saddam. But there was no way to dissuade President Clinton this time. In mid-December, waves of American and British bombers struck at Iraqi military installations and suspected weapons sites in an operation dubbed Desert Fox.

The secretary-general, back in New York, issued a plaintive statement: "This is a sad day for the United Nations, and for the world. . . . It is also a very sad day for me personally. Throughout this year I have done everything in my power to ensure peaceful compliance with Security Council resolutions, and to avert the use of force.

"This has not been an easy or a painless process," he went on. "It has required patience, determination, and the will to seek peace even when all signs pointed to war. However daunting the task, the United Nations had to try as long as any hope for peace remained. I deeply regret that today these efforts have proved insufficient." The statement did not blame anyone—neither the inspectors nor the Iraqis nor the Americans.

Despite the humiliation of the aftermath, Kofi Annan's mission to Baghdad defined his leadership of the UN in several significant ways. Perhaps most important, it established his independence from Washington. Although handpicked by Madeleine Albright and her fellow conspirators against Boutros Boutros-Ghali, Annan refused to act as if he were beholden to her. He regarded her as a friend. He consulted her often. Yet he refused to call off his trip when she deplored it, and he refused to feed her any more information about the proceedings in Baghdad than he gave to the other members of the Security Council.

The mission also demonstrated that he was willing to take chances and move beyond normal bounds in the interest of peace. He was not a histrionic leader. He did not simply rush off to Baghdad. He listened to the advice and demands of many diplomats and fellow workers before he left. He tried to prepare his way carefully. In the end, he left for Baghdad, unsure of the result.

He also showed that he thought and felt with a Third World sensibility. He knew and liked Americans and Europeans. In fact, of course, he was married to a European. But he was an African and, while he understood the conventional wisdom of the Americans and others from the industrialized world, he did not accept it whole. He understood why diplomats such as Madeleine Albright and Richard Butler looked on Saddam Hussein and his coterie as evil. Yet he also felt that the Albrights and the Butlers exaggerated and that you cannot bully a government, no matter how badly it once behaved, if you want to make it do your bidding without force.

Some critics, especially in the United States, looked on him as a soft touch, easily duped by a master such as Saddam Hussein. Kofi Annan, in their view, was a lightweight, foolishly trying to spar with the heavyweights.

But that was not the prevailing view worldwide. In the end, he failed, but he failed with dignity, moral courage, and transparency. He talked frankly with journalists about the session with Saddam Hussein. He explained himself easily in public. He made many people feel he was a secretary-general they could like and trust.

10

Intervention: Kosovo and East Timor

W hile still feeling praise for his mission to Baghdad, the secretary-general delivered a pair of speeches in 1998 that reveal a good deal about his values and thinking. The first, made in the capital of Rwanda, reflected both honesty and courage. The second, made in Britain, was far more important and proposed innovative ways of using UN peacekeepers in a shattering world.

Annan set off on an eight-nation tour of Africa in May. Once again, the specter of the Rwanda massacres dogged him. Even before he reached Kigali, his relationship with Rwanda would erupt in the news again. While in Nairobi during the first stages of the trip, he received the news that the *New Yorker* had just published Philip Gourevitch's article accusing him of failing to raise the alarm during his peacekeeping days about the Hutu plan to wipe out the Tutsis. The accusation did not come from some right-wing publication bristling with contempt for the United Nations. The *New Yorker* was a prestigious weekly with political views generally left of center. It was an unexpected attack, and it was very personal.

"It was hurtful, and I was surprised," he told me several years later. "And besides, I didn't think it was entirely fair, nor was it correct to blame the head of peacekeeping for what happened, particularly when you consider the fact that it wasn't something where the head of peacekeeping had considerable autonomy. I think the role of the [Security] Council and the role of the secretary-general and all that seemed to have been played down [in the article]." He also felt that Gourevitch did not understand the UN's justified fear in those days that all countries would pull out their peacekeepers if they believed there was danger.

"But that kind of analysis is missing in the *New Yorker* article," he said. Then, in an uncertain way, reflective of his willingness to see the best in everyone, he tried to understand the motive of Gourevitch. "But, of course," he went on, "I also see why maybe Philip would write that way to get attention to wake the conscience of the world. I don't know." He paused but then added no more.

The publication of the article did not deter Annan from speaking his mind a few days later while addressing the Rwanda Parliament in Kigali. Discussing the "paroxysm of horror" that had killed several hundred thousand Tutsis, the secretary-general acknowledged that "the world failed Rwanda at that time of evil" and that "the international community and the United Nations could not muster the political will to confront it." But he infuriated the Tutsi leaders of Rwanda by also stating that "it was a horror that came from within."

His words alluded to the murderous relationship between the minority Tutsis and majority Hutus in both Rwanda and Burundi for decades. Annan's words contradicted the catechism of Rwanda's new Tutsi rulers, who blamed outsiders for fostering the killings—the German and Belgian administrators for dividing the Tutsis and Hutus in colonial days, and the UN for failing to prevent the massacres in 1994.

Annan also irritated the Tutsi leaders by telling the Parliament that "you must teach your children that the return from genocide must be paved with tolerance, mercy, and understanding." He spoke barely two weeks after a UN official had criticized the Rwanda government for executing twenty-two people on charges of genocide.

Before Annan spoke, Foreign Minister Anastase Gasana, who had seen an advance copy of the speech, read a long and insulting bill of particulars against the UN. He even berated the UN because its predecessor, the League of Nations, had turned over the German colonies of Rwanda and Burundi to the Belgian colonial administration as mandates. In another insult to Annan, the president, vice president, and prime minister of Rwanda refused to attend a reception that night in honor of the secretary-general. Annan made no friends among the Tutsis with his visit, but he demonstrated his fierce loyalty to the truth, even in the face of fury.

In June, the secretary-general tackled the crucial issue of intervention—in a remarkable lecture to the Ditchley Foundation in Ditchley Park outside Oxford in Britain. Ditchley is a prestigious organization devoted to the study of international affairs, and some of Annan's aides believe that the principles set down in the lecture will rank as one of Annan's most important legacies.

In the lecture, Annan made it clear that he believed in the right of intervention in the internal affairs of a sovereign country to relieve the suffering of people within its borders. He held this view even though the UN Charter forbids the UN from intervening "in matters which are essentially within the domestic jurisdiction of any State."

Annan told the foundation that the Security Council had the "overriding duty to preserve international peace and security" under the UN Charter and that "even national sovereignty can be set aside if it stands in the way" of this overriding duty. The UN has the obvious right, for example, to intervene in civil wars that send refugees to other countries and threaten international peace.

But Annan's lecture took the UN much farther than that. He said that the UN Charter was issued in the name of "the peoples" of the world, not governments. One of the goals of the Charter was "to reaffirm faith in fundamental human rights, in the dignity and worth of the human person." "The Charter protects the sovereignty of peoples," Annan said. "It was never meant as a license for governments to trample on human rights and human dignity. Sovereignty implies responsibility, not just power." The Charter, according to Annan, therefore allowed intervention to save endangered peoples within a sovereign state.

The secretary-general preferred peaceful interventions, perhaps by regional organizations attempting to persuade an offending government to change its ways. But he recognized that military intervention might be necessary. He cited three military interventions that the world had applauded in the past: the Indian intervention in 1971 that ended Pakistan's suppression of East Pakistan (now the independent country of Bangladesh), the Vietnam intervention in 1978 that ended the Khmer Rouge genocide in Cambodia, and the Tanzanian intervention in 1979 that overthrew Idi Amin's regime of terror in Uganda.

But in each case, Annan went on, these interventions had been unilateral—the invaders "had no mandate from anyone else to act as they did." That, he said, set "an uncomfortable precedent." He asked, "Can we really afford to let each state be the judge of its own right, or duty, to intervene in another state's internal conflict?" That kind of chaotic principle, he said, would have legitimized Adolf Hitler's invasion of Czechoslovakia before World War II.

Instead, Annan said, "Surely the only institution competent to assume that role is the Security Council of the United Nations. The Charter clearly assigns responsibility to the Council for maintaining international peace and security. I would argue, therefore, that only the Council has the authority to decide that the internal situation in any state is so grave as to justify forceful intervention."

Theories of intervention are easier to enunciate than to put into practice. This is especially true for a secretary-general of the UN. As Barbara Crossette, the UN correspondent of the *New York Times*, once wrote, "He may be at the pinnacle of world diplomacy, but the throne he occupies is really a hollow box." He has no army of his own, no political power. He has only moral force. That is not a negligible weapon, but it is a limited one. Two crises in 1999—Kosovo and East Timor—tested the usefulness of Annan's Ditchley lecture doctrine in the real world.

As the 1990s came to a close, Kosovo became a prime example of UN impotence. Secretary of State Madeleine Albright was the architect of American policy toward that troubled province of Serbia. President Clinton approved the policy but was distracted by the Monica Lewinsky scandal. He managed to hold on to office, but only after impeachment in the House of Representatives and the ensuing trial in the Senate. Albright did all she could to keep the Kosovo crisis out of UN hands. She insisted she had no choice: Russian leaders had threatened to veto any Security Council resolution that authorized military action against Serbia.

But there were other factors as well. The UN, especially in the eyes of the U.S. Congress, reeked of incompetence, inefficiency, and defeat, and Albright did not want to squabble with Congress about a UN war. Moreover, the UN Security Council had lost the cohesiveness of 1990, when Ambassador Thomas Pickering had crafted unanimous and near-unanimous resolutions condemning Iraqi aggression. That cohesiveness dissipated in the confusion of the Clinton administration's policies toward Bosnia and in the bruising caused by Albright's lone-wolf campaign to get rid of Secretary-General Boutros Boutros-Ghali. Even without the threat of a Russian veto, the United States found working in the Security Council troublesome and slow.

Kosovo was a province of two million people with an area about the size of Connecticut. It had a special place in Serbian history for the Turks of the Ottoman Empire defeated the Serbs there in 1389 and then overran the rest of Serbia, occupying it for almost five hundred years. Despite this tug on Serbian nationalist feelings, perhaps 90 percent of those who lived in Kosovo by the end of the twentieth century were Albanian, not Serb. The United States had warned Serbian president Slobodan Milosević again and again not to persecute these Albanians. But Milosević defied the threats, and Serbian soldiers, police, and paramilitary militias began their odious "ethnic cleansing" in 1998, storming Albanian villages, burning homes, killing many, and pushing others across the borders into Albania, Macedonia, and Montenegro. Milosević defended these brutal assaults as necessary in the hunt for guerrillas of the rebellious Kosovo Liberation Army.

In 1998, the British began circulating a draft resolution in the Security Council that authorized the use of force against Milosević. The British intended this to cover the legality of any future NATO action against him. When Albright got wind of this, she phoned British foreign secretary Robin Cook immediately and told him "he should get himself new lawyers." She did not want to set a precedent that any NATO action required UN authorization, thus giving both Russia and China a veto over NATO. To make matters worse, she wrote later, "if the resolution failed, it would be seen as a victory for Milosević and make it that much harder for NATO to move." The British withdrew their draft resolution.

But the Security Council did condemn Serbian atrocities and asked the secretary-general to document what was going on. In a report to the Council, Annan wrote, "I am outraged by reports of mass killings of civilians in Kosovo, which recall the atrocities committed in Bosnia and Herzegovina." He accused the Serb security forces of using "terror and violence against civilians to force people to flee their home or the place where they had sought refuge." The Serbs insisted they were only trying to separate ordinary Albanians from the guerrillas, but Annan dismissed this excuse as a pretext for ethnic cleansing.

Half a dozen foreign ministers crowded into the VIP lounge of Heathrow Airport outside London in October to discuss action. German foreign minister Klaus Kinkel tried to persuade Russian foreign minister Ivan Ivanov to support a UN resolution authorizing military strikes against Serbia. But Ivanov refused. The Russian insisted military action was unnecessary because Milosević had promised to withdraw some troops from Kosovo. Albright dismissed this. "Milosević is a congenital liar," she said. Ivanov, in later discussions with Albright, acknowledged that while Russia would veto a resolution at the UN, it would not do much else to prevent NATO action.

There were repeated American attempts to persuade Milosević to withdraw from Kosovo. Albright was sure at first that just the threat of bombing would be enough to shock sense into Milosević. But she was wrong. Richard Holbrooke flew into Belgrade to try to repeat his Dayton triumph by cajoling Milosević into accepting the inevitable. General Wesley K. Clark, the supreme commander of NATO, tried to convince Milosević that the threat of bombing was no bluff. "You are a war criminal to be threatening Serbia," Milosević replied. All these attempts at a political settlement failed.

NATO began bombing Serbia on March 24, 1999. The targets were military and other strategic sites in Kosovo and in the rest of Serbia. For the first time, Serbs in Belgrade and elsewhere would feel the effects of one of the wars spawned by Milosević. After the bombing started, Albright's detractors dubbed the conflict "Madeleine's war." The bombing would last for seventy-two days, much longer than she had anticipated. In the end, Milosević caved in. "Well, if it was Madeleine's war," said Joschka Fischer, the new German foreign minister, "it is now Madeleine's victory." But victory did not come until much of Kosovo was destroyed, a million people uprooted, and thousands killed.

The bombing forced a troubling dilemma on Kofi Annan. When the bombing began, Annan could not deny that he believed intervention was necessary. In the Ditchley lecture, in fact, he had warned that Kosovo was presenting "what may be the severest challenge in Europe since the Dayton agreement was concluded in 1995." Albright had phoned Annan before the bombing. He had told her then that the Security Council should be consulted before NATO used force. "We don't agree," she told him. "You are the secretary-general of the United Nations and I am the secretary of state of the United States. That's life. But if we had to put this to a Council vote the Russians would have vetoed it, and people would have continued to die."

Annan did not face the press on the day bombing began but issued a carefully worded statement instead. "I deeply regret," he said, "that, in spite of all the efforts made by the international community, the Yugoslav authorities have persisted in their rejection of a political settlement, which would have halted the bloodshed in

Kosovo and secured an equitable peace for the population there. It is indeed tragic that diplomacy has failed, but there are times when the use of force may be legitimate in the pursuit of peace." Yet, he insisted, NATO should not have acted without authorization from the Security Council.

His statement, despite his misgiving about the lack of Security Council action, was generally regarded as approval. "The Secretary-General Offers Implicit Endorsement of Raids," said a *New York Times* headline. "He supported us," said Assistant Secretary of State James P. Rubin a few years later, "because it was the right thing to do."

Yet, less than two months later, Annan made a speech at The Hague in the Netherlands that reflected his frustration at the refusal of the Americans and Europeans to seek Security Council authorization for the bombing of Serbia. He recognized the difficulty of obtaining Security Council support but insisted that patient and imaginative diplomacy could have achieved this.

"What has been most worrying, in my view," he said, "has been the inability of states to reconcile national interests when skillful and visionary diplomacy would make unity possible."

While this was a rebuke to all on the Council, including the Russians, for their stubbornness, it was obviously aimed mostly at the United States—for lacking the patience and vision to continue negotiations. He sounded a warning: "Unless the Security Council is restored to its preeminent position as the sole source of legitimacy on the use of force, we are on a dangerous path to anarchy."

The Americans not only kept the UN out of the decision to bomb Serbia, they kept the UN out of the peace negotiations as well. Albright feared that she might have to settle for too little from Milosević if she let the UN negotiate the terms for giving in to the bombing.

While Annan was visiting the headquarters of the European Union in Brussels, he received a phone call from Albright admonishing him not to undertake a mission to Belgrade just like his mission to Baghdad. He assured her that he would not. Trying to keep the UN involved, however, he appointed two envoys—former

Swedish prime minister Carl Bildt and Slovakia foreign minister Eduard Kukan—to attempt a peaceful solution to the crisis. The United States and Britain objected. They feared that Milosević would manipulate the envoys to divide NATO. Moreover, Bildt had openly criticized the bombing.

En route to a meeting with Russian president Boris Yeltsin in Moscow, Annan issued a statement deploring that "once again, innocent civilians are paying the price for unresolved political conflict." Albright objected to the statement with its implied criticism of the bombing. Annan replied that "he did not work for the U.S. government" and, as UN secretary-general, "needed room to maneuver."

Yeltsin wrote a letter to President Clinton later proposing that Kofi Annan and former Russian prime minister Viktor Chernomyrdin fly together to Belgrade to try negotiating a settlement with Milosević. But Clinton refused, stating that he would not allow the UN to negotiate on behalf of NATO. Albright instead proposed that Finnish president Martti Ahtisaari take Annan's place. The Russians accepted. Chernomyrdin and Ahtisaari spent a month pleading with Milosević.

Albright, according to a detailed account of the diplomacy by Blaine Harden of the *New York Times*, "was particularly adamant that the United Nations must be kept backstage and out of Belgrade. . . . She distrusted the United Nations because she felt that in the past, its negotiators had been played for fools by Mr. Milosević."

Harden wrote that the secretary of state persuaded Annan to limit the role of Bildt and Kukan, his envoys, to carrying out a peace agreement after it was signed. "She feared that such envoys would complicate and possibly derail the work of Mr. Chernomyrdin and Mr. Ahtisaari," Harden wrote.

After Milosević capitulated and accepted the peace proposals of Chernomyrdin and Ahtisaari, thus ending the bombing, the Security Council passed a resolution authorizing a peacekeeping mission. But there would be no Blue Helmets. NATO—not the UN—would patrol Kosovo with its peacekeeping troops. The UN would be in charge of civilian administration.

Secretary of State Albright balked at Annan's choice for the civilian administrator—Bernard Kouchner, the French minister of health and the founder of Doctors without Borders. She had heard that Kouchner was "difficult." She told Annan that his choice was a mistake. After he heard about this from Annan, Kouchner called on Albright with a bouquet of flowers. "I hear you don't like me," he told the secretary of state. Kouchner charmed her. "I was impressed by his deep convictions, humanity, knowledge, and dedication," she wrote in her memoirs. "I later called the secretary-general to tell him he was right after all."

Throughout the Kosovo crisis, Albright was annoyed by what she regarded as Kofi Annan's prattle and meddling. Yet he made a different impression on many others. In his understated way, he struck many as a man of consistency, reason, integrity, and peace. He believed fervently in patience and talk. "I know some people have accused me of using diplomacy," he told Barbara Crossette. "That's my job. That's what I'm paid for."

Secretary of State Albright did not mind the UN and Kofi Annan handling the East Timor crisis that same year. In fact, she kept herself so far from the troubles there that she does not even mention the crisis in her memoirs. Yet, the terrible news from East Timor monopolized headlines in America for a month. But Americans did not make demands on Washington to intervene. They looked instead toward the United Nations. If Kosovo was Madeleine's war, East Timor was Kofi's crisis, and Madeleine preferred it that way.

Behind the scenes, however, the United States was among those governments that acted as a brake against any headstrong action by the UN. East Timor was regarded by Indonesia as one of its provinces, and Indonesia was a strategically located Pacific nation, with the fourth-largest population in the world. The United States did not want to provoke turmoil, chaos, and anarchy in Indonesia. No Washington official intended Indonesia to be roughed up the way Serbia had been. That factor made it difficult to apply Annan's Ditchley formula to the crisis.

Unlike Indonesia, which had been a Dutch colony before its independence after World War II, East Timor had been held by the Portuguese for three centuries. Although East Timor took up the eastern half of an easterly island in the Indonesian archipelago, its people were almost all Catholic, not Muslim, and spoke a language different from most Indonesians. After the 1974 revolution that ended Portugal's fascist dictatorship, the new leftist government allowed all its colonies, including East Timor, to break away.

But President Suharto of Indonesia coveted what seemed to him like a piece of Indonesian property in the archipelago. That did not bother the United States. Suharto was regarded as a friend and a bulwark against communism. On a visit to Jakarta on December 6, 1975, President Ford was told by Suharto that because of a chaotic situation developing in East Timor, which had just declared itself independent, "we want your understanding if we deem it necessary to take rapid or drastic action." Ford replied, "We will understand and will not press you on the issue." Indonesian troops invaded and occupied East Timor the next day. According to a CIA estimate, 100,000 to 250,000 East Timorese lost their lives during the repressive occupation, which lasted almost twenty-five years—an enormous death toll in a population of less than 1 million.

Neither Portugal nor the United Nations ever recognized the Indonesian seizure and occupation of East Timor, but little could be done about it. Nevertheless, Annan persuaded Indonesia and Portugal to begin talks about the issue in 1997 under the direction of a UN troubleshooter, Jamshed Marker of Pakistan. Annan took an active part, meeting often with the foreign ministers of Indonesia and Portugal.

These negotiations got nowhere until dictator Suharto was overthrown in 1998 and his place taken by the weak vice president, B. J. Habibie. It is not clear why but Habibie decided to let the UN conduct a referendum on East Timor independence. He may have foolishly believed that the East Timor islanders would vote to remain part of Indonesia provided they were allowed a good deal of new autonomy.

Habibie invited the UN to send civilians to East Timor to organize the August 30 referendum but refused to accept UN soldiers in what he regarded as a territory of sovereign Indonesia. Instead, he sent a memorandum to Kofi Annan promising that the Indonesian army would guarantee peace and security and deal swiftly with any troublemakers. It was probably naive of Annan to accept this, but there was little else he could do. The Security Council was in no mood to force Blue Helmets on Indonesia if its president did not want them. Annan told the Security Council that the agreement between Indonesia and Portugal for a referendum "constitutes an historic opportunity for the people of East Timor to shape the future of the territory."

Even before the vote, ragtag militias, organized by the Indonesian army, roamed the streets, trying to intimidate Timorese to vote against independence. If the voters chose independence, militia leaders warned, East Timor would become "a sea of blood." Annan said he was appalled by the disorder and called on the Indonesian army to fulfill the government's pledge to maintain order.

The referendum day proved peaceful, with the militias making no attempt to prevent the vote. Three days later, Kofi Annan announced that East Timor had rejected autonomy and voted for independence by a vote of 78.5 percent to 21.5 percent. The results unleashed the fury of the militias. Hordes of toughs began killing hundreds of East Timorese, hustling tens of thousands of others across the border into the Indonesian territory of West Timor, and destroying buildings, telephone lines, power plants, and other property. It was a scorched-earth campaign at its most terrifying. Indonesian troops did nothing to stop the militias and everything to encourage them. Scores of Timorese took refuge within the UN compound.

Annan was on the phone continually with Habibie, telling the president that the crisis was out of control. Habibie promised again and again that the army would restore order. But it was apparent that he had lost control over his military. In fact, the military commander in Jakarta appeared to have lost control of the military forces in East Timor. Prime Minister John Howard of Australia offered to rush Australian troops to the island. But both China and the United States would not support such intervention unless Indonesia agreed. Habibie refused.

In public, Annan gave Indonesia a chance to restore order itself. "As part of the agreement," he told a news conference, "the Indonesian government undertook to ensure law and order. . . . I am in touch with them, and all of us, the whole international community, is asking them to honor that engagement." He insisted that the time had not come for him to call for the dispatch of UN peacekeepers.

Within a few days, there were calls for intervention. The Security Council rushed the Namibian, Malaysian, Slovenian, British, and Dutch ambassadors to Jakarta for talks with Habibie. Portuguese ambassador Antonio Monteiro accused the Council of stalling. Secretary of State Madeleine Albright warned Indonesia that it had to stop the killing and violence or "let the international community deal with that issue." But she insisted that the United States did not want the UN to send a force to East Timor without permission from Indonesia.

Annan announced that he was giving the Indonesians forty-eight hours to stop the violence. If not, he said, "the international community will have to consider what other measures it can take to assist the Indonesian government in meeting its obligations." He pressed Habibie again and again to accept help. The deadline passed with no change in the Indonesian position. The secretary-general showed his annoyance with what he regarded as the tepid American response to the original violence. He told a news conference that the Americans and others were finally putting pressure on Habibie to call for UN peacekeepers. "I wish the pressure had come sooner," he said.

The secretary-general then issued his direst warning. "I urge the Indonesian government to accept their [the international community's] help without further delay," he said. "If it refuses to do so, it cannot escape responsibility for what could amount, according to reports reaching us, to crimes against humanity." Because of the need to phone Habibie continually and because Jakarta is twelve hours earlier than New York, Annan slept two to three hours a night for a week.

Habibie finally gave in on September 12, almost two weeks after the vote. He asked Annan to send a peacekeeping force into East Timor. On national television, Habibie said in English, "Too many people have lost their lives since the beginning of the unrest, lost their homes and security. We cannot wait any longer. We have to stop the suffering and mourning immediately." Then, speaking in Indonesian, he tried to ease the humiliation of his armed forces by playing down the role of the peacekeepers. "I have decided to invite the international peacekeeping force in order to assist us—together with the Indonesian military, in a cooperative manner—to restore security in the troubled province," he said.

Annan telephoned Habibie to congratulate him on the televised address. It was an emotional phone call. The secretary-general complimented Habibie for his courage. The Indonesian president hailed Annan as a good friend of Indonesia. "May God bless you in your work and me in my efforts to bring peace and human rights and the superhighway of democracy to Indonesia and the region," Habibie told Annan.

The Security Council authorized 8,000 Australian and other troops to enter East Timor. When the first units arrived a little more than three weeks after the referendum, they found a devastated territory. There were huge refugee camps of hungry Timorese on the other side of the border. Many educated Timorese had been killed. As Annan soon reported to the Security Council, "The civil administration is no longer functioning. The judiciary and court systems have ceased to exist. Essential services, such as water and electricity, are in real danger of collapse."

The UN soon took over the administration of East Timor, preparing the territory for full independence. After the Australian-led international force left at the end of October, the UN authorized a peacekeeping force of 9,150 troops and 1,650 police to take over. Sérgio Vieira de Mello, a Brazilian who had specialized in refugee problems, administered the territory for the UN. By May 2002, the East Timorese had elected a new government and gained full independence, joining the UN as a sovereign nation a few months later. But a small UN peacekeeping force remained until May 2005.

Annan looked on East Timor as a qualified UN success story. He told a news conference at the end of 1999, "I deeply regret that we were unable to prevent the senseless bloodshed of August and September. But if we compare the prospect now with that of two years ago [when East Timor was under brutal Indonesian occupation], we see that East Timor is one more case where time and patient diplomacy . . . have brought hope to what had been a hopeless situation."

This was a rather optimistic assessment of a crisis that came to an end too late to prevent a frenzy of despicable havoc. But he was probably right. No government, not even the Australian government, was prepared to take on the Indonesian army for the sake of lives in East Timor. Persuading Habibie to hold the referendum and then to invite foreign troops to quell the disorders was an extraordinary feat of diplomacy. Galvanizing the Security Council into action in only a few days astounded UN-watchers.

A case can be made that the Ditchley formula worked during the East Timor crisis. The Security Council did intervene in a sovereign country to defend the people there from oppressive rulers. But it did so only after the rulers acquiesced. East Timor, in fact, exposed some of the shortcomings of the Ditchley formula. Persuading the Security Council to intervene with force is an extraordinarily difficult task. Persuading a government to accept the intervention without resistance is just as difficult. Annan managed to do both with skill and patience.

There was a good deal of feeling in the Third World, in fact, that Annan and the UN had no right to go any farther than they had in the East Timor crisis. Annan repeated his views on intervention in his speech to the 1999 opening of the General Assembly, which came on the same day that the Australian troops were landing in East Timor. "Nothing in the Charter," the secretary-general said, "precludes a recognition that there are rights beyond borders."

But this drew a sharp rebuke from President Abdelaziz Bouteflika of Algeria, who spoke on behalf of the Organization of African Unity. "Interference can only occur with the consent of the state concerned," Bouteflika said. "We do not deny the right of Northern Hemisphere public opinion to denounce the breaches of human rights where they occur. Furthermore, we do not deny that the United Nations has the right and the duty to help suffering humanity. But we remain extremely sensitive to an undermining of our sovereignty, not only because sovereignty is our last defense against the rules of an unequal world, but because we are not taking part in the decision-making process of the Security Council."

These negative remarks did not surprise Annan. With no more than moral suasion in his arsenal, a secretary-general always finds it easier to lay down principles than to carry them out.

The extended Annan family in 1944 or 1945, when Kofi (lower left) was six years old.

Kofi (top row, second from left) as a student in secondary school in Ghana in the early 1950s.

At Macalester College, Kofi shows his Kente robe to fellow students on International Students Day, 1959.

Breaking the twelve-year-old record for the 60-yard sprint at Carleton Stadium at Macalester College.

Kofi's photo in the
Macalester College
yearbook, 1960.

With fellow students while an MIT Sloan fellow, studying the copper industry in
Zambia, 1971.

Kofi and Nane on their way to be married in New York, 1984.

Secretary-General Annan confers with his spokesman, Fred Eckhard, en route from Namibia to Angola in March 1997.

The secretary-general in 1999.

Kofi and Nane chatting with Rudolph W. Giuliani, mayor of New York City, after the ceremonial "throwing out the first ball" at the 1999 World Series, Game 3, Yankee Stadium.

The secretary-general and his wife, Nane, visiting returned refugees in Timbuktu, Mali, in 1998.

Encounter with a glacier in Norway, 2001.

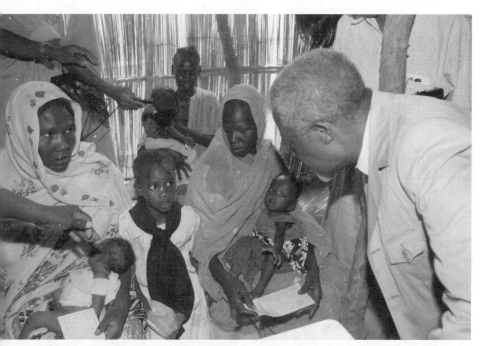

The secretary-general at a clinic in a refugee camp in the Sudan, 2002.

Fishing in Montana, 2002.

Walking on a beach in Mozambique, 2002.

Kofi in Finland, 2003.

Annan, along with joyous Sudanese and other guests, dancing in celebration of the inauguration of Sudan's Transitional Government of National Unity in Khartoum, 2005.

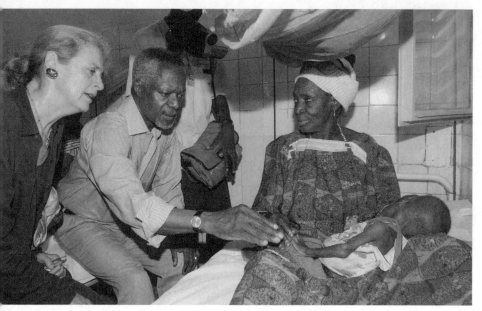

The secretary-general and his wife, Nane, visit the pediatric wing of the Zinder Hospital, Niger, in August 2005.

Secretary-General Annan receives credentials from John Bolton, the new permanent U.S. representative to the UN, at UN headquarters on August 2, 2005.

The secretary-general meets with U.S. president George W. Bush at UN headquarters on the eve of the 2005 World Summit.

In 2005, Annan lays a wreath in memory of former UN secretary-general Dag Hammarskjöld and the staff members who lost their lives with him in a plane crash in present-day Zambia (then Northern Rhodesia) during a peace mission to the Congo (now the Democratic Republic of the Congo) on September 19, 1961.

Annan during the ceremony for the sixtieth anniversary of the United Nations on October 25, 2005, at UN headquarters.

The secretary-general meets with former South African president Nelson Mandela in Houghton, Johannesburg, South Africa, in March 2006.

Annan talking with author Stanley Meisler during a trip to Africa in 2002.

11

The Nobel Peace Prize

After Kofi Annan's mission to Saddam Hussein was deemed a failure in 1998, politicians, especially in the United States, tended to belittle the importance of the United Nations. For most of the 1990s, the UN had been a significant player in the main crises of the era—Iraq, Somalia, Bosnia, and Rwanda. Newspaper front pages often displayed stories about dramatic—and sometimes botched—Security Council actions during these crises. But as the new millennium approached, the UN found itself on the sideline, far from worldwide notice. Secretary of State Madeleine Albright shunted both the secretary-general and the Security Council aside during the Kosovo crisis. While the UN did figure prominently in the East Timor troubles, the crisis in that tiny, underpopulated territory did not loom as large as those earlier crises.

The diminished role of the UN was underscored in an article by Judith Miller in the *New York Times* in March 1999. "In a world with conflicts raging from Angola to Kosovo," she wrote, "the United Nations Security Council, the heart of the world body, finds itself increasingly marginalized." "The Security Council is doing more and more things," David Malone, the Canadian who headed the

International Peace Academy in New York, told Miller. "But the things it is doing seem to matter less and less."

Yet, as the image of the United Nations lost its luster, the stature of its secretary-general grew more and more. It was an odd phenomenon, difficult to explain. But Kofi Annan burnished his reputation as a statesman of moral force in the few years of his administration that the UN stayed out of the news. Perhaps outsiders, uncluttered and unswayed by their passions over major crises, looked at Annan most clearly in those years and marveled over his honesty and disarming goodwill.

He demonstrated his commitment to an open UN in the last two months of 1999. In November, he issued his own report on the fall of Srebrenica and the terrible massacre there during the Bosnian war. A month later he accepted a report on the killings in Rwanda issued by a commission he had appointed. The commission comprised former Swedish prime minister Ingvar Carlsson, former South Korean foreign minister Han Sung-Joo, and retired lieutenant general Rufus M. Kupolati of Nigeria.

Both reports were remarkable documents for an organization that often glories in its secrecy, its diplomats sure that diplomacy needs darkness to flourish. The reports bulged with classified cables, closed-door deliberations, phoned messages, and other secrets. And the reports heaped blame on both the civil servants of the UN Secretariat and the governments that sat on the Security Council. By writing one report and embracing the other, Kofi Annan was trying to open a new era of transparency at the UN.

Spurred by the reports and the controversies over both Rwanda and Srebrenica, the secretary-general asked Lakhdar Brahimi to head a panel that would study the future of UN peacekeeping. Brahimi, a former Algerian foreign minister, is a troubleshooter in the mold of legendary UN figures like Ralph Bunche and Brian Urquhart, who were always ready to take on any UN mission no matter how difficult and complex. Brahimi had already headed UN operations in Haiti and South Africa and had delved into the politics of Zaire, Liberia, Nigeria, and Yemen for the UN as well. After the American rout of the Taliban in Afghanistan, he would run UN operations there, and he would help the U.S. and Iraqi politicians cobble together a government after the American invasion of Iraq.

The Brahimi panel report, which was issued in August 2000, shattered some of the shibboleths of peacekeeping. It agreed that "consent of local parties, impartiality and the use of force only in self-defense should remain the bedrock principles of peacekeeping." But, the panel went on, the UN peacekeepers must not keep treating both sides equally when one side is violating the terms of a peace agreement. At best, that makes the UN ineffective; at worst, that "may amount to complicity with evil." "No failure did more to damage the standing and credibility of United Nations peacekeeping in the 1990s," the panel said, "than its reluctance to distinguish victim from aggressor."

Moreover, the panel went on, peacekeeping forces must be strong enough to defend themselves against attack. And UN Blue Helmets and police "who witness violence against civilians should be presumed to be authorized to stop it, within their means, in support of basic United Nations principles." In short, peacekeepers have the duty to defend civilians, whether or not that action is authorized in the Security Council resolution setting up the mission.

To do all this, the Brahimi panel said, "means bigger forces, better equipped and more costly but able to be a credible deterrent." In complex operations, the Blue Helmets "should be afforded the field intelligence and other capabilities needed to mount an effective defense against violent challengers."

Some of the panel's recommendations, like its admonition to the Secretariat that it "must tell the Security Council what it needs to know, not what it wants to hear," were difficult to put into practice and assess. But all in all, Brahimi and his panel wanted a more powerful and more professional peacekeeping operation, and the secretary-general tried to follow most of their recommendations. The numbers did grow. When Annan took over as secretary-general in 1997, there was little enthusiasm within the UN about peacekeeping. The missions in Bosnia, Somalia, and Rwanda were over and largely condemned by outsiders. But there was a steady and largely unnoticed growth in peacekeeping under Annan. When he began his last year as secretary-general in 2006, the numbers of troops and police in peacekeeping operations had risen to seventy thousand, almost as high as the record totals in the early 1990s. There were eighteen missions.

(But the growth in peacekeeping was accompanied by a burst of sex scandals, with Blue Helmets accused of rape, sex with girls as young as twelve, and the hire of prostitutes. The scandals in the Congo and elsewhere were hardly testimony for enhanced professionalism.)

Annan tried to change the image of the UN in another, more personal way. He allowed himself to become a celebrity in New York. His predecessor, Boutros Boutros-Ghali, was known as a workaholic who rarely took part in New York nightlife. But Kofi and Nane accepted invitations to dinners and parties perhaps three times a week—at least when he was in town. William H. Luers, the former president of the Metropolitan Museum of Art, called Annan "the current social star of New York society." The secretary-general said he accepted the invitations because the city was so vibrant that "on any subject—you name it—you'll find someone to discuss it with or pick their brains." But Kofi and Nane refused all invitations on weekends. That time was reserved for long walks together and outings to the theater, movies, or a concert hall.

Kofi received the ultimate tribute as a celebrity when he was asked to throw out the first ball in October 1999 at a World Series game in Yankee Stadium between the Atlanta Braves and the New York Yankees. He had never mastered baseball in his days at Macalester or since, and his pitch bounced halfway to the plate.

A good deal of praise fell his way. "I found Kofi to be one of the most skillful political animals in the world," said American ambassador Bill Richardson. "His ability to maneuver is incredibly good. He always makes you leave your meeting with him thinking that you've made your point. That's a master skill." Richard Holbrooke, who succeeded Richardson as ambassador during the Clinton administration, described Annan as the best secretary-general in UN history.

The Republican victory in the disputed election of 2000 would eventually embitter relations between Washington and Annan. Relations, of course, had hardly been idyllic under a Democratic administration. President Clinton and his aides had manipulated the UN shamelessly, making the UN the scapegoat for the debacle in Somalia and the impotence in Bosnia and holding the Security Council back from rescuing Rwanda. Moreover, Secretary of State Albright, even though she had led the campaign for his election, had treated Annan with disdain during the Kosovo crisis and made it clear that she regarded him as too soft to negotiate with the big boys.

But Albright and other Clinton officials believed in the UN and wanted it to work—at least in a way that helped them. The new American president, George W. Bush, on the other hand, was surrounded by neoconservative ideologues who did not believe in the UN. They looked on it as an affront to national sovereignty and treated it with contempt.

While the Republicans were out of power, John R. Bolton, vice president of the American Enterprise Institute and a former assistant secretary of state, had made himself the main Republican spokesman on UN issues. When Annan criticized the U.S. Senate for rejecting the Comprehensive Test Ban Treaty in 1999, Bolton said, "I think if he continues down this road, ultimately it means war, at least with the Republican Party."

Bolton's view of the powers of the secretary-general was so narrow that he also castigated Annan for daring to criticize members of the Security Council through the Srebrenica and Rwanda reports. Bolton told the *New York Times*, "This is a growing and serious issue, the illegitimacy of the secretary-general's commenting on the performance of the UN member governments. . . . The issue is whether an international civil servant has or can be given authority to criticize the performance of member governments. . . . All international civil servants in the UN system are employees of member governments. . . . They have no authority to act outside a very limited scope of responsibility. He's well beyond pushing the envelope on that score."

When Bush took office in January 2001, however, his secretary of state was Colin Powell, a booster of the UN who knew Annan well. Bush named a veteran Foreign Service officer, John Negroponte, as UN ambassador. The secretary-general had no problems with either man, and the United States supported Annan for reelection in 2001. Annan had no opposition this time. Some Asian ambassadors had argued that after ten years of leadership by Africans, it was now Asia's turn to take over the job. But no Asian candidate came forward. The Asians had decided they could wait until 2007. Annan was so popular that the unanimous decision by the Security Council to reward him with a second term came six months before his first term ended.

On the morning of September 11, 2001, Kofi Annan was still at his Sutton Place residence when the two planes crashed into the World Trade Center and brought down its twin towers in a terrible fury. Annan hurried to the Secretariat Building and his office on the thirty-eighth floor to confer with aides and prepare a statement. For the next few months, without any hesitation, the secretary-general would move in step with the United States.

"There can be no doubt," he said in a statement that day, "that these attacks are deliberate acts of terrorism, carefully planned and coordinated—and as such I condemn them utterly. Terrorism must be fought resolutely whenever it appears." On the next afternoon, he told an emergency meeting of the Security Council, "A terrorist attack on one country is an attack on humanity as a whole. All nations must work together to identify the perpetrators and bring them to justice." In response, the Security Council passed a resolution condemning the attacks unequivocally and pledging "its readiness to take all necessary steps to respond to the terrorist attacks . . . and to combat all forms of terrorism." In a break with tradition, the Council's fifteen ambassadors rose up and stood in place as they voted in favor of the resolution.

Most important, Annan endorsed the American position that

under the Charter of the United Nations, the United States could invoke "the inherent right of . . . self-defense" to hunt for Osama bin Laden and his al-Qaeda terrorists and bring down the Taliban government protecting them in Afghanistan. Self-defense required no approval from the Security Council. Once under attack, the United States, according to the Charter, simply had to inform the Council that it was invoking the right. When the United States began its bombing of Afghanistan, Annan did not dispute the right but called for an increase in assistance for Afghan civilians "who cannot be held responsible for the acts of the Taliban regime."

On September 24, the secretary-general addressed the General Assembly. At about this time every year, a procession of presidents, prime ministers, kings, princes, and foreign ministers usually began arriving in New York for what was euphemistically described as the General Assembly's annual "general debate." Rather than debate each other, however, the leaders of the world would lay down national policy positions one after another in three weeks of continuous boredom. To ease the security problems of the overworked and grieving New York police after September 11, the UN postponed the annual speechifying for seven weeks in 2001.

Annan thus addressed a General Assembly hall filled only with ambassadors. But the speech attracted notice nevertheless, for he chose terrorism as his topic. "Thirteen days ago—on a day none of us is likely to forget—our host country, and our beloved host city," he said, "were struck by a blow so deliberate, so heartless, malicious, and destructive, that we are still struggling to grasp its enormity. In truth, this was a blow not against one city or one country, but against all of us." He said that the terrorists had struck at everything the UN stood for: "peace, freedom, tolerance, human rights, and the very idea of a united human family."

The secretary-general insisted that terrorism could be overcome only if the nations of the world united to fight it. "This organization is the natural forum in which to build such a universal coalition," he said. "It alone can give global legitimacy to the long-term struggle against terrorism."

He went further than calling for the unity of nations. He said that "all social forces—states, the private sector, institutions of learning and research, and civil society in all its forms" must "unite their efforts in the pursuit of specific, attainable goals." And they must do this under the leadership of the UN. "The United Nations must listen to all these different partners," he said. "It must guide them. It must urge them on."

The speech on terrorism was one of a series that the secretary-general delivered on significant global issues such as intervention, human rights, AIDS, development, disarmament, and the environment during his two terms. They were largely written by Edward Mortimer, the UN's director of communications and a former foreign affairs columnist of the *Financial Times* in London.

According to Fred Eckhard, the process would begin with one of Annan's aides suggesting, "We thought this is the time for you to take a strong position on X." "All right," the secretary-general would reply. "Here are the main ideas I would like to put forward." Mortimer and his crew of speechwriters would consult with UN specialists, show them drafts, and then "come back to the secretary-general with a near-finished draft and the secretary-general would almost always refine that near-final draft." When traveling, Annan might refine the speech even more. He would "sniff the political environment there," Eckhard told the Yale-UN Oral History Project, "and give that speech one last read the night before he was going to give it and then put some finishing touches based on his reading of the political environment. . . . So the speeches go through I can't imagine how many drafts."

The boldness of the ideas pleased many admirers. But the speeches also troubled some critics. A longtime scholar of the UN, Edward C. Luck, director of Columbia University's Center on International Organization, praises Annan for discussing major topics "in a serious and sober way" but then faults the secretary-general for failing to follow through on these ideas and relate them to the work of the UN. On the issue of terrorism, for example, Luck insists that Annan made "courageous, bold, and wise statements for a month or so" and then stopped pushing the issue. Luck describes the speeches as "temporary enthusiasms" that lack "well-worked solutions" to the problems raised.

There is a good deal of merit in Luck's analysis. Kofi Annan is not an intellectual who revels in the rigors of academic thinking. Yet Annan obviously looked on his series of speeches as a sounding of alarms, not as an attempt to propose practical solutions to practical problems. He knew the difficulty of transforming the UN. His call at Ditchley for intervention to save lives became acceptable to the UN only as intervention with the consent of the offending nation. For Annan, that was a practical first step. Much more oratory on the issue might only provoke more opposition. Talking about terrorism at a news conference in Oslo in December, he made it clear that his call for the use of the UN as a cauldron of international cooperation was not proposed as a way of stopping terrorism soon. Instead, he envisioned a much longer fight. "I think the United Nations is laying the foundation for the long-term struggle against terrorists," he said. He was sounding the alarm on the need for international antiterrorist cooperation, and the need, in his view, would be enduring.

There had been rumors in early October 2001 that the Nobel Committee in Oslo was looking closely at Kofi Annan as one of the main candidates for the Nobel Peace Prize. But Kofi's aides had heard those rumors in both 1999 and 2000, only to be disappointed. This year might be more promising. In a recent Scandinavian poll, he had been voted the world's most admired statesman.

On Friday, October 12, the day of the announcements, Eckhard planned to be at the secretary-general's residence on Sutton Place before dawn just in case. He arrived before 5:00 A.M. and found a cluster of TV cameras already on the sidewalk. A Norwegian Broadcasting Service reporter reached Fred on his cell phone just as he entered the building. He told Fred they understood the prize would go to Annan, and he asked for comment from the secretary-general. "Let's wait until it's official," Eckhard said, and the reporter said he would call back.

The residence was dark and quiet. Lamin Sise, one of Kofi's longtime colleagues and advisers, stood in the hallway with a security guard. When Eckhard told them about the call from Norway, the guard phoned and woke the secretary-general. "It was a wonderful way to wake up," Annan told reporters later. "Given the sort of business we are in, usually when you get a call that early in the morning, it's something disastrous."

Annan and his wife emerged about fifteen minutes later. Eckhard's cell sounded again. It was the Norwegian Broadcasting Service. "Here, listen to the announcement," the Norwegian reporter told him. Fred could hear Norwegian words but did not understand a thing. He did hear the name "Kofi Annan," though, spoken with a Norwegian lilt. The reporter explained that the prize was going both to the secretary-general and the UN. "Sir," Fred said, "you are sharing the prize with the UN." "In an organization that can hardly become more than its members permit," the Nobel Committee said in its citation of Annan, "he has made clear that sovereignty cannot be a shield behind which member states conceal their violations."

"I wanted to give him a hug," Eckhard recalled recently. "I gestured toward him and then pulled back. I told myself, 'You can't do that. He is the secretary-general.' There was no jumping up and down. But he and Nane were pleased. It must have been the peak of his career."

Annan, in open-neck shirt, stepped outside the home to talk with the reporters who had gathered. He was asked if the prize would change him or the UN in any way. "I think you've known me long enough," he replied. "I will not change. I hope it will change the organization in the sense that it will energize all of us to do more and to carry on with our work."

When he arrived at UN headquarters, scores of personnel had crowded into the lobby to greet and cheer him. "The world is a messy place," he said, "and unfortunately the messier it gets, the more work we have to do. . . . So, my good friends, let me say congratulations to all of you. Let me say that if the UN has achieved anything it is because of the work you do, and your dedication, and we look forward to many more years of that kind of service. And, who knows, if you keep at it, maybe some of you will see another Nobel Peace Prize." His smiling remark set off a cascade of laughter and cheers. "If you are going to get that next Nobel Peace Prize," he went on, "I think we had better go back to work." He walked toward the elevator amid more laughter, cheers, and applause.

Kofi was in demand during the next few weeks. Before leaving for Oslo in December, he accepted an invitation to tape an episode with the Muppets on the PBS children's show *Sesame Street*. The scene, which aired in February, opens with the Muppets shouting at each other. "I think it's my turn," says one. "What about me?" demands Cookie Monster. "No! Me! Me!" shouts Elmo. "No, Elmo," says another, "it's my turn." In steps Kofi. "Is there a problem I can help you with?" he asks. "Well, that depends," replies Elmo. "Who are you?" "My name is Kofi Annan. I'm the secretary-general of the United Nations." It turns out they are squabbling about who should sing the Alphabet Song. "There is no problem," explains Kofi. "You can all sing the Alphabet Song together." Whereupon he and the Muppets sing the song together.

After the song, the Muppets begin to jostle and lean on the secretary-general as they try to congratulate each other. "I know," says Telly Monster. "Let's do this the United Nations way." "Yeah," says Elmo. "Group hug." The muppets and Kofi all hug each other, and the scene ends happily. The secretary-general performed with aplomb and clearly enjoyed himself. Nane, who had just written and illustrated a children's book, *The United Nations: Come Along with Me!*, stood behind the cameras and laughed at her husband and beamed.

Kofi and Nane arrived in Oslo on Saturday, December 8, for four days of festivities, celebration, and UN business, including a torchlight parade, a dinner hosted by King Harald of Norway, the Nobel Prize presentation at Oslo City Hall, a ball opened by Kofi and Nane dancing alone, a concert by Paul McCartney and others, and a conference of donors pledging funds for East Timor. "It seems almost indecent," Annan told a news conference, "to be accepting a prize for peace, when peace and security are still denied to so many people in different parts of the world—especially on my own continent of Africa and in the Middle East." But, he went on, "I think that also exemplifies the world we live in. The good and the evil unfortunately live side by side. Conflicts will be here with us. What is important is that we do not lose hope and we have the courage to keep working to end conflicts."

Annan made headlines with a comment about the rumors that the Bush administration intended to invade Iraq for its supposed but unproven links to the terrorists of September 11. "Any attempt or any decision to attack Iraq today will be unwise and . . . can lead to major escalation in the region," he said, "and I would hope that would not be the case. . . . Any attempt to take military action in other parts of the world [than Afghanistan] would be something that the Security Council will have to take up. The Council has not authorized any such action."

On late Sunday, Kofi, wearing a decorated white yarmulke, and Nane joined Norwegian foreign minister Jan Petersen and his wife at the Oslo Synagogue for a ceremony lighting the first candle of Hanukkah. The services were attended as well by families of three Israeli soldiers and an Israeli businessman abducted by Hezbollah guerrillas on the Israeli-Lebanon border. One father made an angry speech demanding that the UN pressure Hezbollah into returning the Israelis or, if they were dead, as he suspected, returning their bodies. After the services, Annan met with the families to assure them that he would do whatever he could to help. His sincere manner and comforting words appeared to disarm their anger. At the end, the families thanked him for his help and offered him a bevy of mazeltovs for his Nobel Prize.

The synagogue encounter reflected one of the most perplexing problems for Annan during his administration. Many Israelis and American Jews looked on him as anti-Israel because of UN policies. They resented what they regarded as a UN penchant for acting as a neutral observer even when Palestinian terrorists kill Israeli civilians. They were still rankled by the resolution passed by the General Assembly in 1975 that equated Zionism with racism. Although this was rescinded in December 1991, the critics pointed to many other occasions when the African and Middle Eastern countries of the Third World still ganged up on Israel.

During the Annan years, Israel strengthened its position at the UN. For decades, the Arab nations had shut off Israel from the Security Council and other UN bodies by refusing it membership in their regional grouping. But Israel became a member of the "Western Europe and Others" group, like the United States and Australia, in 2000 and placed itself on track for possible membership on the Security Council in the future. In 2004, Annan organized a UN seminar on anti-Semitism and acknowledged that "the United Nations record on anti-Semitism has at times fallen short of our ideals." The UN commemorated the memory of the Holocaust on January 27, 2006, the anniversary of the liberation of Auschwitz by Allied forces during World War II. Annan, who said this would be an annual observance, did not hesitate to rebut Iranian president Mahmoud Ahmadinejad's repeated denials of the Holocaust. "Holocaust denial is the work of bigots," Annan said in a videotaped address to the General Assembly. "We must reject their false claims whenever, wherever, and by whomever they are made."

Yet the criticism persisted. A 2005 documentary film, *Broken Promises: The United Nations at 60*, narrated by the actor Ron Silver, highlighted UN treatment of Israel as one of the organization's main "broken promises." This kind of attack upset Annan. No secretary-general ever tried harder to fathom the horrors of the Holocaust. Mindful of Nane's relationship to Raoul Wallenberg, Annan and his wife attended every memorial service that they could. It was no accident that he was the only foreign statesman invited to speak at the opening of the new wing of the Yad Vashem Holocaust Memorial in Jerusalem.

"I have tried to push for a peaceful solution of the conflict in the Middle East," he told an interviewer for a PBS documentary in 2002. "I have tried to be very fair speaking out whenever there has been something wrong regardless of who did it. I think we can all agree that neither side has entirely clean hands. Of course, when you say that you get into trouble."

In a discussion with me at about the same time, he showed less patience with the criticism. As secretary-general, he pointed out, he had a responsibility to speak out for the Palestinians and to fulfill obligations under Security Council resolutions. Despite this, he went on, "I have gone into the lion's den of the Arab League and denounced suicide bombing. I have said and I understand that Israel has the right to defend itself. But there is a question of proportionality. I can voice support for Israel a hundred times, but if I criticize Israel once, I am attacked by Israel and American Jewish organizations."

It is not surprising that Kofi wanted his Nobel Prize lecture to be an eloquent statement of all he stood for. But it was not an easy speech to write. To discuss some ideas, he and Edward Mortimer, his chief speechwriter, lunched with Ted Sorensen, who wrote many of President John F. Kennedy's best-known speeches. Kofi wanted to start with the image of "the global village" and what it would look like if the world really were a village of a thousand people: the average income would be six thousand dollars a year, but half the inhabitants would earn only two dollars a day. That idea had been used successfully in the UN's Millennium Report on economic development a year before. Mortimer tried several drafts starting with this theme, but none seemed to work. As the deadline neared, Iqbal Riza, Kofi's chief of staff, brought in Nader Mousavizadeh, a former *New Republic* editor now on Mortimer's staff.

"I sat down to rewrite my draft yet again," Mortimer recalled recently, "while Nader wrote a new one from scratch. I read this and immediately decided it was better than mine—though I persuaded him to add one or two points from mine." Riza approved and sent it to the secretary-general, who approved but still asked for comment from Sorensen and others. Sorensen suggested a paragraph that Annan accepted even though the two main speechwriters didn't like it.

After Annan and Mortimer had already arrived in Oslo, Riza proposed another line: "We have entered the third millennium through a blazing doorway." Mortimer changed this to: "We have entered the third millennium through a gate of fire." That became the most quotable line in the speech.

"So it was mainly Nader's work," said Mortimer about the speech as a whole. "But that was not unusual. He was one of my team—the most junior but also the most fluent." Nader, a Danish national, would leave the UN shortly to join the staff of the international investment banking firm Goldman Sachs.

Annan delivered his Nobel Prize lecture in the Oslo City Hall on Monday afternoon, December 10, 2001, after receiving his medal and certificate from Gunnar Berge, chairman of the Norwegian Nobel Committee. The lecture covered some of the same grounds as his Ditchley Park speech but with more oratorical flourishes and less concern with the limitations of the UN.

After describing the destruction of the World Trade Center as a gate of fire, the secretary-general said, "If today, after the horror of 11 September, we see better, and we see further—we will realize that humanity is indivisible. New threats make no distinction between races, nations, or regions. A new insecurity has entered every mind, regardless of wealth or status. A deeper awareness of the bonds that bind us all—in pain as in prosperity—has gripped young and old."

He then began to steer his rhetoric toward his favorite issue of intervention and sovereignty. "In the twenty-first century," he said, "I believe the mission of the United Nations will be defined by a new, more profound awareness of the sanctity and dignity of every human life, regardless of race or religion. This will require us to look beyond the framework of states and beneath the surface of nations or communities.

"In this new century," he went on, "we must start from the understanding that peace belongs not only to states or peoples, but to each and every member of those communities. The sovereignty of states must no longer be used as a shield for gross violations of human rights."

The secretary-general did not dwell on the limitations of the UN in trying to remove this shield. Instead, in very idealistic terms, he discussed the need for people to accept and understand their differences. "The idea that there is one people in possession of the truth, one answer to the world's ills, or one solution to humanity's needs," he said, "has done untold harm throughout history—especially in the last century. . . . Each of us has the right to take pride in our particular faith or heritage. But the notion that what is ours is necessarily in conflict with what is theirs is both false and dangerous. It has resulted in endless enmity and conflict, leading men to commit the greatest of crimes in the name of a higher power.

"It need not be so," he went on. "People of different religions and cultures live side by side in almost every part of the world, and most of us have overlapping identities. . . . We can love what we are, without hating what—and who—we are not. . . . This will not be possible, however, without freedom of religion, of expression, of assembly, and basic equality under the law. Indeed, the lesson of the past century has been that where the dignity of the individual has been trampled or threatened . . . conflict has too often followed, with innocent civilians paying the price."

Then the secretary-general added, bringing the issue back to intervention without actually saying so, that "when states undermine the rule of law and violate the rights of their individual citizens, they become a menace not only to their own people, but also to their neighbors, and indeed the world."

In a personal historical note, Annan pointed out that exactly forty years before, the Nobel Committee had awarded the Nobel Peace Prize for the first time to a UN secretary-general, Dag Hammarskjöld, who had died while trying to negotiate peace in the Congo, and for the first time to an African, Chief Albert J. Lutuli of South Africa, the leader of peaceful resistance to apartheid. "For me, as a young African beginning his career in the United Nations a few months later," Annan said, "these two men set a standard that I have sought to follow throughout my working life."

12

Interlude in Vienna and Africa

B y all accounts, Kofi Annan's most striking attribute is a personal charm that makes most people like him. Even critics who regard him as weak, muddled, or wrongheaded often like him. This is a difficult side to portray in a political biography. A descriptive interlude of a trip I took with him during the summer of 2002 may help us come to grips with this elusive quality. He had picked up his Nobel Prize half a year earlier, and he was riding high, enjoying adulation, stirring no controversy, and making little news. It was a good time to watch him at work and try to understand the core of his hold on people.

Shortly before the plane took off from New York on July 2, Kofi used an African expression to welcome me. Alluding to the days when I covered the United Nations as a correspondent of the *Los Angeles Times*, he put a hand on my shoulder and said, "It's good to see the old warrior back."

The trip would take Annan, then sixty-four, to Africa—after a vital stopover in Vienna, and he had kindly invited me to come along. Many memories would unfold for me. I had spent ten years in Africa as a Ford Foundation fellow, Peace Corps official, and foreign correspondent, and the secretary-general's African itinerary comprised three countries—South Africa, the Sudan, and Nigeria—that I had not seen in thirty years. Although I had known Annan when he was chief of UN peacekeeping, I had not seen him since his election as secretary-general in 1996.

The old imperial capital of Vienna, the first stop on the tour, attracted the most news coverage because he met Iraqi foreign minister Naji Sabri there. Vienna hosts several UN agencies, and Annan and Sabri negotiated behind closed doors at UN headquarters, a modernist warren of buildings. In two days of formal talks, Annan tried in vain to persuade Sabri to accept the return of UN weapons inspectors to Iraq.

During a break in the talks, the secretary-general returned to his suite at the Bristol Hotel to receive the chancellor of Austria and then embarked on a brisk, forty-minute walk to a city park and through the downtown pedestrian shopping area near the hotel. I ran into him about a block from the hotel. It was a warm day, and the shirts of his bodyguards, beneath their jackets laden with weapons and other equipment, dripped with perspiration. But Kofi looked cool and pleased with himself. He told me that he had just phoned Nane's parents in Sweden and mentioned after greeting them that he was talking while walking in Vienna. "Oh, good," his mother-in-law said, "I was worried and was about to call Nane to tell her that you were out of breath."

On the night before the close of the negotiations, the secretary-general invited Evelyn Leopold of Reuters, Carola Hoyos of the *Financial Times* of London, Richard Roth and Liz Neisloss of CNN, and myself to his suite for half an hour of champagne, canapés, and informal conversation. The half hour lasted for three hours. Accompanied by his spokesman, Fred Eckhard, the secretary-general received us in an elegant sitting room decorated with portraits of what seemed like Hapsburg royalty. The evening made it clear to me that he had not changed much. He was still a man without pretense who spoke in sentences so clear and simple that they seemed, in their understated way, somehow poetic. He struck us as intelligent, thoughtful, politically aware, and sensitive to others. He seemed genuinely interested in finding out what I had been doing since we last met.

He told us that he always spoke with leaders of the opposition on his trips. The UN, after all, is supposed to encourage democracy. But, even more interesting, he told us he tried to seek out leaders who had retired or fallen from power. He had met former chancellor Helmut Kohl in Berlin recently, and the old man had tears in his eyes as he tried to explain why he had refused to name the contributors in the political financing scandal that had brought him down. Annan said he wanted to learn from the former leaders and, if they had made mistakes, he wanted to learn from their mistakes. He had met Lyndon Johnson once after his presidency and was astounded how broken he seemed. "It shows how people can make powerful decisions," Annan said, "and then reveal later that they are fragile human beings."

He thought the White House had been surprised by the worldwide condemnation of its recent decision to withdraw from the treaty creating an International Criminal Court. "Americans want to be liked," he said. "They don't like to be isolated. The French are different. They don't mind standing alone. In fact, when that happens, they feel it is more proof that they are right."

As Eckhard carried a plate of canapés to us, Roth asked, "Do spokesman get an extra 15 percent for doing that?" "No," Kofi replied, "I am just preparing him for his next job." Then he burst out laughing. I thought that some bosses might have sounded cutting, dismissive, or demeaning making a remark like that. Kofi made it sound like a good-natured joke, and Fred took it that way.

On the second and final day of the talks, Annan made it clear to the foreign minister that he would not meet with him again until the Iraqi government accepted the inspectors. He was firm, but as usual his words, according to aides, lacked any bristle of threat or anger. He believed that only soft but reasonable talk could dissipate the Iraqi stubbornness about giving in to American demands that they allow the inspections to resume. He knew, of course, that some

American critics believed he had already wasted too much of his time and prestige talking with the Iraqis. Some accused him of being an appeaser.

When the talks ended, the secretary-general met scores of reporters in the rotunda of the conference center beneath the large flags of the then 189 member states of the UN. He was asked if the Iraqis had said no to inspections. "Well, they haven't said yes yet," he replied. Trying to put the best light on things, he said, "We have come a long way. . . . They have to report back now." But, frank as ever, he could not hide his disappointment. "I would have preferred to have moved further," he said. "I cannot force the issue. I must let them follow their own process."

Iraqi foreign minister Sabri came to the rotunda a few minutes later in a fiery mood. Asked if he were concerned about threats from Washington about an invasion, Sabri replied, "We hear a lot of rubbish. . . . The United States has been attacking us for eleven years." He accused the Security Council led by the United States of violating international humanitarian law by refusing to lift sanctions against Iraq. "We refuse to accept," he said, "that we go ahead accepting these harsh measures while the Security Council evades its commitments. . . . We are the victims of illegal action imposed on the Security Council by the United States."

In light of the continuing crisis with Iraq over inspections and the impending American invasion, the futile talks in Vienna had a good deal of significance, but the journey onward to Africa promised far more excitement and pleasure. We flew in a comfortable, chartered Boeing 737 with a private compartment for the secretary-general and loads of room for the rest of us: advisers, staff assistants, bodyguards, and journalists, a total entourage of fifteen. The UN has no budget for such convenient travel. But the Swiss and Norwegian governments have set aside a fund to rent charter aircraft for the secretary-general whenever commercial flights prove too onerous. Since commercial flights between African countries are infrequent and uncertain, the Swiss and Norwegians approved the trip. A steward confided that the last client for the plane was the rap star Dr. Dre.

Distances are so great in Africa that we had to have refueling stops en route to South Africa. At Libreville, the capital of Gabon, Prime Minister Jean-François Ntoutoume-Emane led us past an honor guard of women soldiers in royal blue kepis and gold-trimmed capes. UN workers gathered around Annan at a reception in the airport and told him about the pressing humanitarian problem of Libreville. Hardwood forests and oil reserves have made Gabon a rich country, and parents from neighboring countries, hoping for a better life for their children, pay smugglers to slip children across the border. There are fifteen thousand to twenty thousand illegal foreign children in Libreville, many roaming the streets in poverty. You cannot escape the harshness of Africa even on a refueling stop.

After the plane left Libreville, Annan, relaxing in a bright red sweater, invited me into his compartment. In the old days, he had a reputation among journalists for a rare frankness. If the question was embarrassing or barbed, he would smile and his eyes would glint as he contemplated the trouble that might engulf him if he replied with all honesty. Yet he would barge ahead and do so anyway. He laughed when I recalled this old trait of his. "You observed me well in those days," he said. But he could no longer speak as frankly as secretary-general. "Words are powerful," he said. "They consume. They can inflame. They can complicate. So given the situations I often deal with, I cannot always speak my mind as I like." Yet it is doubtful that any other statesman in the world speaks with more frankness.

We talked mostly about Africa. A man of medium height with gray, almost white hair and a trim beard, Annan displayed an openness and polite charm and wide-eyed curiosity that must have stamped him even when he was a twenty-one-year-old Ghanian student showing up at Macalester in the cold of Minnesota in 1959. From the vantage of an international civil servant, the downward plight of Africa has been terribly troubling. "There are times when I got angry," he told me. "There are times when I became frustrated and exasperated. If you take my own country, Ghana, it became independent about the same time as Malaysia. I think about the time of independence, we had about the same amount of reserves at the Central Bank. And yet look at the difference—where Malaysia is today and where we are." Yet he has not given up. "I feel passionately about what happens in Africa," he said. "I think Africa has a potential. It is not a lost cause. With lots of effort and hard work, we can turn the continent around."

We arrived in Durban, an industrial city on the Indian Ocean coast of South Africa, for a summit meeting of the Organization of African Unity (OAU). In many ways, South Africa is the continent's main success story. Its transformation during the past decade from a racist, undemocratic, oppressive state to a multiethnic democracy dominated by the African majority has been relatively smooth. The country has enormous problems—poverty, AIDS, crime, stubborn pockets of racism—but the cruel, humiliating and shameful signs of apartheid—the ubiquitous labels "whites" and "nonwhites" on benches and water fountains and elevators, the segregated taxis, the Bantustans, the legislation forcing Africans to live in housing estates outside "white cities," the prisons for political dissidents, the pass laws restricting the travel of Africans—have all disappeared.

When I was last in Durban in 1967, it was inconceivable that the leaders of black Africa would ever meet there. Not only were the heads of fifty-three delegations assembling there now, but also signals of hope and good feelings were all around: I encountered no incident of harshness of one race against another; white, black, and South Asian waiters, none with more authority than the others, served the tables at my hotel restaurant; a white officer led the military band that showed up at the conference's festivities, but most of the musicians were black except for the tuba section, which was, for no reason I could fathom, all white.

The OAU, which was founded in 1963 and never amounted to

more than a theater of overblown oratory, was abolishing itself during four days of meeting and reconstituting as the African Union, patterned somewhat after the European Union. In 1997, during his first year as UN secretary-general, Annan had attended an OAU summit and appealed to the leaders not to grant membership to anyone who came to power through the barrel of a gun. He had been admonished for making such a bold speech.

But Annan's fellow Africans finally accepted his appeal, at least in principle. They designed the new African Union as tough and democratic. According to its charter, it will refuse membership to dictators who come to power through coups or any other unconstitutional way, and it will have the authority to intervene in any country to halt war crimes, genocide, and crimes against humanity. But, as Annan warned the African leaders in a sensible speech, "Let us not imagine that, once proclaimed, our Union will become a reality without further effort."

Annan and the African leaders stayed at the Hilton Hotel alongside the International Convention Center, the site of the conference. An air of bedlam engulfed the hotel. Zulu warriors, wearing sheepskins, gazelle hides, and lion and leopard tails, danced in front of the hotel, plastic conference identification badges bouncing against their bare chests. In the lobby, an African pianist, wearing a touristlike safari hat, his feet tapping on the floor, played wonderful South African and American jazz. Security guards constantly commandeered the elevators so their leaders could move swiftly from floor to floor to meet other leaders. Delegates below the rank of president or prime minister or king sometimes had to wait twenty minutes or more for a free elevator.

Why did Annan spend so much time at so boring and hectic a conference? These meetings allow the secretary-general, especially in private sessions, to learn more about the leaders, listen to their problems, and nudge them toward the right directions. Most leaders made appointments to meet him. Some, such as President Olusegun Obasanjo of Nigeria, showed up to chat about the situation in Africa or in their countries. Others, such as Presidents Paul

Kagame of Rwanda and Laurent Kabila of Congo, came to argue about the causes of the bloody conflict between them.

President Kumba Yala of Guinea-Bissau, wearing a suit and a red stocking cap, and President Yahya Jammeh of Gambia, wearing a gleaming white, flowing robe and an Islamic skullcap, showed up to shout at each other. Their two countries are tiny; neither can boast a population of as much as 1.5 million. But Yala accused Jammeh of training dissidents in Gambia and sending them to Guinea-Bissau to try to bring down the government.

After the accusation was denied, Annan suggested that the Guinea-Bissau president accept an offer from Jammeh to send investigators to Gambia to make sure. The two presidents agreed to return in a few hours to sign a memorandum of understanding authorizing the investigation. They hugged each other in front of press photographers outside the secretary-general's office at the convention center. But neither president showed up later for the signing. "Africa is in trouble with these men in charge," muttered an African official on Annan's staff.

The secretary-general is a kind and generous man, solicitous about the interests of his guests and friends. When Nelson Mandela, wearing his trademark flowered shirt and sporting a cane, visited Annan at the Hilton, Annan decided to call in the three journalists on the UN trip as well—Carola Hoyos of the *Financial Times* of London, the distinguished British author William Shawcross, and myself.

It is odd how even supposedly jaded journalists feel something special and saintly about the presence of Mandela. He endured twenty-eight years of imprisonment; served as the symbol of the struggle against apartheid; preached reconciliation upon his release; helped forge a democratic government; governed as the first South African president ever elected by universal suffrage; and then, in a move rare for African leaders, stepped down from power when his term ended. No one else in Africa, perhaps in the world, can match that record.

My face must have been frozen in awe. After chatting with Shawcross about his father, former British attorney general Hartley Shawcross, then almost a hundred years old, Mandela turned to me, smiled, and teased, "Why do you look so aggressive?" Then he burst out laughing. I had no reply except to laugh with him. When we stepped out of the suite, leaving Mandela and Annan chatting behind us, Shawcross said, pointing backward, "There are only two people with great moral stature in the world today, and both are Africans with grey hair."

Annan next alighted in the Sudanese capital of Khartoum to encourage what seemed like a promising peace process in a country that has been at civil war for most of its forty-six years of independence. The southern Sudanese, who are Christian and animist, had been in continual rebellion against a government dominated by northern Muslims. The war ravaged the south and encouraged the northern-dominated government to waste much of its budget on munitions. Peace talks, ongoing in Kenya, were moving toward some kind of federal solution. The secretary-general turned eloquent at the airport when asked about the war by a Sudanese reporter.

"From Ghana to the Sudan," Annan said, "we did not fight for independence to have starvation. Those of us who fought for independence, all of us, shouted one word: freedom. Now there are many more people hungry than ever before. So where is our freedom? Is a hungry man free?"

I tried to analyze why the secretary-general's words so often seem eloquent. He speaks simply in short sentences that sparkle with clarity and never jar because of a slip in grammar. His measured tones have a slight cadence. His use of words is subtle yet careful. He never postures. And, most important, he projects an air of sincerity that could not possibly be faked.

For the first time on the trip, Annan betrayed some annoyance at UN staff. He was scheduled the next morning to tour a nearby war refugee camp. His officials in Khartoum told him that it was a showcase camp. He spoke softly but pointedly. "So why am I going?" he asked. Informed that the Sudanese government had selected the camp, the secretary-general told them that although he was a guest of the Sudan, "it doesn't mean the government can tell me what to do."

But it was too late to change itineraries, and we set out for the Dar es Salaam refugee camp the next morning. Khartoum lies at the hub where the White Nile and the Blue Nile converge to form the Nile River, and the city is a kind of oasis of some trees, some other greenery, and an occasional breeze in a parched, desertlike area that is baked by the sun in heat of more than a hundred degrees Fahrenheit. We crossed the bridge into the twin city of Omdurman, our cars lifting swirls of sandstorm as we drove ten miles or so.

The camp was set up in 1988 by the government to house southern Sudanese refugees escaping from the war. The refugees looked markedly different from the northerners of Khartoum and Omdurman. They were very dark-skinned, some almost ebony black. Many men wore shirts and trousers, not the standard northern male dress of turbans and loose white robes known as djellabas. The camp included a sparsely decorated Catholic church, not a mosque.

Chanting refugees carried signs that proclaimed in English, "Stop War. We need Development. No for War. Yes for Peace." Refugee leaders, representing different tribes, addressed the secretary-general, calling for peace, invariably ending their orations with the slogan "Sawa sawa." That meant, we were told, something like "We are all together."

The secretary-general toured a medical clinic that was spotless, spacious, orderly, and uncrowded, and then chatted with young girls at a primary school that exhibited samples of its equipment for him: a bench with iron slats for seats, a few books, a leather whip, a rope whip. He later stood in front of the church altar that housed only a small crucifix, two candles, and cloth flowers and told the southerners, "Everywhere I have gone, I have the sense that the people want peace. I think the leaders owe it to you, and you owe it to yourselves, and if we all work together and put the enmities of the past behind us, we should be able to bring peace to this land. Sawa sawa."

In my days as an Africa correspondent, I would savor trips to Khartoum, for it harbored so many vestiges of romantic nineteenth-century British history. In the 1880s, the troops of a rebellious, fundamental Muslim leader known as the Mahdi took over the Sudan and killed the British governor-general, General Charles Gordon, a Victorian hero, by spearing him to death on the outdoor steps of his palace in Khartoum. The victorious Mahdi died a few months later, evidently of smallpox or typhus, but the British did not avenge the death of Gordon until an expedition of British troops led by General Herbert Kitchener defeated the followers of the Mahdi at the Battle of Omdurman in 1898. The whole story forms the backdrop for one of my favorite movies, *The Four Feathers* (the 1939 version starring Ralph Richardson, not the unfortunate remake of 2002).

I took advantage of my return to visit the ornate Tomb of the Mahdi in Omdurman and tour the small museum nearby that includes flags of the Mahdi, robes of his followers, British Gatling guns, and the Mahdi's often-quoted letter to Gordon demanding surrender. The past and present came together a few hours later when Saddick al-Mahdi, a grandson of the Mahdi, met with the secretary-general at his suite in the Khartoum Hilton and then with me and the other journalists in the bar downstairs.

As we sipped tropical juices (alcoholic drinks are prohibited in public places in the Sudan), Saddick, wearing his turban and djellaba, talked about his political career. He had been prime minister until 1989, when military officers overthrew him in a coup and jailed him for six months. The officers, Islamic fundamentalists, thought he was too soft on the south and unwilling to force it to accept Islam. "They said that we inheritors of the Mahdi were betraying the Mahdi," Saddick told us. But, he went on, the military government now realized that its harsh attempts to put down the south had failed. I heard no mention of Darfur at all during the visit to Sudan.

Gordon's old palace is now the presidential palace, and we accompanied the secretary-general there for a ceremonial dinner. While Annan conferred in private with President Omar Hassan

Ahmad al-Bashir, the general who had led the coup against the grandson of the Mahdi, I looked in vain for the outdoor staircase on which Gordon was speared to death. A servant explained that the staircase had been gobbled up by a recent expansion of the palace. He took me to a downstairs room and showed me an indoor wall, perhaps twenty feet tall, that stood in place of the stairs. High on the wall I could see a stone plaque with the name of Gordon and the date of his death.

As we walked to the dining tables in the gardens of the palace, the secretary-general motioned me to his side and introduced me to President Bashir. The president welcomed me to Khartoum. I told him that I had visited the palace thirty years ago and found it greatly changed. "Yes," he said, "we have improved it a lot." I wasn't so sure but agreed anyway.

Our last stop, Abuja, the new capital in the center of Nigeria, is a specially created city, like Brasilia in Brazil, with massive new buildings and wide boulevards, lacking all the confusion and turmoil and crowding of the port of Lagos, the old cacophonic, bustling capital more than three hundred miles to the southwest. "Lagos is very exciting. I love it," Ama Annan told me. "There is nothing happening here." Ama, then thirty-three, wearing a red flowered Nigerian dress, and her brother, Kojo, then twenty-nine and sporting a shaved head, Michael Jordan style, worked in the shipping business in Lagos and had come to Abuja to meet their father. He scheduled no official business that evening and instead dined in private with Ama and Kojo.

Annan came to Nigeria as a sign of support for the nascent democracy in Africa's most populous country. President Olusegun Obasanjo invited the secretary-general and his entourage to breakfast at Aso Rock, the sprawling, fortresslike presidential home built by General Sani Abacha, the paranoid tyrant who ruled Nigeria from 1993 to 1998. When I had last seen Obasanjo, he was the young colonel who commanded the Third Marine Commando Division that won the decisive battle that ended the Nigerian civil war in 1969. Now heavyset and sixty-seven years old, dressed in a

thick yet loose Yoruba robe, he was a democratically elected president, leader of one of the few civilian governments in the history of
independent Nigeria.

Obasanjo sat at the end of a long marble table with a dozen
members of the Nigerian cabinet on his left side, the secretary-
general and his colleagues on the right. The breakfast was partly
British with scrambled eggs, sausages, and baked beans but mostly
Nigerian, featuring *akaras* (savories made from black-eyed peas),
ogi (a corn porridge), fried plantains, fried yams, and beef stew.
Gesticulating with both hands to make his points, Obasanjo talked
about the problems of Africa and of Nigeria. Annan once again
stressed the vital need for democracy in Africa. "In Asia," he said,
"Indonesia collapsed because it did not have a democratic base; it
was built on sand."

The breakfast table discussion covered many issues. The most
memorable came when the minister for youth, a woman, suggested
that Annan hire more women for important positions at the UN.
She had a suggestion. The Nigerian Agbani Darego, who was
selected Miss World of 2001, would make a wonderful UN ambassador of goodwill. "She is very intelligent and very pretty, and she is
my little cousin," said the smiling minister.

Kofi's son, Kojo, arrived at the breakfast an hour or so late. He
excused himself with the foolish grin of a rumpled young man who
had spent most of the night on the town. His father said nothing
but stared ahead with steely angry eyes. President Obasanjo told
Kojo to return that night for dinner; the president had some business to discuss.

During his stay in Abuja, Annan also met with representatives of
what are known in UN parlance as NGOs—nongovernmental
organizations such as women's clubs, civil rights associations, labor
unions, humanitarian aid teams, and other groups that make up
Nigeria's civil society. Some of their words gave us a glimmer of
what Africans outside government feel about the African secretary-
general. "Let me congratulate you, sir," said one Nigerian, "as the
number one civil servant in our turbulent world." "We blacks are

proud of you," said another, "and no matter what you are going through, please keep it up."

At a departing news conference, a Nigerian reporter asked the secretary-general if he would support Obasanjo's bid for reelection in the 2003 presidential election. Annan laughed and replied that he did not have a candidate in the race. "I don't travel around the world to cause excitement," he said.

En route to New York, we stopped on the island of Santa Maria in the Portuguese Azores. International dignitaries often refuel at that airport when flying across the Atlantic in nonjumbo jets. In the small VIP lounge, we found a guest book—a ledger filled with flowery comments signed by many world leaders such as Obasanjo and Cuban president Fidel Castro.

The most florid was that of President Hugo Chavez of Venezuela, who, writing in Spanish, saluted the "warm, sympathetic, marvelous, generous people of the Azores who shared an Iberian heritage" with the Venezuelan people. He hailed the Azoreans as "Latin, Atlantic, and Caribbean" like himself and joined them in wishing for "worldwide peace and justice." He then signed his name in bold script, adding his title, "President of the Bolivarian Republic of Venezuela."

At the urging of a Portuguese official, the secretary-general picked up a pen. There can hardly be an international statesman less flamboyant, less like Chavez, than Kofi Annan. The secretary-general signed the ledger, adding the tiny letters "UN" below his name, and nothing more.

13

Facing the American Juggernaut

In a few weeks, Kofi Annan's energy would be consumed by the impending invasion of Iraq. The war in Iraq would define his ten years as secretary-general. He was the secretary-general who tried, in his own understated way, to stop the American juggernaut. Some critics believe he did not try very hard. But a secretary-general has limited power. He wields only moral force. In any case, Kofi annoyed the Vulcans around President Bush enough to diminish in their eyes. Some felt the need to slap him down.

Annan did not engage in any fiery oratory to dissuade the White House from invading Iraq. Instead, he tried continually to draw the Americans deeper into UN procedures. He preached again and again that any decision for war should be made by the Security Council as a whole, preferably in unanimity. Since both France and Russia were opposed to invasion, unanimity would have probably produced a resolution that fell short of war. Annan wanted the Americans to keep talking and the inspectors to keep inspecting until the Americans stepped back from the brink. That did not happen.

There never was much of a chance to stop the invasion of Iraq. The leading warmongers, like Vice President Dick Cheney, did not want to take the issue to the United Nations. When forced to do so, they treated the UN only as a possible source of validation. In their eyes, the UN had only one use: to stamp the war okay. The peace lobby, including the secretary-general, hoped that the UN would conjure enough diplomatic fog to delay and confuse and finally stop the war. It was only a hope, and it was forlorn.

We now know President Bush was determined to go to war many months before he took the matter to the UN. It is not clear why. He confided to the Palestinian leader Mohammad Abbas that God told him to do it. He mentioned to others the need to avenge the assassination attempt on his father on a trip to the Middle East in 1993. He may have wanted to finish what his father had left undone in the Persian Gulf War. Or he may genuinely have felt that Saddam Hussein and Iraq were a threat to the United States.

In his speeches, the president offered four rationales: that Saddam possessed weapons of mass destruction, that he was linked to the al-Qaeda terrorists who had brought down the World Trade Center, that he was a fiendish tyrant, and that his removal would generate democracy in Iraq and the rest of the Middle East. Only the first—the weapons of mass destruction—mattered to the UN, for Saddam's possession of such weapons would defy numerous Security Council resolutions.

Throughout August 2002 the foreign policy team of President Bush argued vociferously about taking the issue to the UN. The only real opposition to an invasion came from elder Republicans outside the White House who had served with his father. On television and in an op-ed piece in the *Wall Street Journal*, Brent Scowcroft, a former National Security adviser, warned that an invasion "could turn the whole region into a cauldron, and thus destroy the war on terrorism." Lawrence Eagleburger, a former secretary of state, said much the same in private meetings in Washington.

Secretary of State Colin Powell phoned Scowcroft to thank him for opposing the invasion. But Powell did not go as far as Scowcroft in the White House deliberations. His position was more ambiguous. He insisted that the White House had to go to the UN to seek legal sanction for an invasion. Without it, they would not only face worldwide condemnation but also would be undercutting Prime Minister Tony Blair of Britain. They might even risk losing his support. But according to Todd S. Purdum's account in his book *A Time of Our Choosing*, Powell then told his colleagues, "If you take it to the United Nations then you are taking it down a road that will fork. There could be a peaceful solution." In short, while renewed UN inspections of Iraq were necessary to validate an American invasion, they also just might lead to disarmament and peace.

This notion of a peaceful bypath did not strike Powell's colleagues as a satisfactory outcome. Vice President Cheney even made a speech a few days later denouncing inspections. "A return of inspectors," he told a meeting of the Veterans of Foreign Wars, "would provide no assurance whatsoever of his [Saddam's] compliance with UN resolutions." Nevertheless, Bush accepted the advice of Powell and Blair and agreed to seek a resolution at the UN that would surely lead to renewed inspections.

Kofi Annan listened to all the bellicose talk from Washington with alarm and some hope. By the time President Bush arrived at the UN General Assembly a year and a day after the destruction of the World Trade Center, the secretary-general felt that war was more likely than not. "I thought we were getting close," he recalls, "but I was hopeful that it could be averted, that we should do whatever we can to avert it."

Following normal protocol, the secretary-general addressed the opening session of the General Assembly shortly before the president of the United States. But unlike the usual practice, Annan's speech had been released to the press the day before and reported in the morning newspapers before he spoke. Speechwriter Edward Mortimer had suggested the early release so that it would not be ignored by reporters eager to report the words of Bush. Says Annan, "We had discussions . . . and I came down on the side that the message was important and that the message should get out. . . . There was a tendency here when the president comes on the same day . . . the press tends to focus on the president and the message [of the secretary-general] sometimes gets lost." White House aides saw the early release, however, as an attempt to upstage the president, the first of what they regarded as a series of irritants by the secretary-general.

One part of Kofi's message was welcomed by the White House. Calling for the return of the inspectors, he told the General Assembly, "I urge Iraq to comply with its obligations—for the sake of its own people, and for the sake of world order. If Iraq's defiance continues, the Security Council must face its responsibilities."

But he also cautioned against vigilantism by any single state. "I stand before you today," he said, "as a multilateralist—by precedent, by principle, by Charter, and by duty. . . . For any one state—large or small—choosing to follow or reject the multilateral path must not be a simple matter of political convenience. It has consequences far beyond the immediate context."

Then he struck his favorite theme. "Any state, if attacked," he said, "retains the right of self-defense. . . . But beyond that, when states decide to use force to deal with broader threats to international peace and security, there is no substitute for the unique legitimacy provided by the United Nations." As President Bush made clear a few minutes later, he accepted this theory only as long as the UN granted its "unique legitimacy" to what the United States wanted to do.

President Bush's speech was chillingly clear. He first painted a bristling portrait of an Iraq rife with weapons of mass destruction. There were no doubts in Bush's portrait: "The history, the logic, and the facts lead to one conclusion: Saddam Hussein's regime is a grave and gathering danger. To suggest otherwise is to hope against the evidence.

"Iraq has answered a decade of UN demands with a decade of defiance," he went on, setting down the grand challenge of his speech. "All the world now faces a test, and the United Nations a difficult and defining moment. Are Security Council resolutions to be honored and enforced, or cast aside without consequence? Will the United Nations serve the purpose of its founding, or will it be irrelevant?"

Bush then offered cooperation. "My nation will work with the UN Security Council to meet our common challenge," he said. "If

Iraq's regime defies us again, the world must move deliberately, decisively to hold Iraq to account. We will work with the UN Security Council for the necessary resolutions."

A dramatic threat came from the president at this moment. "But the purposes of the United States should not be doubted," he said. "The Security Council resolutions will be enforced—the just demands of peace and security will be met—or action will be unavoidable. And a regime that has lost its legitimacy will also lose its power." In short, if the UN was too powerless or cowardly to act, the United States would do so on its own.

The speech made clear that the Bush administration was prepared for war, but Kofi still found two hopeful signs for peace. The first was the American pledge to work with the Security Council to approve new resolutions. The second was the fact that Bush, unlike Cheney, had not rejected further inspections as a way of disarming Saddam.

Although most diplomats and analysts focused on the words of the president, the American war hawks did not ignore the speech of the secretary-general. They found all its talk about UN legitimacy very unhelpful. Michael Ramirez, the conservative political cartoonist of the *Los Angeles Times*, produced a rather unsubtle cartoon with caricatures of Bush as Winston Churchill and Annan as Neville Chamberlain.

To make matters worse in the eyes of the hawks, Annan in the next few days persuaded Naji Sabri, the Iraqi foreign minister, to change Iraq's policy and accept the return of UN inspectors. Sabri had attended the opening session and heard the speech of Bush. Annan, who had failed to persuade Sabri when they met in Vienna only two months earlier, succeeded this time. In New York, Sabri could sense the mood of war.

But Sabri, Annan recalls, "was in a difficult spot—he was here but his leadership was in Baghdad." Talking back and forth with Baghdad, Sabri came up with "one of those letters which had so many caveats and was couched in terms that you could read any way." Annan was emphatic. He told Sabri "we need a clean letter that invited the inspectors to come back and do their work without any caveats or any conditions."

The final letter, addressed to Annan and signed by Sabri, looked clean. "I am pleased to inform you of the decision of the Government of Iraq," it said, "to allow the return of United Nations weapons inspectors without conditions."

Iraq, the letter went on, wanted "to remove any doubts that Iraq still possesses weapons of mass destruction." Iraq was "ready to discuss the practical arrangements necessary for the immediate resumption of inspections." All Iraq asked, the letter went on, was that the members of the UN respect "the sovereignty, territorial integrity and political independence of Iraq."

A pleased and smiling secretary-general stepped before the press cameras and microphones on Monday, September 16, four days after the speeches. "A lot has happened in this building since Thursday," he told the reporters. First he paid tribute to Bush. "I believe the president's speech galvanized the international community," he said.

He then announced that the Iraqis had accepted the return of the inspectors "without conditions." He thanked the Arab League for its help in persuading Iraq to accept and said he would pass the letter on to the Security Council.

Despite Annan's praise of President Bush, the White House was furious. The simplest gateway to war would be a refusal by Saddam Hussein to admit the inspectors. Now the secretary-general had blocked that. He had persuaded the Iraqis to give in and even helped them write the letter. An administration official, speaking with disdain, told the *New York Times*, "Clearly the hope of the secretary-general was to get out in front of the story before anyone else could." John D. Negroponte, the U.S. ambassador, relayed the White House displeasure to Annan.

The White House insisted that the letter was not as unconditional as Annan claimed. White House spokesman Scott McClellan told reporters, "This is a tactical step by Iraq in hopes of avoiding strong UN Security Council action. As such, it is a tactic that will fail."

Condoleezza Rice, the National Security adviser and future secretary of state, phoned the secretary-general. She berated him for making such a fuss over the letter. It did not strike her as important. She implied it was the usual Iraqi bombast that would end in a lack of cooperation. Annan replied that everyone had been pressing for the Iraqis to let the inspectors come back and do their work, and it is important that they do go back now that the Iraqis have promised to cooperate.

Some Bush administration officials believed Annan had stretched the duties of the secretary-general by helping the Iraqis write their letter to him. "He has overstepped his bounds," said an American diplomat. But Annan insists he worked within the UN Charter. "I think as secretary-general," he says, "it is my job to help whenever I can to assure the implementation of UN resolutions."

Kofi Annan does not have a combative, stubborn or fiercely independent personality. But he has a deep sense of moral integrity, of duty to the United Nations and its charter, and of the need for patience and discussion before action. These qualities would often put him at odds with the Bush White House throughout the Iraq crisis and war.

White House displeasure with Annan would follow a pattern. The fiercest attacks—the true feeling of the White House—would appear in the news as quotes from "senior White House officials" or "senior administration officials" or a similar anonymous source. Ambassador Negroponte would relay a report that his bosses had some concerns. A phone call would follow from Condoleezza Rice or Secretary Powell. They would never scold but would politely leave Annan in no doubt that he had upset the White House.

President Bush himself never voiced any displeasure to Annan. "I must say. . . when the president and I have disagreed," recalls Annan, "he has been quite good about it. He has said, 'Look, this is going to happen. Kofi, you have to do what you have to do, and I have to do what I have to do.' But I'm not sure everyone around him understands that."

Powell and Annan talked often. Annan admired Powell and had felt reassured when President Bush appointed him secretary of state. It was a great disappointment when the secretary-general began to realize that Vice President Cheney and Secretary of Defense Donald Rumsfeld rather than Powell controlled Iraq policy. Whenever Annan upset the White House, his transgression caused Powell special problems. Since the extremists in the White House put Powell and the UN in the same ideological boat, they tended to blame Powell whenever Annan irritated them. That gave Powell an added incentive to try to persuade Annan not to stray.

It took two months for the Security Council to pass a resolution. Since they had no doubt that Iraq bristled with weapons of mass destruction, the most militant Americans wanted a resolution that would trap Saddam Hussein into defiance and trigger war. Vice President Cheney came up with the trap. His proposed resolution would require Saddam to file a detailed declaration of armaments. If he denied having weapons of mass destruction, he would be lying—a cause for war. If he admitted having weapons of mass destruction, he would be confessing—also a cause for war.

Secretary of State Powell had the task of submitting these and other extreme ideas to the Security Council, knowing he could never push them through without moderating them. He and Annan spoke almost every day during these tense days. The secretary-general came to regard Powell as a loyal member of the Bush team, yet different. "Obviously he was a member of a team," Annan recalls. "And he is an honorable soldier and a gentleman. If you are part of a team it is difficult to what extent you can distance yourself and disassociate yourself from the team. But I can say I don't think he was in the same category of those on the team who were gung ho for the war."

Powell did most of his negotiating with the French foreign minister, Dominique de Villepin, a tall, handsome diplomat with a shock of silvery hair. A favorite of French president Jacques Chirac, the forty-seven-year-old de Villepin was sixteen years younger than Powell and had somehow found time during a diplomatic career to write both poetry and history. His postings had included Washington, where he had once served as the press attaché. He knew many American reporters well and spoke English perfectly. De Villepin, supported by most of the others on the Security Council, insisted that the resolution must not trigger war no matter what Saddam did. If he continued to defy the UN, the Council, according to de Villepin, should meet again to set a course of action through a second resolution.

During this period, according to Clare Short, a former member of British prime minister Tony Blair's cabinet, the British intelligence services bugged the offices of Kofi Annan. The secretary-general speaks so softly that it is often difficult to capture his words on an ordinary tape recorder. But assuming the British had equipment sensitive enough to register the conversations in his office, they would have heard him lobbying for a resolution that could win the support of all fifteen members of the Security Council.

Annan believed that a resolution of such significance needed unanimity to be effective. But his campaign for unanimity also strengthened the hand in the Security Council of those who did not want an American-style resolution that provoked Saddam into a defiance that ensured war. Only a somewhat tempered resolution had a chance of winning unanimous support. His opposition to a stringent American resolution reflected his opposition to the American drive to war. Although his public statements were always temperate and indirect, Annan believes his colleagues and the eaves-dropping Bush administration knew where he stood. "I never supported the war," he says. "I didn't think it was wise to go to war."

The vote for Security Resolution 1441 was unanimous. Even Syria, a longtime ally of Saddam Hussein, voted in favor of the resolution. Annan had a major part in this. He phoned President Bashar Assad and told him that unanimity was the best hope of persuading Saddam to comply with the resolution. Compliance by Iraq, Annan argued, was the best chance for averting war. Assad accepted the argument and instructed his ambassador to vote in favor, a vote that surprised all the others on the Council.

The resolution was an artful compromise worked out by Powell and de Villepin. It did have a major drawback. As Annan puts it, "for some of the members it was a fudge. Both sides came away with the sense that the resolution supported their position or gave them the right to do what they wanted to do." Nevertheless, when the resolution was approved, Annan thought "it would give us a chance to move away from war or at least postpone it."

Resolution 1441, passed on November 8, 2002, found Iraq in "material breach" of all past resolutions on disarmament but gave Saddam Hussein's regime "a final opportunity to comply." Iraq was required to allow the inspectors "immediate, unimpeded, unconditional, and unrestricted access to all sites." Cheney's "trap" was there, but it had lost much of its potency. Iraq was required to make the detailed declaration in thirty days. But lying on the declaration was evidently not enough to provoke punishment, certainly not enough to provoke war. Iraq would be declared in "material breach" of Resolution 1441 if it lied on the declaration and if it failed to cooperate with the inspectors. If this happened, the inspectors would report the matter to the Security Council "for assessment." The resolution did not say what would happen next but warned Iraq of "serious consequences" if it did not comply with the resolution.

Annan's hope for peace was based on the lack of a trigger in the resolution. The wording of the resolution implied that war could come only after the Security Council assessed a report of Iraq's transgressions from the inspectors. In Kofi's view, that meant a second resolution. He thought a second resolution "would have led to a discussion, debate, assessment, reassessment of where we are and what the inspectors have achieved or not. And when you get involved in that sort of discussion, where you look at the cold facts, sometimes you walk away from the brink."

After the resolution was passed, Annan no longer played a significant role in the crisis. He was now no more than a commentator, deploring the American onslaught to war but unable to do anything to stop it. His comments were barely noticed, in fact, not even by the White House. The Bush administration focused its venom on the French and the inspectors. De Villepin was trying to rally most of the Security Council against war. And the inspectors were not coming up with any smoking gun to justify war.

The Americans would have had far less difficulty with the Security Council if the Australian diplomat Richard Butler was still the chief inspector. Butler's views were similar to those of the Bush White House. He envisioned his inspecting job as much like that of a chief of police or a district attorney. Whenever the Iraqis denied they had weapons of mass destruction, he knew they were lying. Despite a lack of evidence, he never had doubts. In the year 2000, he had written *The Greatest Threat*, a book that stated without hesitation, "Saddam is back in the business of developing nuclear weapons. (Iraqi defectors say he already has them.) He has also extended the range of his missiles and manufactured chemical and biological weapons." It would not have taken Butler much time to come up with enough evidence and innuendo to accuse Iraq of being in material breach of Resolution 1441.

But the new chief inspector was Hans Blix, a former Swedish foreign minister and a former director-general of the International Atomic Energy Agency (IAEA). Blix looked on himself as a judge sifting evidence, not as a policeman or a prosecutor. In his view, Iraq was neither guilty nor innocent until he and his inspectors amassed enough evidence one way or another. In fact, as director-general of the IAEA, he had led the nuclear inspectors under Butler and concluded that Iraq was no longer a nuclear threat.

Even before Resolution 1441 was approved, Blix and Mohammed ElBaradei, the Egyptian who was now director-general of the IAEA, had visited Washington to discuss inspections. While Bush and Condoleezza Rice received them politely, Vice President Cheney admonished them that inspections could not go on forever and that the United States was "ready to discredit inspections in favor of disarmament." Blix interpreted that to mean that if the inspectors did not find the weapons of mass destruction, "the United States would be ready to say that the inspections were useless and embark on disarmament by other means." Cheney was convinced that Blix was not tough enough to do inspections properly. U.S. intelligence started monitoring Blix's conversations and movements.

As the weeks progressed, the inspectors reported Iraq was cooperating but they were not finding anything significant. They did have an argument with Iraq over long-range missiles. The Iraqis showed the inspectors new missiles that the Iraqis insisted did not violate the UN's limits on range. Blix ruled that they did and ordered the destruction of the weapons. The key evidence against Iraq on other issues was circumstantial and ambiguous. The Iraqis claimed they had destroyed all their chemical and biological weapons. But there was a gap in the records between the amount of chemical and biological agents possessed originally and the amount destroyed. Iraqi scientists insisted their record-keeping was at fault. This later proved correct. But it made the inspectors suspicious. Nevertheless, Blix told the Council that incomplete records were not enough evidence to prove that the Iraqis had chemical and biological weapons of mass destruction.

Annan's relationship with Blix and ElBaradei was far different from his relationship with Butler. The Australian operated independently of the secretary-general, and the two did not get along very well. Annan looked on Butler as a bull who stampeded through Iraq without any regard for Iraqi feelings and then exaggerated what he found. But Annan met with Blix and ElBaradei often. His view about weapons of mass destruction was not the same as that of the White House or of Butler. When Resolution 1441 was passed, a reporter asked him if he believed that Iraq possessed weapons of mass destruction. "I really can't answer that question," Annan replied, "until the inspectors come back."

On January 14, 2003, Annan held a New Year's press conference. He began with a plaintive statement: "We start the year with anxiety—anxiety over the prospect of war in Iraq, over nuclear proliferation in the Korean Peninsula, and over what seems like violence without end in the Middle East." Even the Ivory Coast, he went on, was "now caught in the downward spiral of conflict."

"And yet," he insisted, "I am still an optimist. Today's threats are not the first we have faced. What's more, I believe in the last ten years or so we have been learning to cope with them better."

He recounted successes: the end of war in Bosnia, the rebuilding of Kosovo, the independence of East Timor, the end of horror in Sierra Leone, the end of battling between Ethiopia and Eritrea. Looking ahead, he said, "we are within striking distance of reuniting Cyprus, ending the long civil war in the Sudan, and pacifying the Democratic Republic of the Congo.

"I remain convinced," he concluded, "that peace is possible—in Iraq, in Korea, and even between Israel and Palestine—if states work together on all these problems, with patience and firmness."

There was an enormous flaw in the argument. Annan sounded as if he believed the threat of an Iraq war was just one in a long series of UN crises. But it was far more than that. The Iraq crisis had turned into a behemoth, devouring all before it, threatening the career of the secretary-general and the worth of the United Nations itself. George Bush and the war-bent crew around him had created a monstrous crisis that could not be treated like any other.

Fed up by the failure of Hans Blix and his inspectors to produce what was needed, the White House decided to lay out its own evidence before the Security Council and the world. Colin Powell, the most prestigious figure in the Bush administration, was assigned this crucial assignment. A child of West Indian immigrants, Powell was brought up in the poverty of the Bronx, and his life story had an endearing and romantic air. He was not a West Point graduate but a product of the Reserve Officers Training Corps at the City College of New York. He was chairman of the Joint Chiefs of Staff during the first President Bush's Persian Gulf War. Yet he struck others as a man of war who abhorred war and worked for peace. That is why Kofi Annan and many others were sure he was not a wholehearted member of the cabal of warmongers around Bush.

Powell's presentation on February 5, 2003, was billed ahead of time as his Adlai Stevenson moment at the UN. This was an allusion to the dramatic episode during the Cuban missile crisis of 1963 when Ambassador Stevenson confronted the Soviet ambassador at the Security Council with photographs proving that the Soviets had planted nuclear missiles in Cuba. The confrontation is often regarded as Stevenson's finest act at the UN. But Stevenson also had a humiliating performance at the UN—when he held up photographs during the Bay of Pigs invasion of 1961 and told the Political Committee of the General Assembly that none of the downed planes in the photos was American. Washington, covering up the American sponsorship of the invasion, had not told Stevenson the truth and allowed him to proclaim a lie to the world. In the end, the Powell performance would resemble the Stevenson humiliation of 1961 rather than the Stevenson heroics of 1963.

Powell used tapes of secret Iraqi conversations, satellite photos, flashy visual displays under the rubric "Iraq: Failing to Disarm," and an impressive array of data as evidence that "Saddam Hussein and his regime have made no effort, no effort, to disarm" and "are concealing their efforts to produce more weapons of mass destruction." His claims, he insisted, "are not assertions. What we are giving you," he said, "are facts and conclusions based on solid intelligence." Hans Blix, the chief inspector, wrote later that Powell's presentation "was delivered with bravura by a man who during a long and distinguished military career must have had many more opportunities than ambassadors do to use PowerPoint when briefing demanding audiences."

Blix found some of the claims suspicious. Others had already been checked by the inspectors and discounted. Some claims merited further investigation by his inspectors. Nothing struck Blix as sensational, as the smoking gun catching Saddam red-handed. After the war, the world would find that none of Powell's major assertions would hold up.

Kofi Annan had talked with Colin Powell often during the previous few weeks. But Powell had not briefed him about the details of the impending speech. As he listened to the presentation, Annan felt much like Blix. Annan, after all, had spent a good deal of time talking with Blix and ElBaradei and knew how little evidence had been uncovered. Moreover, during his Vienna negotiations with

Iraq, he had talked with a number of Iraqi scientists and listened to their contention that Iraq was not hiding anything. Despite Powell's claim that he was delivering nothing but facts, Annan knew that most were assertions based on circumstantial evidence.

But Annan realized that the presentation would sound impressive to those who knew less about the inspections than he did. "I cannot say that he was convincing," Annan says, "but he made a powerful presentation." It was, after all, Colin Powell making the speech, and he had put all his prestige behind his recitation and display of evidence. That in itself filled Annan with a sense of foreboding. "It made me feel," he recalls, "that . . . more or less a determining decision must have been made to go to war, and the case was being made preparing the public and the international community." As for the impact on the Security Council, Annan assumed that the White House hoped the speech "would have swung some members of the Council to support the action." The evidence in Powell's presentation may have been weak, but that was less significant than the identity of the prestigious official making the weak case. There was little doubt now that Bush was going to war.

The Bush administration attempted to wrest a second resolution from the Security Council that would castigate Saddam Hussein for failing to disarm and authorize a war against Iraq. But this proved difficult, mainly because France objected and led a campaign within the Council to oppose the American resolution. At this point the White House directed its anger far more at President Chirac and Foreign Minister de Villepin than at Annan and Blix.

France, which sought time for more inspections, proved a formidable foe, for it had world opinion on its side. Diplomats and UN civil servants burst into applause when de Villepin told the Security Council, "In this temple of the United Nations, we are the guardians of an ideal, the guardians of a conscience. This onerous responsibility and immense honor . . . must lead us to give priority to disarmament through peace."

Since France was one of the five permanent members of the Security Council, it had the power of veto, and President Chirac vowed to use it against any resolution authorizing war. This infuriated the Americans, who became even more angry when de Villepin flew to Africa to campaign for Angola, Cameroun, and Guinea to vote with France against the United States. The White House regarded the de Villepin foray as somehow unfair and underhanded, even though the United States was applying its own pressure on members of the Security Council.

The secretary-general also played a hand in this maneuvering. Chile and Mexico feared economic reprisals if they defied the Americans. Behind closed doors, Annan urged Mexican ambassador Adolfo Aguilar Zinser and Chilean ambassador Juan Gabriel Valdés to maintain their resistance. We do not know if American intelligence discovered this encouragement. If it did, the White House would have felt even more justification for its contempt for Annan.

Despite the French threat of a veto, the United States, with British and Spanish support, decided to press forward with the resolution. Without a veto, a resolution needs the votes of nine of the fifteen members of the Security Council to pass. The White House hoped to win the support of at least nine on the Council. If the resolution then failed because of a French veto, the White House intended to claim a moral victory, proclaiming that only French intransigence prevented the Security Council from working its will. But by mid-March the White House realized that it probably would fail to get the nine votes.

The United States withdrew the resolution. The White House decided to go to war without the resolution and claim it was doing so on the strength of a host of other resolutions including Resolution 1441. Kofi Annan told reporters outside the Security Council, "If this action is to take place without the support of the Council, its legitimacy will be questioned, and the support for it will be diminished." A week earlier, he had told a news conference in the Netherlands, "If the United States and others were to go outside the Council and take military action, it would not be in conformity with the Charter." These admonitions were ignored by the White House.

At 8:00 P.M. on March 17, 2003, President Bush, in a televised address, said, "The United Nations Security Council has not lived up to its responsibilities, so we will rise to ours. . . ."

"All the decades of deceit and cruelty have now reached an end," Bush went on. "Saddam Hussein and his sons must leave Iraq within forty-eight hours. Their refusal to do so will result in military conflict, commenced at a time of our choosing."

Neither Saddam nor his sons left Iraq, and planes began to bomb Iraq two days later. The war had begun.

The secretary-general then issued a resigned and wistful statement. "Despite the best efforts of the international community and the United Nations," Annan said, "war has come to Iraq for the third time in a quarter of a century. Perhaps if we had persevered a little longer, Iraq could yet have been disarmed peacefully, or—if not—the world could have taken action to solve this problem by a collective decision, endowing it with greater legitimacy, and therefore commanding wider support, than is now the case."

The protest within these words was subtle and nuanced. In fact, they sounded less forceful than his admonitions before the war began. It was as if he saw little point in crying out now that the deed was done. Some critics believe he should have reacted differently—that he should have thundered against this war with all the moral force within him.

Marrack Goulding, for example, the official who was replaced by Annan as the chief of peacekeeping more than a decade earlier, insists that Annan should have immediately declared the war illegal. "I compare him with Hammarskjöld," says Goulding. "Hammarskjöld would have said loud and clear, 'This is a violation of the Charter. The Charter requires that the parties settle their differences peacefully. Only the Security Council can authorize military action.'"

Brian Urquhart, the former undersecretary-general who is a biographer of Hammarskjöld, agrees with Goulding. "Dag Hammarskjöld would have made a different statement, and he would have been right," says Urquhart. Urquhart cites the Suez crisis of

1956, when Hammarskjöld condemned Britain and France for invading Egypt.

In the Suez crisis, however, the United States supported Hammarskjöld and joined him in condemning Britain and France. In the Iraq war, Kofi Annan would have had to defy the United States, not Britain and France. He surely would have endangered his organization if he had dramatically condemned the country that hosts the United Nations headquarters, funds 22 percent of the regular budget, pays even a higher percentage of peacekeeping costs, and wields enormous influence as the world's only superpower.

In any case, a histrionic outburst would have been out of character for Kofi Annan. "I think it is easy in hindsight after the event for one to stand by and do—what do you call it here?—Monday morning quarterbacking?" says Annan. ". . . Obviously some people may say I should have made a big speech condemning, but I had said enough and quite a bit for everyone to know where I stood on this issue. I don't think there was anyone in this organization who had any doubt that I was not in favor of war. . . . I was very clear."

But when the war began, the secretary-general says he was concerned about the division within the UN caused by the conflict between the United States and France. He explains, "The split was so deep already. . . . I was worried about that. When an organization is split and you are trying to help pull it together, it is not the time for you to go and make a big speech which deepens the rift.

"But," he goes on, "not having made a big pronouncement or proclamation, no one could say that they did not know where I stood. The administration knew where I stood. And I think everybody else did."

14

Relevance and Melancholia

A few days after the American-led invasion of Iraq, Richard A. Perle, an American defense specialist and guru of neo-conservatism, wrote a commentary for the *Guardian* newspaper in Britain. "Saddam Hussein's reign of terror is about to end," Perle wrote. "He will go quickly, but not alone; in a parting irony he will take the UN down with him." Perle then hedged a bit. He did not really mean "the whole UN." "Good works" would survive. So would the bleating "chatter box" in New York with all its boring speeches. What would die would be "the liberal conceit" that there is "safety through international law administered by international institutions." In short, the heart of the UN would go. The *Guardian* headline writer understood the point of Perle's piece. The headline read, "Thank God for the death of the UN."

Gloom had descended upon the UN early in 2003. It began once Secretary Powell made his elaborate presentation to the Security Council. Many diplomats and international civil servants did not believe him. Many lost faith in a man they had once admired immensely—a man of great moral strength and inner peace, much like the secretary-general. Powell had shattered their illusion. But it did not matter what they now felt about Powell. The speech had made them realize that President George W. Bush was bent on war, and nothing, certainly not the UN, could stop him. When the war came, Bush deepened the gloom by throwing his triumphalism in their faces. He was forced to act, he said, because the UN had not lived up to its responsibilities. As he had warned months before, the UN was now irrelevant.

Despite Bush's assertion, an argument can be made that the invasion had proven the relevance of the UN. Bush had been forced by political pressures to go to the UN and lay out his evidence for war. The fragility of his case had galvanized world public opinion against his invasion. Protesters filled the streets of capitals throughout the world, even in capitals such as London and Madrid, where the governments supported him. Without a UN to test Bush's case, protests might have been confused and aimless. He might even have gone to war without anyone knowing beforehand. The UN had exposed the mendacity and weakness of his case. To go to war, he had to defy the will of the Security Council. The UN had maneuvered him into near-isolation.

In Paris, Claire Tréan of *Le Monde* pushed this kind of argument in a news analysis. All the enormous pressure by the powerful United States had failed to change a single vote in the Security Council. A majority of the members of the Security Council and of the UN in general remained in opposition to the war, and they did so, Tréan wrote, "in the name of defending their principles." In the long run, this moral position would bound to the advantage of the UN.

But these were not very satisfying arguments. They provided a weak reed to lean on. They paled against the enormity of what had happened. Bush had launched an illegal and unwarranted war against Iraq, and the UN and Kofi Annan had proven too weak to stop him.

I asked the secretary-general during his last year in office if it were true that Condoleezza Rice, then the National Security adviser, had phoned him soon after the invasion and promised that the UN would have a vital role in the reconstruction of Iraq.

"Not just Condi Rice," Annan replied. "All of them. They used words like 'vital role of the UN,' 'central role of the UN,' 'major role of the UN.' And even today we still hear about a central role of the UN in Iraq."

But no matter what euphemism they used, the Americans always meant that the UN would have a subordinate role. The Bush White House could only envision American victory, American occupation, American glory, American triumph. At most, the Americans wanted the UN to serve as a cover, as a sop to those who felt better about an American occupation if the UN were around helping out. There was little room for a vital UN in this vision.

"In fact, after the war," Annan said, "I thought there was a missed opportunity for bringing the international community together." The United States, according to Annan, could have said: "Let's forget our debate before the war. Let's forget our differences. We have a situation in Iraq, which is an important part of the Middle East. It's a region that has great economic significance at a crossroads, and we must all work together to stabilize it and get it right.

"But, of course," he went on, "working together would also have meant not just sharing the burden but sharing the decision-making. . . . I don't think the mood in Washington was ready for that. It was they have won the war, they are victorious. There was a certain hubris. We won the war. The secretary-general of the UN did not support us. Why should we bring in the UN?"

In the face of this American contempt, Annan had to decide how much help the UN could offer the occupation. To do so, he had to deal with the demoralized mood of his organization. Like Annan, his immediate staff opposed the war. So did practically everyone else who worked in the UN Secretariat. Yet, as Edward Mortimer, Annan's chief speechwriter, puts it, they saw "no virtue in rending your garments." Crying out against Bush and his White House was pointless now. UN civil servants wanted to prove that they were relevant and could be helpful, even vital, in Iraq, but they wanted to do so without looking like patsies pushed around by the United States.

Two points of view developed among the senior staff. Civil servants working in the field of humanitarian assistance wanted the UN to return to Iraq as soon as possible. Under the oil for food program before the war, the UN had been the main source of food for most Iraqi families. War had halted this work. As soon as embassy staffs and private relief workers returned after the fall of Baghdad, the UN humanitarian staff wanted to go back.

But others in the senior staff urged caution. They said that the return had to be slow as long as Iraq and especially Baghdad remained insecure. Politics colored this view somewhat. The United States wanted the UN back as a sign of normalcy and a sign of cooperation. UN aides were reluctant to give the United States that satisfaction and cover—even though they knew that the secretary-general wanted to demonstrate the relevance of the UN.

The secretary-general also had to deal with his own melancholy. Many on his staff noticed that he seemed very distant. He often did not speak unless spoken to. "When he came into the conference room," recalls Fred Eckhard, his spokesman, "it seemed to me he wasn't there. He seemed spiritually void. It was as if his soul had traveled to another place for guidance." Annan began to develop bouts of laryngitis.

His mood was understandable. "It looked like the end of the UN," says Eckhard. "The United States didn't need anyone else. It didn't need to share ideas with anyone else. The United States and its friends would be the real organization. This was something real to be depressed about. As head of the UN, no one should be more depressed."

Iqbal Riza, Annan's chief of staff, scheduled more vacation time for the secretary-general and Nane and more time for him to relax during a workday. The staff saw gradual improvement. But the secretary-general had to make some important decisions while wrestling with his melancholy.

This mood evidently escaped the notice of most of the press corps. I cannot find any American publication mentioning it until a

New York magazine profile appeared two years later. The secretary-general managed to control the mood enough to deal normally with many associates. Catherine Bertini, the undersecretary-general for management, heard all the rumors about depression but found no evidence herself. "When I was in a room with him," she says, "he was always extremely focused on whatever issue. If I showed him a memorandum of some kind, he would absolutely focus on it and would not need to be reminded of the issue."

For a few months, members of the Security Council argued about a resolution. Opponents of the invasion, like France, did not want to bless Bush's adventure. At the same time, the French were not foolish enough to ignore the reality of what had happened—Iraq was under American-led occupation, and Bush was not going to remove his troops anytime soon. The ambassadors also argued about the role of the UN, even though they knew that no matter what the final resolution said, the UN would have no greater role than the main occupying power allowed.

The word "vital" bobbed up again and again, even as politicians and diplomats strangled all meaning out of it. Bush and British prime minister Tony Blair met in Northern Ireland on April 8 and promised that "the United Nations has a vital role to play in the reconstruction of Iraq." But Bush, in the news conference that followed the pronouncement, offered only a vague notion about what he had in mind.

"I view a vital role as an agent to help people live freely," said Bush. "That's a vital role. That means food. That means medicine. That means aid. That means a place where people can give their contributions. That means being, you know, a party to the progress being made in Iraq. That's what that means."

Secretary of State Powell told Annan that the Americans would be pleased if the UN appointed Sérgio Vieira de Mello as the official in charge of the UN mission to Iraq. Vieira de Mello, a fifty-five-year-old Brazilian, was then the UN high commissioner for Human Rights, a position he had held for less than a year. Educated at the

Sorbonne in Paris and fluent in five languages, Vieira de Mello belonged to a stellar class of sophisticated, efficient, and dedicated international civil servants, ready to head anywhere, who have graced the United Nations for more than sixty years. Often working with refugees, he had been assigned to Cambodia, Lebanon, Cyprus, Bangladesh, and elsewhere, and he had led the UN missions in Kosovo and East Timor. But he was hesitant about going to Iraq.

"Initially, Sérgio didn't want to go," says Annan, "and I didn't want him to go. I recall my several conversations with Secretary of State Colin Powell telling him he has a job and an important job, the high commissioner for human rights . . . and I cannot spare him, and I don't want to create the impression that the [human rights] assignment is so unimportant that you can move him in and out." Moreover, as Sérgio told his friend *New York Times* foreign correspondent Steven Erlanger, it was not clear what the Security Council expected him to do in Iraq. "The mandate, as far as I can tell, does not look right to me," he e-mailed Erlanger. That made him even more hesitant.

Vieira de Mello finally gave in to the American pressure and told Annan he was ready to go if it were an assignment for only four months. "He was one of our best," says Annan. "He has been in so many of our missions that he set up. . . . And so when the idea came up of setting it up for four months and then coming back, I said all right. But I wasn't entirely comfortable pulling him out of the [human rights] job."

Sérgio requested and Annan agreed to assign Nadia Younes, a fifty-seven-year-old Egyptian, as his chief of staff. Nadia, a tough-talking, rapier-witted, chain-smoking UN civil servant, had served as Annan's chief of protocol for most of his administration. For the past eight months, she had been the executive director for external relations of the World Health Organization in Geneva. One of the recurring jokes in the corridors of the UN in New York centered on how Nadia managed to hide her addiction to cigarettes from the World Health Organization. Annan had plans to appoint her as an assistant secretary-general in New York after her tour in Iraq.

In late May, the Security Council, under American pressure, passed Resolution 1483, which recognized the United States and its allies as the occupying powers of Iraq and outlined "a vital role" for the UN in humanitarian relief, reconstruction, and, most important, "the restoration and establishment of national and local institutions for representative governance." The resolution authorized Vieira de Mello to help the occupation powers create an Iraqi interim administration that would lead Iraq toward elections and sovereignty. With 1483, the Security Council and thus the UN gave the occupation a cloak of legality.

At a news conference, in which he introduced Vieira de Mello as the chief of the new UN mission to Iraq, Annan had to deal with a pointed question: Didn't the resolution legitimize "the results of an illegal war" and prove once again that the UN "is unable to stop the unilateral action of a powerful state"? In reply, the secretary-general said, "I do not think that the resolution . . . is going to change the history of the recent past." In short, it did not legitimize the American invasion. What the resolution did, Annan insisted, was give the UN "a solid and a legal basis for our operations in Iraq, and I think . . . if we pursue our actions on that basis, we will be able to make a difference."

Before he left for Baghdad, Vieira de Mello e-mailed Erlanger that he was still troubled by the assignment, "but it's only for four months. All the very best, my friend," he closed, "and please pray for me."

L. Paul Bremer III reigned in Iraq then as a kind of American viceroy. He was the head of the Coalition Provisional Authority— the ponderous name for the nonmilitary branch of the American-led occupation. He did not relish the idea of dealing with Vieira de Mello. According to George Packer's account of the occupation, *The Assassins' Gate: America in Iraq*, Bremer rolled his eyes whenever anyone brought up the UN at a meeting. He looked on talk about the UN as a waste of his time. In his own memoir, *My Year in Iraq*, he makes it clear that he feared the UN would get in his way. When Vieira de Mello called on him just a week after Annan had announced the appointment, Bremer told a member of his staff, "Damn, I didn't think the UN would get its act together so quickly."

But Vieira de Mello charmed Bremer. "I liked him immediately," Bremer wrote. The UN official promised to be helpful and assured Bremer they could work well together. "That was a relief to hear," said Bremer in his memoir. "The last thing we needed in the very complicated political minuet we were dancing was to have the Iraqis feel that they could play the UN off against the Coalition."

Vieira de Mello helped Bremer put together a Governing Council that would serve as a shadow Iraqi government until elections were held. Bremer was limited by his dependence on Kurds and former Iraqi exiles for advice about Iraqi politics. The most powerful Shia cleric, the Grand Ayatollah Ali el-Sistani, refused to meet with Bremer or any other official of the occupation. But he did meet with Vieiro de Mello. UN officials also made their way into the strife-torn Sunni areas to talk with political and religious leaders there. The UN staff included a good number of Arabs who understood Iraqi politics and could converse easily in the Arabic of Iraq. Vieiro de Mello told Packer that the UN was responsible for selecting about half of the twenty-five members of the Governing Council.

After the appointment of the Governing Council, Bremer had little use anymore for the UN. Vieira de Mello found his relationship with the viceroy cooling and little of substance left to do. Annan, who was vacationing with Nane on an island off Norway, phoned Sérgio on August 18. In a little more than a month, the special assignment would end. The secretary-general said he would like to meet with Sérgio in Europe sometime before the Annans returned to New York. Annan said he would phone the next day to propose a meeting place.

Kofi never made the call. Sérgio was sitting in his office with several visitors and staff on the afternoon of August 19 when a suicide bomber sped his flatbed truck down the access road to UN headquarters in the Canal Hotel. A one-ton bomb exploded, and Sérgio's office plunged two stories to the ground, a mass of debris and concrete trapping Sérgio below. He was still alive, responding weakly to UN colleagues, while American soldiers tried to loosen the boulders. By the time they reached him, he was dead. Nadia died in the blast as well as twenty others.

When Bremer phoned President Bush with news of the explosion, the president said, "I hope the UN will stay the course." According to Bremer, Sérgio had a similar thought just before he died. Bremer said an American soldier reported Sérgio's last words as "Don't let them pull the UN out." Kofi Annan quickly contributed to this melodramatic finale.

A day after the bombing, the secretary-general addressed all the employees of the UN through a video message. "How can we thank our lost colleagues for their life's contribution?" said Annan. "Only by vowing to work on, every day, to complete the work that they began. So let me send this message to all of you, dear colleagues, as well as to the people of Iraq. We will not be deterred. We will go on doing whatever we can to help build a better future for the Iraqi people."

This statement of fiery defiance—which resembled the bursts of machismo that often came from the George W. Bush White House—amounted to a total rejection of a plea from the UN Staff Council, the union of UN employees.

As soon as news of the bombing reached New York, the Staff Council's Standing Committee on the Security and Independence of the International Civil Service had issued a statement calling on the secretary-general "to suspend all operations in Iraq and withdraw the staff until such time as measures are taken to improve security." The committee also demanded "a full investigation to determine why adequate security was not in place to prevent such a horrifying act."

It is clear now that the Staff Council was right and the secretary-general in error. Annan would rectify his mistake, but the delay shook some of the faith that the staff had placed in their hero—the first secretary-general to rise from the ranks.

Kofi Annan was torn in several directions as he tried to decide on the future of the UN after the bombing. The death of Sérgio had left him with bouts of shock, guilt, remorse, and fury. When he discussed Sérgio with me two and a half years later, his voice bristled at times with bitter anger. "It was very difficult," said the secretary-general. "Here's someone—and it was not only him but Nadia, the others. I had spoken to him the day before . . . and the next day he was gone. In those situations, you cannot help having a sense of guilt, a sense of doubt, a sense of questioning. Did he go because I asked him? Would he have done it otherwise? Because he was a very loyal person and a very good international civil servant.

"And, of course," the secretary-general went on, "what was also difficult is then you also ask yourself why did he die and what did he die for? Here, having done everything to avoid a war, having never supported the war, and yet feeling at the end that we need to help clean up Iraq, otherwise the whole region can become very dangerous, and so I took the mandate the [Security] Council gave us very seriously, and you send in some of your best people who are friends and they get killed for trying to sort out the aftermath of the war that you didn't support, you can imagine my discouragement and melancholy. It was tough."

He had to balance two forces: his fury at the United States for creating a catastrophe that killed his friends, against his hope that he could still assert the relevance of the United Nations by helping to clear away the debris from the catastrophe. To many of the international civil servants, however, his actions looked like kowtowing to the United States.

On September 22, a month after the killing of Sérgio and the others, another suicide bomber exploded his car in a parking lot 150 feet from the Canal Hotel, which was still used as UN headquarters. His target was probably UN personnel coming to work at that time, but the bomb killed a UN security guard and two Iraqi police instead. The secretary-general's security and policy advisers then urged Annan to pull the UN out of Iraq, but he refused. Instead, Annan reduced the numbers of staff in Iraq and called on an outside panel led by former Finnish president Martti Ahtisaari to investigate the bombings and UN security in Iraq.

The UN staff was upset over the secretary-general's refusal to withdraw completely. Anger intensified as evacuees came back with lurid tales of UN workers huddling in their hotel rooms in fear. The anger was exacerbated by the feeling that the UN was placing itself in danger only to please President George W. Bush with his catastrophic war. Some civil servants were in defiance; they would refuse to serve in Iraq from now on.

Ghassan Salamé, the Lebanese-born political adviser to Sérgio, had survived the blast on August 19 and had spoken with Sérgio as he lay trapped and dying. After his return to New York, Salamé told Colum Lynch of the *Washington Post,* "What are we doing there? If our role is central, you take the risk even if the risk is high. If your role is peripheral and the risk is high, you don't take risks. As far as I am concerned, I will not go [back] to Baghdad."

The panel's report, issued on October 20, was crushing. It said that UN management and staff had failed to comply with standard security precautions in Baghdad and thus left the UN vulnerable to attack. The UN had behaved as if it were sure terrorists and insurgents would always respect the UN flag. American military forces had tried to protect the Canal Hotel by stationing soldiers on the roof, a truck on the access road, and anti-aircraft crews in front. But the UN staff felt uncomfortable about this closeness to the occupying forces and asked the United States to remove the protection.

The report did not identify who decided to spurn American military security. But it was typical of Sérgio Vieira de Mello to disdain anything that would put the UN in a cocoon. After all, the one great advantage that the UN had over the United States was its ability to travel everywhere in Iraq and talk to everybody. Sérgio, according to the report, even refused to move to another office when told by security officers that he was working too close to the access road.

The rush by various UN agencies to return to Iraq after the invasion was so hectic, according to the Ahtisaari panel, that the UN did not even know how many non-Iraqi staffers were in the country. A number had entered Iraq but had failed to register with headquarters at the Canal Hotel. The UN had withdrawn its 387 international staff when Bush announced the impending war in March. In June, after the return began, UN security officers said they could provide safety for no more than 200 in Baghdad. But by the time of the August bombing that killed Sérgio, the UN estimated there were 350 foreign staff in Baghdad. The report said that independent sources put the figures much higher, with some estimates reaching a total of 550 foreign staff in Baghdad and 900 in the country as a whole.

Faced with this stark report, Annan withdrew all non-Iraqi UN staff from the country. He called it a temporary suspension of work. But despite continual entreaties and even insults about UN cowardice from Washington, the secretary-general never revived the mission. He seemed to feel comfortable now accepting an outsider's role for the UN in Iraq. At the most, he allowed a limited number of staff people from time to time to take part in a temporary activity such as organizing elections. And these interventions came when it was obvious that the United States needed special help from the UN and needed it badly. As Annan puts it, "We decided to do only those things where the UN had comparative advantage—that if we didn't do it, nobody else could do it."

By the end of 2003 Bremer, the American civilian boss of Iraq, was mired in a political standoff. Some of the problem probably stemmed from his own personality and style of management. Bremer, who liked to flit about in a suit with combat boots, often behaved like a British governor in colonial Africa. He had a tendency to treat Iraqis like unruly children. He liked to lay down rules and bully Iraqi leaders into accepting them. He preferred talking to listening. His memoir brims with condescending maxims. "Bremer's Iron Law of Iraqi Politics," he writes, is "that no two of the three major groups [Shia, Sunni, and Kurd] would ever be tranquil at the same time." "Bremer's First Rule of Life in Iraq," he says, is "If you get what appears to be good news, it usually means you're not fully informed."

In mid-November, Bremer pressured the Governing Council into accepting his latest plan for the political future of Iraq. The United States would turn sovereignty over to Iraq by the end of June 2004. Through a series of caucuses throughout the country, an interim assembly would be selected to rule Iraq until elections in early 2005. The elected parliament would then write a new constitution.

But Grand Ayatollah Ali el-Sistani, the most important religious figure among the majority Shia, did not like the plan, and Bremer had no means of bullying el-Sistani into accepting it. El-Sistani would not even talk with Bremer, and the American viceroy communicated with the grand ayatollah by sending Iraqi emissaries. Like many other Iraqis, el-Sistani suspected that the confusing caucuses provided a way for the United States to control the makeup of the government. He demanded direct elections before sovereignty was transferred on June 30, and he sent tens of thousands of protesters into the streets to back up his demand. Bremer insisted that it was too late to organize elections for June, but the grand ayatollah did not trust Bremer. Through an emissary, Sistani announced that he wanted to hear what the UN had to say about elections.

The grand ayatollah's intervention demonstrated the true value of the UN. Despite failures such as Srebrenica and Rwanda, the United Nations, especially when led by an admired secretary-general, has a moral force and disinterested stance unmatched by anything or anyone else in a crisis-strewn world. Bremer, of course, did not philosophize about this in his memoir. He was in a political jam and needed the UN to help him get out of it. So he and the Iraqi Governing Council rushed letters out to the secretary-general, asking for help.

Annan summoned the pleaders to meet with him in New York on January 19, 2004. They met in a conference room in the basement of the Secretariat Building. Bremer arrived with several leading members of the Governing Council; Robert Blackwill, who monitored Iraqi politics for the National Security Council in the

White House; and Jeremy Greenstock, a former British ambassador to the UN who now represented Britain in Iraq. Bremer, according to his memoir, told Annan that he and the Coalition Provisional Authority "welcomed the opportunity to reestablish a long-term partnership with the UN." He promised to do everything possible to give the UN representatives in Iraq "appropriate security." He also told the secretary-general that he believed Grand Ayatollah el-Sistani wanted a democratic Iraq.

Bremer, who had the reputation of ruling Iraq with dictatorial pronouncements, sounded almost obsequious in his politeness. Edward Mortimer, the UN director of communications, one of several aides who accompanied Annan, says "you couldn't help savoring the irony of the moment." "Remember," says Mortimer, "that these were people who had elbowed the UN aside as they charged into Iraq, and then had grudgingly allowed it back in an advisory or ancillary role, very imprecisely defined, for which Sérgio and the others had paid with their lives. And here they were . . . pleading with us to come back because el-Sistani had said he wouldn't believe you couldn't have elections before June 30 unless the UN came and told him so."

Annan told Bremer and the others that he would consider sending a technical team to Iraq to study the feasibility of elections. But he would have to satisfy himself about their usefulness and their security. There was a good deal of suspicion at the UN. An ambassador to the Security Council told the *Washington Post* that the United States needs "to find a scapegoat to take the blame in case this fails." At a news conference that day, Annan was asked why he would want "to pull America's chestnuts out of the fire." He replied, "I think I have had a chance to state time and time again that the stability of Iraq should be everyone's business."

In the end, he dispatched more than a technical team. He sent Lakhdar Brahimi as well. Brahimi, then seventy, had just completed a two-year assignment as the chief of the UN mission to Afghanistan. He had impressed American officials with the way he guided the Afghans toward democratic elections, and the United States asked for him in Iraq. Annan agreed only after he was assured that Brahimi would play a significant role in helping the Iraqis move toward sovereignty.

Not everyone in the Bush administration liked the idea of Brahimi coming to Iraq. Both Vice President Dick Cheney and Secretary of Defense Donald Rumsfeld objected to him because he had strongly opposed the invasion of Iraq. Of course, it would have been difficult to find a UN official who had a different view of the war. Condoleezza Rice, the National Security adviser, pointed to his useful work in Afghanistan and suggested he could be helpful in Iraq provided he persuaded Grand Ayatollah el-Sistani that elections before June 30 were impossible and came up with alternatives. "But we have got to be prepared," Bremer told a White House meeting, "to confront el-Sistani if the UN comes up with a credible alternative consistent with our objectives and timeline and el-Sistani still rejects it." Despite the objections from Cheney and Rumsfeld, the White House endorsed Brahimi.

Bremer met Brahimi a few days later. "The Iraqi people want sovereignty back," Bremer told Brahimi. "And we have to show that we're not going to be pushed around by [Grand] Ayatollah el-Sistani." Brahimi, according to Bremer, replied that he did not believe Iraq's government should be run by "people with black turbans." "As Rice had suggested," Bremer wrote in his memoir, "Brahimi was an insightful thinker. I liked him, and was confident we would work together effectively."

Annan announced later that he had agreed to send a team of electoral experts to Iraq but did not mention Brahimi. Brahimi's departure for Iraq was a surprise, even to the team of experts. They did not realize he would join them until he showed up in the departure lounge in Paris in early February before the flight to Baghdad. Brahimi, in fact, had resisted the assignment but accepted after extraordinary White House pressure, including pleas from President Bush in two meetings.

"The Brahimi mission was a diplomatic astonishment," wrote foreign affairs columnist Jim Hoagland of the *Washington Post*.

"Annan has been under enormous pressure from his staff to avoid further UN involvement in Iraq while occupation continues. His willingness to take the risks inherent in sending Brahimi and his team to Baghdad shows the secretary-general's concern for Iraq and for the world body's relations with Washington."

Brahimi made three extensive visits to Iraq during the next four months and swiftly demonstrated the advantages of acting in the name of the United Nations. He conferred with Grand Ayatollah el-Sistani immediately and persuaded him that there really was not time enough to organize elections before June 30. But he also agreed with the grand ayatollah that caucuses made no sense. That plan was abandoned by Bremer. Instead Brahimi, after conferring with many Iraqis, proposed that he would put together a provisional government based on suggestions from the influential Iraqis that he planned to meet. It would rule Iraq (under the shadow of the American-led military forces, of course) until elections in December 2004. Bremer and the grand ayatollah accepted the plan.

Much like Kofi Annan, Brahimi was a listener. He told the Security Council he had sought out "politicians, civic and religious leaders, women's groups, academics, intellectuals, businessmen and merchants, among others." He traveled to Mosul, Basra, and other cities, but many Iraqis came to him in Baghdad. "We were humbled," he said, "by the many Iraqis who faced the perils of travel in today's Iraq and even inside Baghdad in order to meet with us." He said the Iraqis told him they wanted a caretaker government "comprised of honest and technically qualified persons." It would be possible to identify a list of qualified people "representative of Iraq's diversity" by the end of May, Brahimi said, and "the United Nations can certainly help the Iraqi people in that process, as requested, by meeting with as many of them as possible and identifying where points of consensus could be forged."

The importance of the UN mission was demonstrated by Bremer's fears that Brahimi would throw up his hands and give up. He almost did because of the Battle of Fallujah. On March 31, insurgents in the Sunni city of Fallujah killed four American contractors, mutilated their bodies, and strung them up. President Bush put on his macho air and threatened, "I want heads to roll." A U.S. Marine division was ordered to attack the city. This assault for revenge was sure to cause many civilian deaths, and Brahimi was furious. He was also upset by the attempt to suppress an uprising in the Shia areas by Moqtada al-Sadr and his Mahdi army. Bremier had precipitated this by closing down Moqtada's newspaper and arresting his chief lieutenant.

Bremer pleaded with Brahimi to stay on and asked Secretary of State Powell to pass the same plea on to Kofi Annan. Brahimi was invited to a military briefing on the two insurgencies. Brahimi listened but told Bremer that many Iraqis opposed the suppression of Moqtada. In any case, Brahimi was more concerned about bloodshed in Fallujah. At the end of the session, Brahimi, who was in continual phone contact with Annan, said he would stay on "for now."

As the marines fought in the center of Fallujah, several members of the Governing Council threatened to quit. Brahimi started to waver again. Bremer could cobble together a government without Brahimi and the Governing Council, but he knew it would not have credibility. That would make it difficult to turn sovereignty over on June 30 as planned. "Therefore to lose both the Governing Council and the UN would mean losing the June 30 date—with no clear way to get a credible political process revived and no idea of how long that would take," Bremer wrote.

After discussing the problem with Washington, Bremer met with the U.S. military commanders in Iraq and told them, "Brahimi is neuralgic about Fallujah and could pull up stakes if we're not careful." Faced with this threat from the UN, the military called off the assault on Fallujah. The Shia crisis also passed without the arrest of Moqtada.

In the end, Brahimi did not get the kind of provisional government he had envisioned. He wanted a government, mainly of technocrats, headed as prime minister by Hussein al-Shahristani, a Shia nuclear scientist who had been imprisoned for many years by

Saddam Hussein. But Brahimi was not making his decisions by fiat. He discussed his cabinet choices with a team made up of Bremer, Blackwill, and three members of the Iraqi Governing Council.

The Americans knew little about al-Shahristani. When Bremer brought up his name in a telephone call to Washington, President Bush said, "It's important to have someone who's willing to stand up and thank the American people for their sacrifice in liberating Iraq. . . . I want someone who will be grateful. Does al-Shahristani want the job? Will he support us?" Bremer and Blackwill dined with al-Shahristani and decided he did not meet White House requirements. They pushed instead for Ayad Allawi, a Shia politician with one big drawback: he and his exile political party had received CIA funding for many years.

According to Bremer, Brahimi concluded on his own that al-Shahristani was not suitable and finally settled on Allawi as the candidate must likely to have widespread Iraqi support. Brahimi told the Security Council later that al-Shahristani had "provoked opposition from almost all quarters." Brahimi said he had then informed the Americans and the Iraqis on the selection team that "we were ready to respect the emerging consensus on Dr. Ayad Allawi as prime minister and that we were ready to work with him in the selection of the cabinet."

Brahimi's spokesman, Ahmad Fawzi, an Egyptian-born UN official with many years of experience as a television journalist in Europe, said that Allawi was chosen by a process of elimination. All candidates, Fawzi explained, encountered rejections from some of the many factions in Iraq, but Allawi had the least of all.

When he announced the choice of Allawi and the thirty-one other members of the cabinet in early June, Brahimi told reporters, "the whole slate is a compromise between the main actors, the Governing Council, a lot of Iraqis, and the Americans." He said the press had been mistaken in thinking that he was picking the cabinet single-handedly. After talking with several thousand Iraqis, he had met with the two Americans and three Iraqi politicians to narrow the choices.

He said, "It's actually true that I have been under a lot of pressure. . . . I sometimes say—I'm sure he doesn't mind me saying that—that Bremer is the dictator of Iraq. He has the money. He has the signature. Nothing happens without his agreement in the country. . . . I would remind you that the Americans are governing this country, so their point of view certainly was taken into consideration. Whether Dr. Allawi was their choice, whether they maneuvered to get him . . . you better ask them. The thing is there were a number of candidates and then the common denominator at the end was Dr. Allawi, and he's now the prime minister."

The Brahimi mission could count several major achievements. It had loosened a political logjam and set conquered Iraq on a path to sovereignty and eventual elections. Brahimi's anger was a major force in pressuring Bremer to persuade the military commanders to stop their assault on the city of Fallujah. Practically every member of the new cabinet had been selected by Brahimi. Yet, as Fawzi put it, "The mission was not a UN triumph. It was an exercise in frustration." The obvious American preference for Allawi had left the impression that the UN had been manipulated by the United States into serving the occupation. "We were perceived," says Fawzi, "as being used by the Americans to clean up their mess."

That unfortunately reinforced the neoconservative notion that the UN has only one use: to serve as an instrument of American policy. Another White House might have drawn a different lesson from the experience. It might have concluded that the UN has an inner strength, molded by its moral force, neutral leadership, and worldwide standing, that merits respect and deserves to be taken into account—not just used—by American foreign policy. But this idea did not fit the ideology of the Bush White House.

As the year 2004 went on, the Bush administration returned to its natural disdain for Kofi Annan and the UN. In fact, relations worsened, and the White House began to look on the secretary-general as far more than an annoyance. In Washington's view, he was behaving like a dangerous enemy.

In September, a persistent BBC reporter, Owen Bennett-Jones, managed to cajole Annan into saying exactly what he felt about the legality of Bush's invasion of Iraq. Until then, the secretary-general had always described the invasion as an act "not in conformity with the UN Charter." That phrase had the sniff of illegality but stopped short of actually saying so. Bennett-Jones pressured him to say so.

The transcript catches the pressure:

Bennett-Jones: Are you bothered that the United States is becoming an unrestrainable, unilateral superpower?

Annan: Well, I think over the last year, we've all gone through lots of painful lessons. I'm talking about since the war in Iraq. I think there has been lessons for the United States and there has been lessons for the UN and other member states and I think in the end everybody is concluding that it is best to work together with our allies and through the UN to deal with some of these issues. And I hope we do not see another Iraq-type operation for a long time.

Bennett-Jones: Done without UN approval—or without clearer UN approval?

Annan: Without UN approval and much broader support from the international community.

Bennett-Jones: I wanted to ask you that—do you think that the resolution that was passed on Iraq before the war did actually give legal authority to do what was done?

Annan: Well, I'm one of those who believe that there should have been a second resolution because the Security Council indicated that if Iraq did not comply there will be consequences. But then it was up to the Security Council to approve or determine what those consequences should be.

Bennett-Jones: So you don't think there was legal authority for the war?

Annan: I have stated clearly that it was not in conformity with the Security Council—with the UN Charter.

Bennett-Jones: It was illegal?

Annan: Yes, if you wish.

Benentt-Jones: It was illegal?

Annan: Yes, I have indicated it was not in conformity with the UN Charter, from our point of view and from the Charter point of view it was illegal.

After the interview, Annan asked his spokesman, Fred Eckhard, "What do you think?"

"'Illegal' will cause trouble," Eckhard replied.

"It's in effect what I have been saying all along."

"But you have never put it so bluntly," said Eckhard.

Eckhard was right. Bush and his aides, in the midst of a presidential reelection campaign, were furious. They, of course, did not read the transcript of the interview to discover how the word "illegal" had been wheedled out of a secretary-general who does not like to dissemble. As far as Bush aides were concerned, Annan had issued a pronouncement stamping the Iraq invasion illegal, and he had done so to help the Democratic candidate, John F. Kerry, defeat Bush.

"I think it is outrageous," Randy Scheunemann, a former aide to Secretary of Defense Donald Rumsfeld, told the BBC, "for the secretary-general, who ultimately works for the member states, to try to supplant his judgment for the judgment of the member states. To do this fifty-one days before an American election reeks of political interference."

In October, American military forces in Iraq again tried to assault the city of Fallujah. This upset Annan and senior aides such as Brahimi and Kieran Prendergast, the British under secretary-general for political affairs. Brahimi had been able to help stop an assault six months earlier. But he and the UN had political leverage then. Now the UN could rely on no more than an appeal to reason and good sense.

Away on a weekend meeting with other UN officials at the

Greentree Foundation estate on Long Island, the former home of the late John Hay Whitney, once the owner of the now defunct *New York Herald Tribune*, Annan phoned Prendergast to discuss Fallujah. Prendergast proposed that Annan call Colin Powell and British foreign secretary Jack Straw to outline his objections to the assault. But Annan said he intended to write letters instead. Prendergast suspects that the secretary-general felt his arguments were too complex for a phone call. He might be cut off with a negative response before he had a chance to set down all his reasons for deploring an attack. With the help of aides, the secretary-general wrote letters on October 31 to President Bush, British prime minister Tony Blair, and Iraqi prime minister Allawi, asking them to call off the offensive against Fallujah.

Annan wrote that he was worried "about the negative impact that major military assaults . . . are likely to have on the prospects for encouraging a broader participation by Iraqis in the political process, including in the elections."

While he understood the need to restore security within Iraq, Annan wrote, "the problem of insecurity can only be addressed through dialogue and an inclusive political process." He warned that "the threat or actual use of force not only risks deepening the sense of alienation of certain communities, but would also reinforce perceptions among the Iraqi population of a continued military occupation." In short, Annan was saying, an assault on Fallujah would not only alienate the Sunnis in that part of Iraq but also would arouse sympathy among the majority Shias elsewhere and turn them against the Americans.

No one at the UN disagreed with the logic, but many were surprised to find the sentiments set down in letters. Iqbal Riza, who was Annan's chief of staff then, says, "there were so many other ways of doing it," including private telephone calls. The letters were drafted and dispatched on the weekend. When Riza arrived back in New York on Sunday evening, "it was too late to stop them."

Annan assumed that the letters would be treated by Bush, Blair, and Allawi as private and confidential and never find their way into newsprint. But Maggie Farley of the *Los Angeles Times* obtained a copy of one letter and wrote a story about it a week later.

The reaction to Farley's worldwide scoop was swift and noisy. The *Washington Post* reported that Bush administration officials described themselves as "livid." Again, they suspected electoral bias. Even though Farley's story was published after election day, the letter had been sent two days before the election.

Asked about the letter, State Department spokesman Richard Boucher said, "Frankly, we differ. The Iraqi government has made very clear that they do have a strategy for resolving the problems of these towns like Fallujah. . . . It's a strategy of reaching out politically to local leaders, of reasserting Iraqi government control and of moving militarily where that needs to be done, Iraqis and coalition forces together." Secretary of State Powell, whose colleagues sometimes castigated him as an apologist for Annan, phoned the secretary-general to complain about the timing of the letters, sent on the eve of the American elections. John C. Danforth, the American ambassador to the UN, came to the secretary-general's office to complain about the timing as well.

Disdainful comments came from the British and Iraqis. Emyr Jones Parry, the British ambassador to the UN, said, "[I]t's easy for those not in Iraq to underestimate the overwhelming concern the Iraqis have for security. There cannot be an area as big as Fallujah which is allowed to be a base for terrorism."

Iraqi prime minister Allawi ridiculed Annan's plea to solve the Fallujah security problem through dialogue and the political process. "I don't know what pressure he has to bear on the insurgents," Allawi said contemptuously. "If he can stop the insurgents from inflicting damage and killing the Iraqis, then he's welcome—we will do whatever he wants."

Annan defends both the substance of the letter and his right to speak out. "I was quite concerned," he says, "that, aside from civilian casualties, it is a bit like kicking the hornet's nest. The terrorists . . . in Fallujah . . . would spread all about Iraq, and it would be difficult to get a hand on them and under control."

Since the UN was organizing the Iraqi elections in January, Annan believed he had every right to speak out about Fallujah, for the military assault might persuade many voters to stay at home. "We were worried," he says, "that it would have a negative impact on the elections and the political process . . . and, in fact, it did. The Sunnis boycotted the elections." Bush, Blair, and Allawi did not bother to reply to Annan's letter.

It was now open season on Annan at the White House. On top of his Fallujah letter and his talk about an illegal invasion, the Americans also found Annan infuriating because, citing the lack of security, he allowed no more than thirty-five UN election officials to go to Iraq to organize the January elections. As if looking for a potential scapegoat, the Bush administration accused the UN of botching the job of preparing the vote. An American official, just back from meetings at the White House, told UN correspondent Warren Hoge of the *New York Times*: "We're beyond anger. We won reelection. Kofi's term is up in '06 and though we have been asking him to define the UN role in Iraq, he is thumbing his nose at us." When the elections, despite American worries, proceeded smoothly in January, President Bush, in his State of the Union address, congratulated the Iraqi people and the American military, not Kofi Annan.

The secretary-general had to deal with many issues other than Iraq during this era: Darfur, the southern Sudan, Cyprus, the Congo, HIV/AIDS, and the Ivory Coast, to name a handful. But Iraq loomed over all else, and Annan's decisions on Iraq mattered more than anything else. He may have made some wrong choices. Perhaps he should have denounced the American invasion with heat and flourish. Perhaps he should not have sent the letter on Fallujah. He surely should have pulled the staff out of Iraq sooner than he did. But all his decisions were made with honesty, moral grounding, loyalty to the universal spirit of the United Nations, and a deep aversion to bloodshed. He cannot be faulted for that.

15

Oil for Food and Kojo

On November 24, 2004, as his plane headed toward Ouagadougou, Burkina Faso, for the annual summit of Francophonie, the association of French-speaking countries, the secretary-general announced to his staff that he wanted to cancel the visit. He had just spent two days at Sharm el-Sheikh in Egypt for an international conference on the future of Iraq. He was fatigued, he had lost his appetite, and he did not feel like seeing anyone. His aides finally prevailed upon him to stop in Ouagadougou briefly. They did not want him to insult President Blaise Compaoré of Burkina Faso. When Annan arrived, one of the officials who welcomed the secretary-general described him as "tired, depressed, absent." Annan attended the official dinner hosted by President Compaoré and then flew out of Ouagadougou before dawn the next morning. In New York, Fred Eckhard, his spokesman, reported that the secretary-general had cut short his visit "to deal with pressing business here." Ibrahima Fall, the UN official in charge of the mission in the Great Lakes region of Africa, read Annan's prepared speech to the conference.

According to Philippe Bolopion, who reported about the shortened visit to Ouagadougou six months later in the French weekly newspaper *Le Journal du Dimanche*, President Jacques Chirac of France soon heard about the incident and phoned Annan to lift his morale. "You must pull yourself together," Chirac said.

The secretary-general's unusual behavior on this trip signaled a relapse—the start of his second bout with melancholia or depression. He had been battered for many months. The White House lashed at him continually. Even when he tried to cooperate with the American occupation of Iraq, he could not erase what the White House regarded as his fatal flaw—he had opposed the invasion. While he tried to deal with this problem of relations with the most powerful member of the UN, he found another problem looming over him—the so-called oil for food scandal. To make matters worse, his son, Kojo, was mired in the scandal, taking a job in what looked like a tawdry scheme to cash in on his father's station and influence.

Not everyone realized it, but the oil for food troubles were magnified and manipulated by his antagonists to punish the secretary-general for his opposition to the war. The pressures on him were enormous. "They were attacking his honor, his character, his reputation, and his fatherhood," says Iqbal Riza, his former chief of staff. Annan's good friend Julia Preiswerk said, "He had been turned into a black pope a few years ago, and now he was turned into a common criminal." Annan himself told a news conference at the end of 2004, "There is no doubt that this has been a particularly difficult year, and I am relieved that this annus horribilis is coming to an end."

Many friends and colleagues were very worried over the relapse. One friend passed on to him the name of a doctor who treated clinical depression. Annan began to speak hoarsely and sometimes lose his voice again. "People were saying," Riza recalls, "that the S-G is so passive now. He has to lift himself up and be decisive." A diplomat told Meryl Gordon of *New York* magazine, "There were weeks when Kofi seemed disturbed, bothered, unfocused." When she interviewed Annan early in 2005, she said, "the overall impression he left was that of a man at the center of a mael-strom, coping by the hour."

Fred Eckhard was less worried than he had been during the first period of melancholia. He recalled the secretary-general's speech about his days at MIT when he felt lost among so many overachievers (see chapter 2). Kofi had walked along the Charles River, thought matters through, and then resolved to continue in his own way. "I imagined him now taking walks along the Charles in his mind," says Eckhard, "and finding the strength to continue. Things were getting him down, yes, but that was to be expected. I felt he was coping."

Eckhard was right. Annan broke out of the funk after several months. When I interviewed him at the end of 2005, I found that he still had his old focus, his confidence, his thoughtfulness, his alert mind, his grasp of a myriad of issues, his careful and articulate speech, his engaging sense of humor, and his uncanny ability to listen carefully to others. What seemed missing was that wonderful sense of joy that once infused him and his work. The White House, oil for food, and Kojo had beaten that out of him.

So much has been made of the oil for food failings that the nuts and bolts of the program need to be examined carefully and hon-estly. The details are not really very complex. But all the wild accu-sations and exaggerations about oil for food have befuddled the issues and made them seem too convoluted to comprehend. News accounts have too often neglected the details and simply abbrevi-ated everything by labeling the program a UN scandal, with thiev-ery costing billions of dollars. The secretary-general appointed a commission headed by former Federal Reserve chairman Paul Volcker in April 2004 to investigate the matter. The commission did lay bare all the facts, but it took a year and a half to do so, plenty of time for the scandal to batter Annan again and again.

Oil for food came out of an American proposal to ease the sanc-tions that were strangling Iraq. The sanctions were imposed in 1990 soon after the Iraqi invasion of Kuwait and were kept in place even after American-led forces dislodged the Iraqis from Kuwait and chased them back toward Baghdad. The sanctions were probably the most onerous imposed on a defeated nation since the shackling of Germany after its defeat in World War I. According to UN resolutions, the Iraqi sanctions would be lifted whenever UN inspectors were satisfied that Iraq had been shorn of all its weapons of mass destruction and all its programs to produce them.

But the hurdle was raised by American insistence that it would never allow the lifting of sanctions, no matter what Iraq did, as long as Saddam Hussein remained in power. This attitude, combined with the Iraqi reluctance to cooperate with UN inspectors, seemed to presage a long era of sanctions. But sanctions were devastating the well-being of the masses of ordinary Iraqis. There were stories of babies dying for lack of food. Many governments were growing restive about sanctions. France and Russia even suggested there was enough evidence of Iraqi disarmament to justify lifting the sanctions.

So American ambassador Madeleine Albright proposed allowing Iraq to sell enough oil to purchase food, medicines, and other necessities for its population. Thus the sanctions would have a conscience. But Saddam Hussein did not like all the restrictions on his sales and purchases in the proposed program, and he delayed his agreement until 1996. A memorandum was then signed between the Iraqis and UN secretary-general Boutros-Ghali stating that the Iraqis accepted the oil for food program as set down in Security Council Resolution 926.

Boutros-Ghali, however, takes no credit for his part in implementing the program. "The reality," he told me recently, "is that the memorandum of understanding was devised by a British-American team. They want to say Boutros-Ghali did it. But she [Ambassador Albright] boasted that Resolution 926 was written word by word by an American team."

Kofi Annan inherited the oil for food program when he succeeded Boutros-Ghali as secretary-general, and he inherited some of his predecessor's attitude toward it as well. Annan tended to look on oil for food as a creation and responsibility of the Security Council, especially of two of its permanent members, the United

States and Britain. The Security Council had a Sanctions Committee, known as the 661 Committee (named after the resolution that imposed the sanctions), which monitored Iraq's compliance with sanctions, and Annan assumed it would bear the burden of making sure that Iraq's purchases fit all requirements.

The secretary-general was making a distinction that was real but nevertheless lost to many headline writers. The United Nations is an organization of governments that make their most important decisions through the Security Council. The UN also has a Secretariat headed by the secretary-general that carries out the orders of the Security Council. When the UN fumbles a mission and is attacked in print, as it was in Rwanda, readers usually think the secretary-general is at fault, even though the Security Council may be the culprit.

Annan appointed a veteran UN official, Benon Sevan of Cyprus, as executive director of oil for food. Neither Annan nor Deputy Secretary-General Louise Frechette monitored Sevan's work very closely. Both assumed that as long as the Security Council did not complain, he must be doing an excellent job.

Under the oil for food program, which lasted seven years, Iraq sold more than $64 billion worth of oil and purchased $37 billion worth of food and other basic goods. The excess of sales over purchases was used by the UN to pay for administration of the program, for distribution of the food, and for reparations that Iraq owed Kuwait for damages in the invasion. There is no doubt that the oil for food program saved many lives and prevented widespread hunger and malnutrition. But by doing so, it also strengthened Saddam Hussein's hold on power.

The commission headed by Volcker found that Saddam Hussein was able to skim $1.8 billion of illegal income out of the oil for food program while the $101 billion of oil sales and food purchases were going on. Since the program allowed him to choose both the customers for his oil and the suppliers of food and other basics, he could charge customers a premium for buying the oil and solicit kickbacks from suppliers.

In addition, Saddam earned more than six times as much illegal revenue from smuggling that had nothing to do with the oil for food program. Thousands of trucks and other vehicles transported oil from Iraq to Jordan and Turkey and brought goods back. Iraq also broke sanctions by pumping oil out on a pipeline to Syria. Saddam sold $10.99 billion worth of illegal oil outside the oil for food program, according to the Volcker commission. But the United States and other members of the Security Council winked at these shenanigans, especially in the case of Jordan and Turkey. Since both were traditional trading partners of Iraq, they had been hurt unjustly by the UN sanctions. Smuggling gave them a chance to recoup some of their losses.

Although oil for food was labeled a UN scandal, its kickbacks and premium payoffs for the most part did not involve UN officials. Almost all bribes were paid by foreign customers and suppliers to Iraqi officials. There was one major exception, and it embarrassed Kofi Annan greatly. The Volcker commission accused Annan's old colleague Benon Sevan, the executive director of oil for food, of evident corruption.

Since he had the right to choose oil purchasers, Saddam Hussein often issued oil allocations to diplomats and officials whom he wanted to influence. The recipient could then buy oil himself or turn the allocation over to someone else. Sevan received allocations that he turned over to a friend with connections to an oil company. The Volcker commission said that $147,000 was then deposited in the bank account of Sevan and his wife in New York. Sevan, the commission concluded, "corruptly benefited" from the oil allocations. Annan then forced Sevan to resign. In the only other case of UN corruption uncovered by the Volcker commission, a UN procurement officer was accused of soliciting a bribe.

For Annan, the cold facts of Iraqi oil smuggling tended to assign blame far more to the Security Council and its leaders than to the Secretariat and himself. As he told a conference of former UN correspondents and retired UN spokesmen in April 2005, most of Saddam Hussein's illicit money was made "on the American and British watch." Alluding to American and British naval boats and other military patrols, Annan said, "They were the ones who had interdiction. Possibly they were also the ones who knew exactly what was going on, and the countries themselves decided to close their eyes to smuggling to Turkey and Jordan because they were allies."

But this kind of logic did not figure in the bruising attacks mounted against Annan during 2004 and 2005. While the roles of the United States and Britain were ignored, he and the UN were lambasted as scandalous and incompetent. Annan described the incessant denigration as a "politicized campaign." By that expression, Undersecretary-General Shashi Tharoor explained, Annan meant that the campaign was "engineered and orchestrated by people out to get the secretary-general." There is no doubt that many of his critics were conservatives angered at him for opposing the war in Iraq.

In early June 2003, for example, Ahmad Chalabi, the Iraqi exile leader who had been a source for some of the fanciful news stories that described Saddam Hussein's Iraq as a land awash in weapons of mass destruction, met Edward Mortimer at the bar in the Millennium UN Plaza Hotel, across the street from the UN complex. Mortimer, a former columnist of the *Financial Times* of London who was now UN director of communications, had known Chalabi for more than a decade. In fact, Mortimer had joined Chalabi as one of the founders of the International Committee for a Free Iraq in 1991. Chalabi had returned to Iraq after the American invasion and would soon become a member of the Iraq Governing Council. Back in the United States to attend his daughter's college graduation, he phoned Mortimer, proposing the meeting.

It was not surprising that Chalabi, like all those who had agitated for the forcible removal of Saddam Hussein, disparaged the UN. The Security Council, after all, had refused Bush's demand for a second resolution authorizing the invasion, and there was no doubt that the secretary-general opposed the invasion. But Chalabi now told Mortimer he was just as furious over the profits Saddam Hussein had raked in under the UN oil for food program. When

Mortimer replied that "such payments were made without the knowledge or approval of the UN," Chalabi countered that the "payments were notorious" and that Kofi Annan "should have made greater efforts to expose them or at least insisted that companies state whether or not they had made them." Chalabi warned Mortimer that he was "going to initiate a public campaign against the United Nations for having enabled the Iraqi regime to make substantial profits under the program."

Mortimer alerted Annan and also wrote a note to Sérgio Vieira de Mello in Baghdad about the conversation. "You can see what the line of attack will be," he wrote Sérgio, "and you may want to guard against it—particularly in your public appearances and statements."

Chalabi is often vilified for misleading the Pentagon and the press before the war about the plethora of weapons and the cheering populace that the Americans would find in Iraq. We do not know, aside from the chat with Mortimer, how strong a hand Chalabi played in igniting the oil for food scandal. But much of the early cries of scandal from Congress and the press were based on information from sources in Iraq. Brian Urquhart, who served with the UN for forty years and has written about its problems with great perception for twenty years afterward, believes Chalabi's influence was considerable. "He seems to have been remarkably successful in pursuing this campaign, especially with his neoconservative friends in Washington," Urquhart wrote in the *New York Review of Books*.

In any case, it would not have taken much to orchestrate an anti-Annan campaign. The secretary-general had angered the White House, Republican congressmen, and right-wing pundits with his antiwar comments, and they wanted to punish him. As evidence of wrongdoing mounted from Iraq, it was easy for the anti-Annan cabal to strike out at him.

Judith Miller, who had depended on Chalabi for some of her inflated stories about weapons of mass destruction, was one of the chief *New York Times* reporters churning out scandal stories about oil for food. After Miller resigned from the *Times* in a brouhaha over her reporting about Iraqi weapons and over her sources, a former colleague, Barbara Crossette, urged a closer look at her reporting about oil for food.

Crossette, who had headed the *Times* bureau at the UN from 1994 to 2001, set down her case in a letter to Jim Romenesko, who manages a media Web site for the Poynter Institute, a journalism school and research center in St. Petersburg, Florida. "Judith Miller," said Crossette, "also wrote a series of damaging reports on the 'oil for food' scandal at the United Nations—in particular, personally damaging to Secretary-General Kofi Annan because the reports were frequently based on half-truths or hearsay peddled on Capitol Hill by people determined to force Annan out of office."

Interest in the scandal sometimes lagged in mainstream publications like the *Washington Post* and the *New York Times*. But conservative publications like the *Weekly Standard* and conservative columnists like William Safire and Robert Novak fanned the story continually. When Republican congressmen picked up the cause and made it their own, press coverage intensified.

The stories and speeches were marked by a characteristic that made them misleading. Headlines and lead paragraphs always emphasized an oil for food scandal, even though smuggling outside the program accounted for far more chicanery. At the most, some writers called it an oil for food and smuggling scandal. The writers usually explained deep in the stories that the smuggling side of the scandal was far worse than the oil for food side. But they never called the scandal what it really was—a Bush administration smuggling scandal or a U.S.-British smuggling scandal or a Security Council smuggling scandal. By focusing on the smallest side of the scandal, oil for food, they could punish Kofi Annan.

On top of this, many journalists and congressmen exaggerated the total cost of the smuggling and the oil for food bribes, often coming up with a figure almost twice the $12.8 billion found by the Volcker commission. Safire, a columnist for the *New York Times*, wrote, "Never has there been a financial rip-off of the magnitude of the UN oil for food scandal."

The campaign reached a climax on December 1, 2004, when Senator Norman Coleman, a Republican from Minnesota, wrote an op-ed piece in the *Wall Street Journal* that began, "It's time for UN secretary-general Kofi Annan to resign." Coleman, who headed a subcommittee investigating the issue, insisted that Saddam Hussein had pocketed $21 billion "through abuses of the oil for food program and UN sanctions." But Coleman never broke this figure down between oil for food bribes and sanctions-busting. Since he cited oil for food as the problem throughout the rest of the article, he gave the false impression that almost all the illicit $21 billion stemmed from abuses of the oil for food program.

"If this widespread corruption had occurred in any legitimate organization around the world," Coleman wrote, "its CEO would have been ousted long ago in disgrace. Why is the UN different?" Similar calls came from the *Wall Street Journal* editorial page itself, the *New York Sun*, and Safire. One Republican congressman, Representative Scott Garrett of New Jersey, went farther. "To me the question should not be whether Kofi Annan should be in charge," said Garrett. "To me the larger question is whether he should be in jail at this point in time."

Annan says there never was any chance that he would resign. Whenever he thought about the concept of resignation in a general way, he told me in May 2006, he realized that "it would be easy to resign." But, he went on, "it would have been the wrong thing to do because of the nature of the campaign against me. It would have been giving in to them."

The campaign against Annan became so fervent and so conservative-based that many analysts assumed the White House was behind it. President Bush reinforced that idea with a lukewarm, ambiguous response when a reporter asked him whether he thought Annan should resign. Bush replied that "there ought to be a full and fair and open accounting of the oil for food program" so that Americans will "feel comfortable supporting the United Nations."

The suspicion about the White House prompted a worldwide backlash of support for Annan. British prime minister Tony Blair praised him. Annan received a standing ovation from the delegates to the UN General Assembly. David Hannay, a former British ambassador to the UN, likened the anti-Annan crowd to a "lynch mob." This cascade of support for Annan may have prompted the White House to change course.

In any case, John C. Danforth, the American ambassador to the UN, tried in mid-December to deny a White House role. "Some have suggested to me that what the United States wants is to force the resignation of the secretary-general," Danforth told reporters outside the chambers of the Security Council. "It is important for us, the United States, to clarify our position. We are not suggesting or pushing for the resignation of the secretary-general. We have worked well with him in the past. We anticipate working with him very well in the future for the time to come." Later, he told reporters, "No one, to my knowledge, has cast doubt on the personal integrity of the secretary-general—no one. And we certainly don't."

In an interview by Charlie Rose on PBS television, Annan described the campaign as "very painful to watch." He acknowledged that he should have paid more attention to what was going on. "But when it comes to corruption and fraud," he said, "I daresay the problem was with the capitals and the companies, because . . . only one staff member is presumed to have taken $150,000. All the others were the companies sitting in their capitals making deals with Saddam."

Kofi Annan might have withstood all the accusations over the oil for food program without much damage to his reputation if it were not for the involvement of his son, Kojo. But Kojo created a murky cloud of suspicion that proved too tenacious to clear away. He caused a terrible shame that made it difficult for the secretary-general to explain and defend himself. Despite his frankness about UN policy, his desire to conduct UN operations with transparency, and his genuine kindness and warmth, Kofi Annan is a very private person who does not talk about personal problems with any ease. Many friends who admire and love him describe him as a man of great reserve. There is an inner Kofi they can never reach. Badgered about Kojo by reporters, the secretary-general grew irritable and evasive.

The British press liked to call Kojo a member of "the international rat pack" because of his association with wealthy youth such as the son of Sheikh Yamani, the former oil minister of Saudi Arabia. Kojo, a standout rugby player in British boarding school, was graduated from Keele University in central England in 1995 at age twenty-two and took advantage of his family connections to obtain a job at a Swiss firm, Cotecna. The firm specialized in inspecting cargo on ships entering and leaving ports. Michael Wilson, the son of an old Ghanian friend of his father, was in charge of Africa marketing for Cotecna and arranged for Cotecna to hire Kojo to work in its Lagos office. The Wilsons were so close to the Annans that Michael, following Ghanian custom, regarded Kofi as his uncle.

At the end of 1998, Cotecna won a contract from the UN to inspect cargo coming to Iraq under the oil for food program to make sure it contained only food and other necessities. A month later, the *Sunday Telegraph* in London published an article raising the issue of an apparent conflict of interest, since the UN had awarded a contract to a company employing the son of the secretary-general.

Kojo told the *Sunday Telegraph* reporter, "I would never play any role in anything that involves the United Nations, for obvious reasons. I would appreciate if you would make that very clear. I never have done and I never will do." Cotecna, in letters to the *Sunday Telegraph*, insisted that Kojo had not been involved and, in any case, had resigned from the company at the start of the contract bidding process. When the British newspaper inquired at the UN, the secretary-general phoned both Kojo and Michael Wilson for information and was told the same: Kojo had nothing to do with the contract and had left the company.

After the publication of the *Sunday Telegraph* story, the UN Secretariat looked into the matter in a perfunctory way. Iqbal Riza, the chief of staff, asked Joseph Connor, the undersecretary-general for management, to review whether the procurement staff was aware of Kojo's association with Cotecna when the contract was awarded. Connor was annoyed that the matter had been sent to him rather than the legal or auditing departments. He assumed that Riza wanted some quick answers for the press, not a long and thorough investigation. Connor's staff prepared a memo that same day stating that Cotecna had won the contract because it submitted the lowest bid and that procurement officers had not known of or been influenced by Kojo's association with the company. That ended the in-house investigation.

Kofi Annan's colleagues looked into the impending scandal in a slipshod way because they could not imagine him or his family involved in such dirty dealings. Annan told the Volcker commission he had repeatedly warned his children that "they shouldn't try to do business with the UN or get involved with the UN business" and that they should "try and stay away from any business that will bring them so close to the UN that it would seem like conflict of interest."

Kofi Annan has never enriched himself the way many American politicians do. "I've always lived quite a straight life," Kofi told Meryl Gordon of *New York* magazine. "I'm not one of those who is in a hurry to get rich. It's not my way of life or desire."

The Volcker commission confirmed the straightness of his life when it examined his financial records. "The secretary-general's financial records reflect that his primary source of income was his United Nations salary and rental income," said the commission in its final report. "He lives within his means and has accumulated a retirement fund through savings. The secretary-general contributes heavily to charity and to the support of his extended family. For example, when he was awarded the Nobel Peace Prize in 2001, he donated all of his prize money—$481,265—to the United Nations. The records produced do not raise concerns about the secretary-general's financial stability nor do they reveal any payments or transactions that appear suspicious or improper." (As of 2006, the secretary-general's annual salary was $397,245, less a staff assessment of $83,275, the UN equivalent of taxes.)

Unfortunately, the image of Annan family honesty cracked with the revelations that Kojo's version of Cotecna events was largely false. Kojo had not severed his connection with Cotecna before it tried to win a UN contract in 1998. The Volcker commission found that Cotecna had kept paying him until 2004, sometimes hiding the payments by channeling them through other companies. In all, Kojo received $195,894 from Cotecna and possibly more. Moreover, Kojo "used his contacts at the United Nations to assist Cotecna's effort to obtain the Iraq inspection contract," the commission said. He did so, according to the commission, by placing several calls to family friends in "the procurement department at critical times in the bidding process."

The Volcker commission did not find the secretary-general guilty of any wrongdoing. It concluded that "no credible evidence exists that the secretary-general influenced, or attempted to influence, the procurement process in 1998 leading to the selection of Cotecna."

But Kofi had also insisted that he did not even know that Cotecna was trying to obtain the inspection contract. The commission was far less emphatic about endorsing this assertion. "The evidence is not reasonably sufficient to conclude that the secretary-general knew that Cotecna had submitted a bid on the humanitarian inspection contract in 1998," the Commission said.

This lukewarm finding did not completely clear the secretary-general of the possibility that he knew something about the adventure of his son. In an interview a month after the commission's final report was issued in September 2005, Paul Volcker was asked by Maggie Farley of the *Los Angeles Times* whether he thought the secretary-general knew about Kojo using his father's connections to help Cotecna, Volcker replied, "To this day, I still don't know."

The Volcker commission also delved into another byway of Kojo embarrassment. In 1998, young Kojo attended an auto show in Geneva and decided to buy a Mercedes that attracted him. His friend Michael Wilson put down $3,000 as a deposit, and Kojo finagled a discount price for the car by pretending it was for his father. Mercedes cut $6,541 off the price as a special deal for the secretary-general and sold the car to Kojo for $39,056. Kojo then persuaded a family friend working for a UN agency in Ghana to arrange for his father's car to be imported duty-free. That saved Kojo $14,103 in import duties. From Ghana, it was an easy drive to Kojo's home in Nigeria.

The secretary-general had sent Kojo a check for $15,000, but the commission concluded he had no idea that Kojo had invoked his father's name to hoodwink Mercedes into a discount and Ghana Customs into allowing the car to enter Ghana duty-free.

Almost every comment from the secretary-general about Kojo for more than a year sounded like a cry of anguish. When he believed that his son had severed the Cotecna connection long ago, he implored reporters in June 2004, "We need to be patient and allow the investigation to go forward. And I think some are being very impatient and jumping to conclusions without facts, without evidence, and seem to know the truth and want to go ahead. It is a bit like lynching actually." When he realized his son had lied, Annan told reporters, "I did talk to him, but I really don't want to get into this. . . . Naturally, I was very disappointed and surprised."

The secretary-general was at his frankest in a long conversation with Meryl Gordon of *New York* magazine in April 2005. "He has apologized," Annan told Gordon. "He is extremely embarrassed. . . . I have talked to him about coming clean with everything he knows, no surprises." Kojo had refused to meet again with Volcker commission investigators but would do so a few months later. "I have no theories," the secretary-general went on. "You know, it's incredible when you see these little children. You carry them in your arms and lead them along the way. And over time, they develop their own personalities and become their own person." After reading the Volcker commission's interim report detailing Cotecna payments to Kojo, the secretary-general told Gordon he was so angry he cut short one phone conversation with his son. "He was sorry that he hadn't leveled with me," Annan said.

But the secretary-general did not break with his son. He kept up contact and from time to time they would meet in Europe or New York. "I think he's been a caring father," Nane told Gordon. "Of course, this is very painful to him as a father and as a secretary-general. It's difficult. It's difficult. This is so unfortunate."

It was also very painful for Nane. "She was very hurt by the accusations," the secretary-general told me. "She is a very private and gentle person. I was able to go about my work during all these accusations. But she was a bystander. It was difficult for her."

When Julia Preiswerk, his good friend for more than forty years, met him in August, he did not want to talk much about the problem. But he told her, "I'm very upset about Kojo." In March 2006, PBS interviewer Charlie Rose remarked that some critics insist he should have known what his son was up to. The secretary-general replied defensively, "I hope those who are saying that, they all have sons and children, that they know everything their sons do when you are living thousands of miles apart. . . . I'm not so sure that is how it happens in the real world."

In the last few weeks of 2004, some of his colleagues decided they needed a private meeting with him to shake him out of his low feelings and to help him defend the UN against the swirl of attacks over oil for food. His chief of staff, Iqbal Riza, was delegated to broach the idea with him. Annan agreed, and the aides met with him at the apartment of Deputy Secretary-General Louise Frechette. The session was supposed to be hush-hush. But at lunch that day, Catherine Bertini, the undersecretary-general for management, was shocked when an ambassador stopped at her table and asked, "Are you going to the meeting today?"

Shashi Tharoor, the undersecretary-general for communications, prepared a memorandum ahead of time outlining for Annan what Tharoor had heard from "a number of well-placed figures in the American media." Many said they themselves had found the oil for food issue too intricate to analyze properly but that the anti-UN critics had succeeded in leaving the impression that "something was rotten." As for the Kojo issue, Tharoor said, the UN's refusal to say much about it had left the impression that "we had something to hide." Tharoor reported that journalists had told him the UN could change the negative view of Washington opinionmakers only by being more active and visible in Iraq—the one issue that mattered to the Bush administration. "If you help pull the United States' chestnuts out of the fire in Iraq," a columnist told Tharoor, "it will change the American debate about the UN."

Annan listened impassively to all that was said during the evening and commented little. The session pleased his aides. "Real issues were discussed," says Bertini, "and we talked about them with the boss." The mood was broken when one participant received word by cell phone that a newspaper was reporting Kojo had lied about his payments from Cotecna. One of those present told *Time* magazine later that "a look of surprise and dismay" crossed Annan's face and "his jaw started clenching and unclenching." Then the secretary-general said, "Let's get on with the agenda."

Another private meeting was hosted by Richard Holbrooke a few days later in his New York apartment. This one would have more dramatic results than the Frechette meeting. Holbrooke, a UN ambassador during the Clinton administration, had been regarded as the most likely choice for secretary of state had Senator John F. Kerry defeated Bush in the 2004 presidential election. Holbrooke's small group included Leslie H. Gelb, the former president of the Council on Foreign Relations; Timothy Wirth, the former Democratic senator from Colorado who now headed the United Nations Foundation; John G. Ruggie, a Harvard professor of international relations who had served as Kofi Annan's assistant secretary-general for strategic planning; and Nader Mousavizadeh, the Danish national who had helped write Annan's Nobel Prize speech and now worked for the international investment banking firm Goldman Sachs.

Holbrooke and his group were worried about the strained relations between Annan and Washington. They were determined, as one told the *New York Times*, "to save Kofi and rescue the UN." "We talked about the fact that the UN could not succeed if it was in fundamental opposition to the United States," Holbrooke told Charlie Rose of PBS. "The United States needs the UN and the UN needs the United States. It's as simple as that." Holbrooke said Annan and the UN must recognize the election results and "not only live with but work with the administration."

Holbrooke's group came up with the usual Washington prescription for an institution in trouble—shake it up with some major personnel changes. In the most important, Annan accepted the resignation of Iqbal Riza, who had asked to leave a couple of years earlier, and replaced him as chief of staff with Mark Malloch Brown of Britain. Riza, a distinguished UN civil servant who had worked with Annan for many years, liked to operate quietly behind the scenes. But Brown, administrator of the United Nations Development Program, the main UN aid agency, and a former journalist and World Bank vice president, preferred the limelight to obscurity and prided himself on his skills as a communicator.

"Certainly, I am going to be more than a chief of staff," Malloch Brown told Nora Boustany of the *Washington Post*. "Can you bring someone in who has run a staff two-thirds the size of the UN, with a much bigger and more complex agency than others, and have him just manage the secretary-general's appointments? I am a reform-oriented manager and someone who has been involved in communications."

Malloch Brown, who knew the Washington scene well and had good relations with Washington officials, was evidently expected to lend some pizzazz to the UN cause and burnish its image with his communication skills. But his first attempt backfired. That came after the Volcker commission issued an interim report about Kojo and Cotecna in late March 2005. "There is no evidence," the report said, "that the selection of Cotecna in 1998 was subject to any affirmative or improper influence of the secretary-general." But the commission also said that "the evidence is not reasonably sufficient" to show that Kofi knew that Cotecna had submitted a bid for the contract. And the commission chided Annan for his inadequate investigation of the Kojo affair once he found out about it.

At a news conference, Annan put the best light on the findings and called them an "exoneration." Some reporters did not agree, and one asked the secretary-general if he felt "it's time for the good of the organization to step down." Annan replied, "Hell, no." After a few more words, the secretary-general walked off the stage as planned, leaving Malloch Brown behind to field the rest of the questions. That move was supposed to allow Malloch Brown to show off his skills. But the correspondents were furious. They wanted the secretary-general to reply to their questions, not his chief of staff. It looked like the secretary-general had run away from them. They peppered Malloch Brown with aggressive, almost nasty questions. When Malloch Brown sputtered, "He's not a crook," a reporter snapped, "That's what Richard Nixon said, too." The session was a public-relations disaster. Malloch Brown never again attempted to substitute for Annan at a news conference.

The secretary-general, who once basked in the admiration of journalists, did not turn his back on the press just because their questions had turned tough. Mort Zuckeman, the publisher of the New York *Daily News* and editor in chief of *U.S. News & World Report*, invited Kofi and Nane to dinner in June mainly with editors and journalists. The session at Zuckerman's Fifth Avenue apartment was informal—nothing said was for attribution—and Annan replied frankly to questions about oil for food, Kojo, Iraq, and relations with the White House.

One of the guests was Diego Arria, a former Venezuelan ambassador to the UN and a former Caracas newspaper editor. The questions were pointed, but, according to Arria, Annan retained his usual "noble bearing and sense of dignity that makes him different." When the dinner ended, Arria joked to the secretary-general, "That wasn't a free lunch." "No," Annan agreed, "I paid for that dinner."

The Volcker commission issued a final report on September 7, 2005. Its criticism of Annan was scathing but not because of any corruption. Slipshod management was the harsh complaint. While recognizing that the Security Council and its Sanctions Committee shared the blame, the commission castigated the secretary-general for failing to keep watch on the oil for food program.

Annan told the Security Council that the report "had shone a harsh light into the most unsightly corners of the organization." He accepted its conclusions and reform proposals, such as the creation of a chief operating officer at the UN and an Independent Oversight Board to audit all aspects of UN operations. But he said most of the reforms would require approval by the UN General Assembly.

The final report did not end the press's interest in the story of Kojo and his discounted Mercedes. The Volcker commission had examined the case only because it suspected at first that the Mercedes might be a payoff by Cotecna to Kojo. That proved erroneous. In fact, the Mercedes incident amounted to a bit of fraud committed by a foolish kid just out of college. But the fraud was committed in the name of the UN secretary-general, and that made it news.

Although the spokesmen for the secretary-general insisted for months that there was no further information, James Bone of the *Times* of London kept peppering the UN for more details. Bone is a tall, long-serving UN correspondent with a boyish face and a good eye and ear for color and gossip, no matter how trivial. He is in the tradition of British journalism's eternal quest for the titillating tale. A good yarn counts more in that tradition than worldly significance. The more the UN stonewalled, the more Bone persisted.

In November, for example, Bone asked deputy spokesman Marie Okabe, "Did this Mercedes have diplomatic license plates?" and "Does it still have diplomatic license plates?" When Marie directed him to Kojo's lawyer for answers, Bone countered that "it's a question about the United Nations and whether there's a Mercedes with UN diplomatic plates tooling around in Ghana at the moment, and the implication being that if it hits anybody, the UN might be liable, for instance, to pay the insurance." But Marie still had no answer. (A partner of Kojo's lawyer in London told the *New York Times* a couple of months later that the Mercedes "had been damaged beyond repair as a result of an accident" during the same month that Bone asked his question. That, of course, would not have halted his questioning. In fact, it probably would have set off more questions.)

Bone's continual questioning about the Mercedes became the joke of the daily news briefings from the spokesman's office and the bane of the briefers. The spokesman's office was severely handicapped because Annan had drawn the line: He regarded Kojo's guile over the Mercedes as a personal problem that the secretary-general would not share with others.

Bone stood up at the secretary-general's year-end news conference on December 21 to ask once more about the Mercedes. "Some of your own stories—your own version of events," the *Times* correspondent said, "don't really make sense. I'd like to ask you particularly—"

He was interrupted by the secretary-general: "I think you are being very cheeky here."

"Well, let me, sir, let me ask my question."

"No, hold on, hold on," said Annan. "Listen, James Bone. You have been behaving like an overgrown schoolboy in this room for many, many months and years. You are an embarrassment to your colleagues and to your profession. Please stop misbehaving, and please let's move on to a more serious question."

Bone still tried to ask his question about the Mercedes.

But the secretary-general said, "No. Move on to serious journalists," and he called on another correspondent.

The outburst was so shocking and so unusual for the secretary-general that CNN ran the incident on television all day with the headline "Annan Loses His Cool." At the end of the news conference, Jim Wurst, president of the United Nations Correspondents' Association (UNCA), told the secretary-general, "On behalf of the . . . association, I have to tell you that James Bone is not an embarrassment. He's a member in good standing of UNCA. He had every right to ask the question."

"No, I agree with you," Annan replied. "He has a right to ask questions, and I came here to answer questions. But I think we also have to understand that we have to treat each other with some respect. . . . There are ways of asking questions and ways not to ask questions. . . . You know what has been going on in this room. You know how my spokesmen have been badgered, mistreated, insulted. They have been professional. They have stood there and taken it. . . .

You have the right to ask all the questions you want to ask. I reserve the right to refuse to answer questions I don't want to answer. But there is a certain behavior and a certain mutual respect which we have to expect."

Stéphane Dujarric, who had succeeded Fred Eckhard as the secretary-general's spokesman, and his staff feared that the outburst would deal another blow to the UN's relations with the press. Their fears were justified, of course. As Maggie Farley of the *Los Angeles Times* told me months later in an e-mail message, "His televised rebuke to James Bone was seen as a damaging moment of loss of control that ironically elevated Bone and diminished the S-G."

And yet there may have been a positive side as well. When Kofi Annan won the Nobel Peace Prize in 2001, Shashi Tharoor, who had worked alongside him for many years, wrote a tribute to his boss in the *Hindu*, an Indian newspaper. "He has an extraordinary inner calm," Tharoor wrote. "No one has seen him angry, depressed, excited, or in a panic. I once compared him to an Indian yogi—a human being who seems to walk on a different plane, with a strong, still center to him in which he is deeply anchored and from which he faces pressure and pleasure with absolute confidence that neither can overcome him."

The image of a yogi has appealed to several magazine writers who quoted Tharoor in their profiles of Annan. Yet the image has always troubled me. It made Kofi Annan seem more than real—as if he wore the mask of a yogi to somehow hide his inner self. It did not seem very healthy or admirable. But Iraq and oil for food and Kojo battered him so much that he could not hide his depression and melancholy any longer. His outburst at James Bone—played out on television—displayed his anger for all to see. He was still a yogi, but a yogi who could sometimes lose his cool. That enhanced the reality of his image. Losing his cool made him more human and easier to accept and understand.

16

The Year of Summing Up

K ofi Annan entered the last of his ten years as secretary-general of the United Nations with his old equilibrium and self-confidence fully in place. There was an easy and assured calm about him as he thought about his legacy and his future. Nane, who had stopped painting when he assumed the post in 1997, returned to the Art Students' League over the Christmas holidays in 2005. She wanted to work more at painting the human face and had sought help from an instructor there. She and Kofi had decided to live in both Ghana and Europe after the UN but had not yet chosen where in Europe.

The furor over oil for food had subsided, and Annan never doubted that he had been the unfair victim of a political campaign set off and fanned by right-wing ideologues who had contempt for the UN. He even tended, as most fathers would, to judge his son less harshly. He was pleased that Kojo had won a civil suit against the *Sunday Times* of London for falsely accusing him of taking part in a deal to sell two million barrels of Iraqi oil to a Moroccan company. Although relations between father and son had been strained, Kofi had never broken the relationship. "There was never a break between us," says Kofi. "It is difficult for a father and son to break apart." They talked by phone and met occasionally throughout the ordeal.

In mid-April 2006, Kojo came to New York and conferred with his father at the residence. "He has learned a lot, and he has grown," Kofi told me a couple of weeks later. The secretary-general deplored that Kojo's "name had been dragged through the mud." When I pointed out that Kojo had hid his continued association with Cotecna from his father, Kofi agreed. "It is true that he withheld information from me," he said. "He caused me lots of grief."

The secretary-general kept up his usual heavy schedule of worldwide travel. In March and April, for example, he was traveling a third of his time. With Nane, he embarked on a twelve-day African trip to South Africa, Madagascar, the Congo Republic, the Congo, Gabon, Equatorial Guinea, and Ghana. And, again with Nane, he spent eight days in Spain and the Netherlands. He also flew to St. Paul, Minnesota, in late April to inaugurate the Institute for Global Citizenship at his alma mater, Macalester College.

His staff steadied at the beginning of the last year. When Louise Frechette resigned as deputy secretary-general, he named Mark Malloch Brown to take her place. It was a more sensible role for the outgoing and energetic Malloch Brown than overblown chief of staff.

But Annan had to work with a constant irritant. Since August 2005, the American ambassador at the UN had been John R. Bolton, an ideologue who, as discussed in chapter 11, had spent many years demeaning and chastising the United Nations. He had once said that several floors of the UN Secretariat Building could be sliced off without being missed. Appointing Bolton ambassador was an insult to both the UN and its secretary-general.

President Bush and Secretary of State Condoleezza Rice, however, were less concerned with insulting the UN and Annan than in finding a suitable place for Bolton and appeasing the far right. Bolton, the undersecretary of state for arms control and international security, was regarded as the White House's neoconservative mole in Colin Powell's State Department during Bush's first term. His time at the State Department was noteworthy for a pugnacious and tough stance against Iranian and North Korean nuclear bomb development that accomplished nothing and for bullying subordinates who did not seem conservative enough for his tastes. Rice knew she would have had a rebellion in the ranks if she had succumbed to the blandishments of the far right and named Bolton to the job of deputy secretary of state. Sending him to the UN amounted to prestigious damage control.

When she announced the nomination of Bolton in March 2005, Secretary Rice proclaimed that he would serve in the tradition of our best ambassadors "with the strongest voices." She cited Daniel Patrick Moynihan and Jeane Kirkpatrick as the models. President Bush echoed her comparisons. But the Bolton nomination hardly fit any historical tradition.

Both Moynihan, who served in the mid-1970s, and Kirkpatrick, who served in the early 1980s, faced a UN at the nadir of its fortunes. It was an object of contempt for many Americans and Europeans, not all of them conservative. The Cold War had paralyzed the Security Council. No issue of significance could be solved there as long as the United States and the Soviet Union were prepared to veto each other.

Most of the noise at the UN in those days came from the General Assembly, controlled by the many formerly colonized nations of the Third World. The General Assembly was a nearly powerless body of incessant talk. Many small countries took advantage of the Security Council's paralysis to attract attention by denouncing the United States and other rich countries in the General Assembly. That satisfied their pride but brought disdain down on the UN.

Some American policymakers hoped then that the tart tongues of Moynihan, appointed by President Ford, and Kirkpatrick, appointed by President Reagan, might shake some sense into the UN. That strategy really didn't work. The infamous Zionism is racism resolution, for example, was passed by the General Assembly on Moynihan's watch. The nomination of Bolton as another

Moynihan or Kirkpatrick was a strong indication that many Bush administration policymakers still had the same contempt for the UN that their predecessors had in the 1970s and 1980s. But that, of course, ignored history. It ignored the enormous changes in the UN since the end of the Cold War and the realization of the Security Council that it could now exercise power.

For almost five months, Bolton failed to win confirmation by the Senate. He was opposed by Democrats and some Republicans for holding extremist views and for bullying subordinates. On August 1, while Congress was in recess, President Bush sent Bolton to New York under what is known as "a recess appointment." The president can appoint anyone to office without Senate approval if the appointment is made while Congress is not in session. That appointment, however, lasts only until the term of the Congress is over. In the case of Bolton, that meant he could serve as ambassador until the end of 2006. The terms of Annan and Bolton would thus end at the same time.

While circumventing the Senate, President Bush said he was sending Bolton to New York "to provide clear American leadership for reform" at the UN. This brought an admonition from Annan. "I think it is all right for one ambassador to come and push," he told reporters, "but an ambassador always has to remember that there are 190 others who will have to be convinced—or a vast majority of them—for action to take place."

Annan's relationship with Bolton was somewhat cold and correct. That surprised Annan. He has always tried hard not to allow political viewpoints to interfere with his personal relations. His friendship with William Shawcross, for example, remained close despite the British writer's fervent endorsement of the American-led invasion of Iraq in a book that shocked Shawcross's friends, including Annan. Since he is not an ideologue, Annan is not so wedded to his own point of view that he cannot bear to hear others. He admired both John Negroponte and John Danforth, Bolton's predecessors as the Bush administration's UN ambassadors, and talked about both with great respect.

But he found Bolton, as the secretary-general put it, "awkward"—a man ill at ease with others. Bolton knew how to demand but not how to cajole. He knew how to pontificate but not how to compromise. Despite eight years in the State Department, Bolton was not very proficient as a diplomat. The lack of interpersonal skills was a trait of Bolton that surprised Annan.

Bolton's announced assignment—reforming the UN—was a phantom task. No amount of reform would ever satisfy the UN's fiercest American critics. The calls for reform had become political cant over the years. They had become as automatic and meaningless in American political life as praising fallen soldiers or waving the flag. The UN had been reforming itself for many years. But the calls for reform never ceased.

Kofi Annan never denied that the UN needed reform. He had proposed and enacted reforms almost every year of his tenure. But UN reform needed to be put into perspective. Many institutions and processes needed reform. The U.S. Electoral College needed reform. So did the American system of casting and counting votes. So did many American corporations, as well as the FBI and the CIA. Secretary of Defense Donald Rumsfeld insisted that the U.S. military needed reform. And everyone seemed to agree that American public schools needed reform. But the clamor for UN reform was different. It was incessant, very loud, and very suspicious.

It came too often from American ideologues who wanted to paint a false image of the UN as corrupt, slovenly, wasteful, inefficient, and anti-American. The attacks never took into account the wonderful diversity of the UN. There were 192 member states in 2006 and six official languages: English, French, Spanish, Chinese, Russian, and Arabic. The civil servants came from an incredible variety of cultures. To avoid misunderstanding in the same office, they needed to show great sensitivity and tread carefully with each other. That might slow work a bit and foster some inefficiency, but it was one of the glories of the UN.

The brouhaha over the Human Rights Commission illustrated the secretary-general's difficulty in dealing with reform while

Bolton charged around this way and that. The commission had long been a UN disgrace. Countries such as China, Zimbabwe, the Sudan, Saudi Arabia, Libya, Nepal, and Cuba successfully maneuvered to become members so they could block any investigator from looking at their abuses. Annan said the "declining credibility and professionalism" of the commission cast "a shadow on the reputation of the United Nations system as a whole."

To remove the disgrace, Annan proposed that the fifty-three-member commission be abolished and replaced by a new forty-three-member Human Rights Council elected by two-thirds vote of the General Assembly. The members of the commission had been elected by a majority vote of the obscure and impotent UN Economic and Social Council. Since this council has only fifty-four members, in the past a human rights abuser could win a seat on the Human Rights Commission with the approval of only twenty-eight members of the UN.

Annan expected strong support from Bolton on this issue. Bolton, after all, blustered a good deal about reform from the sidelines. In November 2005, he issued a dire warning to the UN as part of a talk he gave in the Jesse Helms Lecture Series at Wingate University, North Carolina. "Being practical," he said, "Americans say that either we need to fix the institution or we'll turn to some other mechanism to solve international problems." But he took little part in the negotiations in the General Assembly over replacing the Human Rights Commission.

He did try tossing off one bold and futile proposal in December. He called for the UN to grant automatic seats on the Human Rights Council to the United States and the four other permanent members of the Security Council. Since this might shield from prying eyes China's longtime abuse of political dissidents, Russian president Vladimir Putin's restrictions on democracy, and the Bush administration's treatment of "unlawful combatants" and other detainees, the proposal struck many inside and outside the UN as hypocritical and self-serving. Bolton withdrew it.

Bolton, in fact, did not act in any significant way again until

March 2006, when Jan Eliasson of Sweden, the president of the General Assembly, brokered an agreement with the key players in the General Assembly for the establishment of the Human Rights Council. Eliasson's compromise dropped the two-thirds requirement for election and replaced it with election by an absolute majority on a secret ballot. A candidate government would need 97 votes, no matter how many of the 192 members took part in the election. This was far more than the 28 votes required for Human Rights Commission membership in the past. To ensure that members of the new council not use their seats to escape scrutiny, all would have to submit to a human rights investigation during their three-year terms.

But this did not satisfy Bolton. "Based on conversations with other governments," he said, "the strongest argument in favor of this draft is that it is not as bad as it could be." Annan, in contrast, accepted the compromise. "Obviously the proposal isn't everything I asked for," he said. "There are enough good elements on this to build on." Support came from the leaders of human rights organizations, and from a group of Nobel Peace Prize laureates that included Jimmy Carter and Desmond Tutu.

"It's an open question," said Kenneth Roth, executive director of Human Rights Watch, "whether Bolton's throwing all the cards up in the air is meant to improve the council or to prove that the UN can't reform itself and therefore should be abandoned."

When the vote came on March 15, Bolton stood in virtual isolation. The General Assembly approved establishment of the Human Rights Council by a vote of 170 to 4. Bolton voted no, joined only by Israel, the Marshall Islands, and Palau. Belarus, Iran, and Venezuela abstained. Bolton insisted that he found the retreat from the two-thirds electoral proposal unacceptable.

His high-minded stance was suspicious. "All too often," said Swiss ambassador Peter Maurer, "too-high-minded ambitions are cover-ups for less noble ambitions and are aimed not at improving the United Nations but at weakening it."

After all his maneuvering to try to push the United States onto the council, Bolton finally announced that the United States would not seek election during the first year. Bolton had a number of excuses for this, but most diplomats assumed the United States feared that the tales of torture of prisoners from the Afghanistan and Iraq wars would dash any American chances for election in a secret ballot.

Reform proposals also pushed Annan into a confrontation with the UN staff union. In March, the secretary-general, insisting on the need for "a radical overhaul of the United Nations Secretariat," called for the General Assembly to enact a series of employment changes that infuriated the staff. He proposed moving staff from headquarters into missions throughout the world, hiring staff on short-term appointments, offering buyouts to one thousand staff members, and outsourcing some work, such as translations. At an anger-filled session, union members voted that they no longer had any confidence in their secretary-general.

Workers anywhere react with fury over proposals that might threaten their jobs. But the vote of no confidence shocked aides close to Annan. It would have been unthinkable for the staff to have reacted that way three or four years earlier. Annan, after all, was the first secretary-general to rise from the staff.

But the relationship soured. Most of the staff did not want to go into Iraq after the American-led invasion because they were wary of giving cover to the Bush administration. After the car bomb murder of Sérgio Vieira de Mello and the others in Baghdad, the secretary-general's refusal to pull everyone out right away had angered the staff. For the past three years, many UN civil servants felt that Annan gave in too easily to American pressure, and they looked on his reform proposals in 2006 as an example of kowtowing to Bolton and the Bush administration.

Many staffers had a feeling as well that Annan did not reach out to them any more and was more concerned with protecting the top ranks than ordinary members of the Secretariat. This was epitomized—in the eyes of the staff—by Annan's handling of the Ruud Lubbers case.

Lubbers, the UN high commissioner for refugees, was accused

by two women of sexual harassment at his offices in Geneva. Although investigators found evidence supporting the accusations, Annan concluded the evidence was too weak to hold up in any legal proceeding against Lubbers, a former prime minister of the Netherlands. Annan sent a letter to the staff in July 2004 admonishing Lubbers but clearing him of the charges. The furor and adverse publicity lasted so long that Annan, taking the advice of Mark Mollach Brown, his new chief of staff, called Lubbers to New York in February 2005 and forced him to resign.

Annan understood the anger of the staff, but he could not assuage it. He believed that his proposed reform of UN employment practices was vital. Unlike many of his ideological adversaries in Washington, he really did believe in reform. He wanted to leave a UN system that operated with more efficiency and good sense than it had in the past. That, in Annan's view, would be part of his legacy.

He also believed that he would be judged in the future on how well he managed the terrible crisis in Darfur during his last year. In the public mind, Darfur conjured memories of the wanton slaughter in Rwanda and of the feeble international response to it. The crisis had erupted in 2003 when African rebels in the western Sudan rose up against the Arab-dominated government in Khartoum. To suppress the rebellion, the Sudanese rulers armed Arab militias on horseback and camels and dispatched them on raids in the Darfur countryside. The militias, known as the Janjaweed, plundered villages, burned fields, murdered civilians, and raped women in their hellish strikes—often mounted with the help of the Sudanese army and air force.

In three years, more than two hundred thousand civilians died and more than two million fled to refugee camps along the border with Chad. President Bush called the suppression "genocide" but did not rally his allies to rush troops there to halt it.

The Darfur crisis raised the issue of intervention once again. The killings took place within the sovereign territory of Sudan. Neither the United States nor any other military power wanted to intervene without the approval of Sudan. As a result, President

Omar Hassan Ahmad al-Bashir had to be persuaded by Annan, fellow African leaders, Bush, and European leaders to accept some kind of intervention. He rejected UN intervention but agreed in 2004 to an African Union force of seven thousand troops. Financed by the United States, Britain, Canada, Japan, and the European Union, this force proved too small and ineffectual to stop the Janjaweed slaughter and plunder.

Annan and the UN were called in as major players in May 2006. After a fragile peace agreement between the rebels and Khartoum was brokered by the African Union, the Security Council passed a resolution instructing the secretary-general to prepare the way for UN peacekeepers to take over the Darfur operation in a few months.

There was a danger in this for Annan. Since the United States and other members of the Security Council did not intend to invade Sudan, Bashir still had to be persuaded to accept UN intervention. By September, in fact, Bashir's resistance stiffened. If Annan failed to persuade him or if UN peacekeepers failed to quell the killing, Washington would surely blame Annan. If the mission succeeded, however, Washington would take credit.

The Israeli-Lebanon crisis in midyear drew Annan into renewed controversy and prominence. On July 12, soldiers of Hezbollah, the militant Shia militia in Lebanon, crossed the border into northern Israel and kidnapped two Israeli soldiers and killed three others. Israel launched a massive counterattack, bombing Lebanon relentlessly while Hezbollah rained rockets on the towns of northern Israeli daily.

There was no hesitation by Annan. The crisis was almost a textbook model testing his values as a statesman for peace. From the beginning, he denounced Hezbollah for its rockets and for its unprovoked attack that started the crisis. But he denounced Israel even more for what he regarded as a disproportionate response. The Israeli bombing was killing hundreds of Lebanese civilians, many of them children. The secretary-general called again and again for a cease-fire.

These calls angered President Bush and the Israeli government, for both had deluded themselves into believing that the Israel Defense Forces could wipe out Hezbollah in a week or two. Bush's irritation was made obvious at a summit meeting of the Group of Eight in St. Petersburg, Russia, a few days later when he was overheard telling British prime minister Tony Blair that Annan, instead of calling for a cease-fire, should pressure Syria, a patron of Hezbollah. "What they need to do," Bush said, "is get Syria to get Hezbollah to stop doing this shit, and it's over." The secretary-general also found himself under fire from American Jewish groups.

In the end, Annan proved wiser than his detractors. Israeli troops bogged down in southern Lebanon and failed to destroy Hezbollah. The crisis, in fact, transformed Hezbollah into the heroes of the Middle East. After a month of bloodshed, the Security Council passed a unanimous resolution calling for a cease-fire and authorizing a force of fifteen thousand UN peacekeepers to join the Lebanese army in patrolling southern Lebanon. In his statement to the Security Council, Annan could not resist chiding the United States for standing in the way of a cease-fire for a month. "I would be remiss," he said, "if I did not tell you how profoundly disappointed I am that the council did not reach this point much, much earlier."

After the resolution was approved, the secretary-general swiftly assumed the role of the major diplomatic player. He persuaded Israel and Lebanon to accept the cease-fire, cajoled Europe into supplying the bulk of the new UN force, and toured the capitals of the Middle East to shore up the cease-fire. It was kind of a heroic climax to his last year as secretary-general. He had defied the Bush administration for a month and then served as the main broker of peace.

As might be expected during a last year in office, Annan mulled over the quality of his legacy—and how it might be affected by his role in crises such as those of Darfur and Lebanon. But he was not very good talking about it. Asked about his legacy by Charlie Rose on public television in early March, the secretary-general was unusually vague. "So I hope it will be said when they look at the record," he said, "that not only did I try to, in my own reform efforts, make the UN an effective instrument, but I have put the individual at the center of everything the UN is about. When you look at our program, it is about the individual, his dignity, his health, education of a child. . . . And I hope it would also be said that the UN is functioning better than it did ten years ago."

But he was keenly interested in what others had to say. He assembled forty academics, diplomats, journalists, and UN officials for a retreat at the Whitney estate on Long Island during the last weekend of April to talk about the UN during his ten years as secretary-general. He sat in on almost every session. I was there as well, and the informed discussion, on top of a year of conversations with others who know the UN well, helped me reach some conclusions about the secretary-general's record.

There is no doubt that his administration can be credited with an impressive handful of major achievements. First of all, he established the principle of the right of the international community to interfere when a government abuses its own people. That has proven difficult to enforce. But the principle—that people are more important than sovereignty—is accepted even by those who insist the offending government must consent to the intervention. Even Sudan has accepted the legitimacy of African Union soldiers protecting Sudanese on Sudanese soil.

Annan also revived a weakened peacekeeping department and increased the deployment of troops to near-record levels. During his administration, the UN started seventeen new missions. The increase reflected major successes in negotiating cease-fires and the end of wars, especially in Africa. The mission in southern Sudan, for example, enforced a peace agreement that ended forty years of war. All this was accomplished with a minimum of fanfare.

The UN's role as the main coordinator of international relief was solidified under Annan. He created the Office for the Coordination of Humanitarian Affairs and later appointed the outspoken Jan Egeland of Norway as its chief. Egeland, who shocked the White House by calling its first offering "stingy," took charge of worldwide relief for the Asian victims of the tsunami in January 2005. Tsunami relief made it obvious that the UN is the only organization able to organize humanitarian assistance on such a scale.

Annan called a summit meeting of the UN in September 2000 that set a series of "millennium development goals." The leaders of the world pledged that by the year 2015 they would halve the numbers of people in extreme poverty, achieve universal primary education, reduce child mortality by two-thirds and maternal mortality by three-fourths, reverse the spread of malaria and HIV/AIDS, and fulfill several other pressing goals. Annan succeeded in spotlighting these problems, but it will take another decade before the lofty goals are either reached or exposed as meaningless talk.

Finally, Annan created an atmosphere of transparency and openness unique in UN history. Although he was reluctant to talk about what he regarded as private matters such as the machinations of his son, Kojo, Annan replied to press questions with more frankness and detail and frequency than any other secretary-general. His aides produced an array of reports exposing past mistakes and predicting problems ahead. Annan tried hard to clear the mystery and secrecy out of UN diplomacy. His successors will find it difficult to backtrack.

These achievements, however, may end up as footnotes in history. The ten years of Annan's administration were overwhelmed by the crisis in Iraq. From his disappointment in the inspections of Richard Butler, to his meeting with Saddam Hussein in Baghdad, to his failure to rein in George W. Bush with diplomacy, to his attempt to carve out a role for the UN after the invasion, to his battering in the so-called oil for food scandal, Annan had to wrestle with the enervating problem of Iraq. When historians look at this era in the future, they will surely see and write about little else but Iraq.

Kofi Annan will be judged favorably. The invasion of Iraq was one of the most catastrophic events of our time. The act looks more and more like an unfortunate spasm of adolescent machismo egged on by ideologues and exiles. The death tolls and suffering caused by the adventure are numbing. George W. Bush will surely be judged harshly by historians, and Kofi Annan credited for opposing him.

But Annan will not be regarded as a major player in the crisis. President Bush's foray into the Security Council was a sham. He came not to negotiate but for a stamp of approval. When he could not get it, he shunted Annan and the UN aside and invaded. The secretary-general was powerless to prevent him. The UN did make some significant contributions afterward toward creating a stable, sovereign, and democratic Iraq, but these may lose significance if the country fails to emerge from its fearsome violence.

Annan's most critical achievement during the Iraq war may have been his ability to carry the United Nations through the crisis with honor. He and the UN were castigated by the White House for many months, and the weaknesses of the UN were made obvious. But he maintained his popularity throughout the rest of the world. Even more important, at the end of his tenure, Annan presided over an organization that could not be described as irrelevant. Even President Bush found it necessary during the year 2006 to act through the UN on matters like Darfur and Lebanon.

In assessing the performance of Annan, an analyst is struck by a sense of what might have been. I discussed this early in 2006 with eighty-six-year-old Brian Urquhart, the dean of all UN-watchers and commentators. "He had the bad luck," said Urquhart, "to be secretary-general when Washington was run by a band of ideologues. . . . If the United States had been on his side, he would have been regarded as in the class of Dag Hammarskjöld."

In a sense, the reign of Kofi Annan represents a lost opportunity. The UN works best when the United States and the secretary-general are in harmony—a wedding of great American power with a moral force reflecting the needs and desires of the rest of the world. Annan was the first secretary-general educated in the United States. He had many American friends and shared many American attitudes. He was African and understood the demands and posturing of the Third World. Married to a Swede, he also understood Europeans and their annoyance at American administrations that tried to barrel ahead without them. He was independent but not stubborn. He was accommodating but not servile. He was honest but not arrogant. He had all the traits Americans admire in a partner. Yet the Bush administration turned its back on him and the UN, shattering any chance for harmony.

The sixty-eight-year-old Annan did not intend to retire into leisure and rest after he departed the UN at the end of 2006. He and Nane planned to spend half the year in Ghana and half the year either in Sweden near Nane's family or in Switzerland near Nina and their two grandchildren.

Annan will devote himself to a pair of African problems: the low level of women's education and the poor state of agriculture. "Africa is the only continent that has not had a Green Revolution," he says, "the only continent that cannot feed itself." He will try to either create and run a foundation devoted to these problems or join some foundation or institution already involved.

After we talked about his future in African development in May, he phoned me the next day. He told me, "I am going to be part of this. . . . There is nothing tentative about this. I am definite." Working in African development will fulfill the promise he and other young African students had made in the early days of independence. They had pledged, as Annan once put it, to get education, learn a trade, and then come back to make a contribution.

KOFI ANNAN'S NOBEL
PEACE PRIZE LECTURE

H ere is the lecture delivered by Kofi Annan in Oslo, Norway, on December 10, 2001, upon receipt of the 2001 Nobel Peace Prize:*

Your Majesties, Your Royal Highnesses, Excellencies, members of the Norwegian Nobel Committee, ladies and gentlemen:

Today, in Afghanistan, a girl will be born. Her mother will hold her and feed her, comfort her and care for her—just as any mother would anywhere in the world. In these most basic acts of human nature, humanity knows no divisions. But to be born a girl in today's Afghanistan is to begin life centuries away from the prosperity that one small part of humanity has achieved. It is to live under conditions that many of us in this hall would consider inhuman.

I speak of a girl in Afghanistan, but I might equally well have mentioned a baby boy or girl in Sierra Leone. No one today is unaware of this divide between the world's rich and poor. No one today can claim ignorance of the cost that this divide imposes on the poor and dispossessed who are no less deserving of human dignity, fundamental freedoms, security, food, and education than any of us. The cost, however, is not borne by them alone. Ultimately it is borne by all of us—North and South, rich and poor, men and women of all races and religions.

Today's real borders are not between nations, but between powerful and powerless, free and fettered, privileged and humiliated. Today no walls can separate humanitarian or human rights crises in one part of the world from national security crises in another.

Scientists tell us that the world of nature is so small and interdependent that a butterfly flapping its wings in the Amazon rain forest can generate a violent storm on the other side of the earth. This principle is known as the "butterfly effect." Today we realize, perhaps more than ever, that the world of human activity also has its own "butterfly effect"—for better or for worse.

Ladies and gentlemen, we have entered the third millennium through a gate of fire. If today, after the horror of 11 September, we see better, and we see further—we will realize that humanity is indivisible. New threats make no distinction between races, nations, or regions. A new insecurity has entered every mind, regardless of wealth or status. A deeper awareness of the bonds that bind us all—in pain as in prosperity—has gripped young and old.

In the early beginnings of the twenty-first century—a century already violently disabused of any hopes that progress towards global peace and prosperity is inevitable— this new reality can no longer be ignored. It must be confronted.

The twentieth century was perhaps the deadliest in human history, devastated by innumerable conflicts, untold suffering, and unimaginable crimes. Time after time, a group or a nation inflicted extreme violence on another, often driven by irrational hatred and suspicion, or unbounded arrogance and thirst for power and resources. In response to these cataclysms, the leaders of the world came together at midcentury to unite the nations as never before.

A forum was created—the United Nations—where all nations could join forces to affirm the dignity and worth of every person, and to secure peace and development for all peoples. Here states could unite to strengthen the rule of law, recognize and address the needs of the poor, restrain man's brutality and greed, conserve the resources and beauty of nature, sustain the equal rights of men and women, and provide for the safety of future generations.

We thus inherit from the twentieth century the political, as well as the scientific and technological power, which—if only we have the will to use them—give us the chance to vanquish poverty, ignorance, and disease.

In the twenty-first century I believe the mission of the United Nations will be defined by a new, more profound, awareness of the sanctity and dignity of every human life, regardless of race or religion. This will require us to look beyond the framework of states, and beneath the surface of nations or communities. We must focus, as never before, on improving the conditions of the individual men and women who give the state or nation its richness and character. We must begin with the young Afghan girl, recognizing that saving that one life is to save humanity itself.

Over the past five years, I have often recalled that the United Nations' Charter begins with the words "We the peoples." What is not always recognized is that "we the peoples" are made up of individuals whose claims to the most fundamental rights have too often been sacrificed in the supposed interests of the state or the nation.

A genocide begins with the killing of one man—not for what he has done, but because of who he is. A campaign of "ethnic cleansing" begins with one neighbor turning on another. Poverty begins when even one child is denied his or her fundamental right to education. What begins with the failure to uphold the dignity of one life, all too often ends with a calamity for entire nations.

In this new century, we must start from the understanding that peace belongs not only to states or peoples, but to each and every member of those communities. The sovereignty of states must no longer be used as a shield for gross violations of human rights. Peace must be made real and tangible in the daily existence of every individual in need. Peace must be sought, above all, because it is the condition for every member of the human family to live a life of dignity and security.

The rights of the individual are of no less importance to immigrants and minorities in Europe and the Americas than to women in Afghanistan or children in Africa. They are as fundamental to the poor as to the rich; they are as necessary to the security of the developed world as to that of the developing world. From this vision of the role of the United Nations in the next century flow three key priorities for the future: eradicating poverty, preventing conflict, and promoting democracy. Only in a world that is rid of poverty can all men and women make the most of their abilities. Only where individual rights are respected can differences be channeled politically and resolved peacefully. Only in a democratic environment, based on respect for diversity and dialogue, can individual self-expression and self-government be secured, and freedom of association be upheld. Throughout my term as secretary-general, I have sought to place human beings at the center of everything we do—from conflict prevention to development to human rights. Securing real and lasting improvement in the lives of individual men and women is the measure of all we do at the United Nations.

It is in this spirit that I humbly accept the Centennial Nobel Peace Prize. Forty years ago today, the prize for 1961 was awarded for the first time to a secretary-general of the United Nations—posthumously, because Dag Hammarskjöld had already given his life for peace in central Africa. And on the same day, the prize for 1960 was awarded for the first time to an African—Albert Lutuli, one of the earliest leaders of the struggle against apartheid in South Africa. For me, as a young African beginning his career in the United Nations a few months later, those two men set a standard that I have sought to follow throughout my working life.

This award belongs not just to me. I do not stand here alone. On behalf of all my colleagues in every part of the United Nations, in every corner of the globe, who have devoted their lives—and in many instances risked or given their lives in the cause of peace—I thank the members of the Nobel Committee for this high honor. My own path to service at the United Nations was made possible by the sacrifice and commitment of my family and many friends from all continents—some of whom have passed away—who taught me and guided me. To them, I offer my most profound gratitude.

In a world filled with weapons of war and all too often words of war, the Nobel Committee has become a vital agent for peace. Sadly, a prize for peace is a rarity in this world. Most nations have monuments or memorials to war, bronze salutations to heroic battles, archways of triumph. But peace has no parade, no pantheon of victory. What it does have is the Nobel Prize—a statement of hope and courage with unique resonance and authority. Only by understanding and addressing the needs of individuals for peace, for dignity, and for security can we at the United Nations hope to live up to the honor conferred today, and fulfill the vision of our founders. This is the broad mission of peace that United Nations staff members carry out every day in every part of the world. A few of them, women and men, are with us in this hall today. Among them, for instance, are a military observer from Senegal who is helping to provide basic security in the Democratic Republic of the Congo; a civilian police adviser from the United States who is helping to improve the rule of law in Kosovo; a UNICEF child protection officer from Ecuador who is helping to secure the rights of Colombia's most vulnerable citizens; and a World Food Program Officer from China who is helping to feed the people of North Korea. Distinguished guests, the idea that there is one people in possession of the truth, one answer to the world's ills, or one solution to humanity's needs, has done untold harm throughout history—especially in the last century. Today, however, even amidst continuing ethnic conflict around the world, there is a growing understanding that human diversity is both the reality that makes dialogue necessary, and the very basis for that dialogue.

We understand, as never before, that each of us is fully worthy of the respect and dignity essential to our common humanity. We recognize that we are the products of many cultures, traditions, and memories; that mutual respect allows us to study and learn from other cultures; and that we gain strength by combining the foreign with the familiar. In every great faith and tradition one can find the values of tolerance and mutual understanding. The Qur'an, for example, tells us that "We created you from a single pair of male and female and made you into nations and tribes, that you may know each other." Confucius urged his followers: "When the good way prevails in the state, speak boldly and act boldly. When the state has lost the way, act boldly and speak softly." In the Jewish tradition, the injunction to "love thy neighbor as thyself" is considered to be the very essence of the Torah. This thought is reflected in the Christian Gospel, which also teaches us to love our enemies and pray for those who wish to persecute us. Hindus are taught that "truth is one, the sages give it various names." And in the Buddhist tradition, individuals are urged to act with compassion in every facet of life. Each of us has the right to take pride in our particular faith or heritage. But the notion that what is ours is necessarily in conflict with what is theirs is both false and dangerous. It has resulted in endless enmity and conflict, leading men to commit the greatest of crimes in the name of a higher power.

It need not be so. People of different religions and cultures live side by side in almost every part of the world, and most of us have overlapping identities which unite us with very different groups. We can love what we are, without hating what—and who—we are not. We can thrive in our own tradition, even as we learn from others, and come to respect their teachings.

This will not be possible, however, without freedom of religion, of expression, of assembly, and basic equality under the law. Indeed, the lesson of the past century has been that where the dignity of the individual has been trampled or threatened—where citizens have not enjoyed the basic right to choose their government, or the right to change it regularly—conflict has too often followed, with innocent civilians paying the price, in lives cut short and communities destroyed.

The obstacles to democracy have little to do with culture or religion, and much more to do with the desire of those in power to maintain their position at any cost. This is neither a new phenomenon nor one confined to any particular part of the world. People of all cultures value their freedom of choice, and feel the need to have a say in decisions affecting their lives.

The United Nations, whose membership comprises almost all the states in the world, is founded on the principle of the equal worth of every human being. It is the nearest thing we have to a representative institution that can address the interests of all states and all peoples. Through this universal, indispensable instrument of human progress, states can serve the interests of their citizens by recognizing common interests and pursuing them in unity. No doubt, that is why the Nobel Committee says that it "wishes, in its centenary year, to proclaim that the only negotiable route to global peace and cooperation goes by way of the United Nations." I believe the committee also recognized that this era of global challenges leaves no choice but cooperation at the global level. When states undermine the rule of law and violate the rights of their individual citizens, they become a menace not only to their own people, but also to their neighbors, and indeed the world. What we need today is better governance—legitimate, democratic governance that allows each individual to flourish, and each state to thrive.

Your Majesties, Excellencies, ladies and gentlemen, you will recall that I began my address with a reference to the girl born in Afghanistan today. Even though her mother will do all in her power to protect and sustain her, there is a one-in-four risk that she will not live to see her fifth birthday. Whether she does is just one test of our common humanity—of our belief in our individual responsibility for our fellow men and women. But it is the only test that matters. Remember this girl and then our larger aims—to fight poverty, prevent conflict, or cure disease—will not seem distant, or impossible. Indeed, those aims will seem very near, and very achievable—as they should. Because beneath the surface of states and nations, ideas and language, lies the fate of individual human beings in need. Answering their needs will be the mission of the United Nations in the century to come.

Thank you very much.

CHRONOLOGY

1938

April 8   Kofi Atta Annan is born in Kumasi, Ghana, to Henry Reginald and Victoria Annan. He is named Kofi because it is a Friday and Atta because he is a twin. Henry Reginald is a manager for the multinational corporation Unilever.

1953

Kofi enters Mfantsipim, an elite boarding school founded by British missionaries. The headmaster is a Ghanian, Francis Bartels, who is a friend of Kofi's father.

1957

March 6   Ghana, the former British colony known as the Gold Coast, becomes independent, the first colony in tropical Africa to do so. Kwame Nkrumah is prime minister and later president.

Kofi enters the Kumasi Institute of Science and Technology and studies economics there.

1958

Annan is elected vice president of the Ghana national students' union.

1959

Annan enters Macalester College in St. Paul, Minnesota, as a junior. His education there is sponsored and paid for by the Ford Foundation.

1961

Annan graduates from Macalester.

Annan enters the Institut Universitaire des Hauts Études in Geneva under a grant from the Carnegie Endowment.

1962

Annan joins the World Health Organization as an administrative and budget officer. His rank is P1, the lowest in the UN system.

1965

May   Annan and Titi Alakija, a Nigerian, marry at Holy Trinity Anglican Church in Geneva.

September   Annan is assigned to Addis Ababa, Ethiopia, as an administrative officer in the personnel section of the UN Economic Commission for Africa.

1966

February 24   Nkrumah is overthrown in a military coup.

1968

April   Annan is named special assistant to the head of administration of the Economic Commission for Africa.

November   Annan goes to New York for a year's special training at UN headquarters.

1969

October   Annan is named acting chief of the Economic Commission's personnel section.

November   Ama, the daughter of Kofi and Titi, is born in Lagos, Nigeria, the home of Titi's family.

1970

June   Annan is promoted to chief of the Economic Commission's personnel section.

1971

June   Annan takes sabbatical leave to attend Massachusetts Institute of Technology on an Alfred Sloan fellowship.

1972

January 13   A second military coup in Ghana overthrows the civilian government that was installed after the first coup. Lieutenant Colonel Ignatius Kutu Acheampong (later a general) rules the country for more than six years.

June   Annan receives an M.S. in Management from the Massachusetts Institute of Technology. He returns to Addis Ababa.

August   Annan is assigned to Geneva as an administrative management officer.

1973

July   Kojo, the son of Kofi and Titi, is born in Geneva.

1974

May   Annan is assigned to UN Emergency Force in Egypt, with headquarters in Cairo and later Ismailia, as chief personnel officer for civilians working with the UN peacekeeping mission there.

November   Annan leaves the UN and takes a position in Ghana as managing director of the Ghana Tourist Agency.

1976

September   Annan returns to the UN as a personnel officer in New York.

1978

September 1   Annan serves as deputy chief of staff services in the office of personnel services of the UN in New York.

1980

August 1   Annan is appointed head of personnel of the office of the UN High Commissioner for Refugees (UNHCR) in Geneva.

Annan and Titi separate.

1981

Annan meets Nane Lagergren, a Swedish lawyer who is also working for the UNHCR.

1983

April 1   Annan is named director of administrative management of the UN in New York.

September 1   Annan is named director of the office of the undersecretary-general for administration and management.

Annan and Titi are divorced.

1984

January 9   Annan is named director of the budget division of the office of financial services.

September 10   Annan and Nane are married at the Church Center for the United Nations in New York.

1987

February 1   Secretary-General Javier Pérez de Cuéllar appoints Annan the assistant secretary-general in charge of human resources.

1990

August 2   President Saddam Hussein of Iraq sends his troops across the border to invade and seize Kuwait.

September 1   Pérez de Cuéllar appoints Annan the assistant secretary-general in charge of program planning, budget, and finance, and the controller of the UN.

September   Pérez de Cuéllar sends his chief of staff, Viendra Dayal, and Annan to Iraq to negotiate the release of UN staff people held as hostages. The UN staffers are released. Annan also arranges an airlift of several hundred thousand Asian and African workers out of Iraq.

1991

January 17   Bombing of Baghdad begins as the United States leads a coalition in a successful war to oust Iraqi troops from Kuwait. The war ends on February 27. The Security Council imposes a harsh peace on Iraq, keeping sanctions in place until it eliminates all weapons of mass destruction. UN inspectors are assigned to make sure this disarmament is carried out.

1992

January   Boutros Boutros-Ghali of Egypt assumes office as the sixth secretary-general of the UN.

January   Annan heads a team of UN negotiators trying to negotiate an agreement with the Iraqis for an oil for food program. Tariq Aziz heads the Iraqi delegation. The talks fail.

February   After Bosnia votes to secede from Yugoslavia, Serbian troops join Bosnian Serbs in civil war against the Bosnian Muslims. Serbs engage in bloody "ethnic cleansing" of Muslim areas of Bosnia. The UN sends peacekeepers to protect relief convoys in Bosnia.

March   Annan, still holding the rank of assistant secretary-general, is named deputy chief of the department of peacekeeping operations.

December   President George H. W. Bush, under UN authority, sends American troops into Somalia to avert a humanitarian catastrophe there.

1993

February   Boutros-Ghali promotes Annan to undersecretary-general in charge of peacekeeping operations.

October 3–4   Eighteen Americans die and two Black Hawk helicopters are downed in Mogadishu in a UN firefight with a warlord. President Clinton announces that he will withdraw American troops from Somalia within five months.

1994

January 11   General Roméo Dallaire, chief of the peacekeepers in Rwanda, sends a cable to a fellow Canadian, General Maurice Baril in New York, warning of Hutu extremist plans to exterminate Tutsis. Reply from New York, written by Iqbal Riza and approved by Annan, asks Dallaire to inform President Habyarimana in hopes that he will regard the message as a warning to halt extremist plans.

April 6   President Habyarimana and the Burundi president die when their plane is shot down by rockets. Hutu militants go on a rampage, beginning killings that lead to several hundred thousand Tutsi deaths.

May 17   The Security Council authorizes a force of fifty-five hundred to be assembled, after a two-week delay, and sent to Rwanda to quell the killings. But governments never volunteer enough troops to fill the force.

July   France launches Operation Turquoise and leads French and Senegalese troops into Rwanda to prevent further killing. This is resented by General Paul Kagame and his rebel Tutsi army, since he has already taken control of most of the country.

1995

July   The Bosnia crisis reaches a climax with the massacre of several thousand Bosnian men after Serbs overrun the UN safe area of Srebrenica. The atrocity galvanizes the United States and European powers into a change in strategy. NATO bombing of Serb forces is unleashed.

November   Richard Holbrooke brokers an agreement at Wright-Patterson Air Force Base in Dayton, Ohio, that ends the Bosnian war.

November   Boutros-Ghali sends Annan to the former Yugoslavia as the secretary-general's special representative in charge of the missions to Croatia and Bosnia.

1996

April   Annan returns to his position as undersecretary-general in charge of peacekeeping.

May 20   Iraq agrees to an oil for food program; the agreement is signed by Boutros-Ghali and Iraqis.

November 19   American ambassador Madeleine Albright vetoes the bid of Boutros-Ghali for a second term as secretary-general. The vote in the Security Council is fourteen to one in his favor.

November   The Security Council authorizes a Canadian-led force to protect Hutu refugees in the eastern Congo from the Tutsi army of Kagame, but the force is never dispatched after the United States claims refugees have returned to Rwanda. UNHCR and other humanitarian sources insist the United States is mistaken.

December 13   After France withdraws its objection, the Security Council nominates Kofi Annan of Ghana as the seventh secretary-general of the UN.

1997

January 2   Annan assumes the post of secretary-general. The General Assembly agrees to his proposal to create a new position of deputy secretary-general to strengthen UN management. Louise Frechette of Canada is named to the position.

April   The new secretary-general issues a report on Africa. He tells Africans to stop blaming their ills on colonialism. Africa must look at itself, he says.

May   Laurent Kabila takes over Zaire (soon to be the Congo again) and prevents UN investigation of massacres during the war.

July   Annan calls on the Organization of African Unity to stop tolerating governments that come to power through military coups.

July   Annan appoints Richard Butler of Australia as the chief inspector searching for weapons of mass destruction in Iraq.

October   Iraq proclaims that it will no longer allow Americans on inspection teams to enter the country. A crisis is avoided when the Russians persuade Iraq to back down.

1998

January   Iraq announces that it will not allow inspections of presidential palaces. The United States threatens to bomb Iraq.

February 20   Secretary-General Annan arrives in Baghdad to discuss inspection issues with Saddam Hussein. After meeting with Saddam, Annan signs an agreement with Tariq Aziz that allow inspections. The United States calls off the bombing.

May   While traveling in Africa, Annan receives word of the first *New Yorker* article criticizing his role in Rwanda. He addresses the Rwandan parliament and angers Rwandan politicians by saying that the 1994 horror in Rwanda "came from within."

June   Annan delivers a lecture at Ditchley Park, Britain, in which he makes the case for UN intervention into a country if that is the only way to protect people from repression by their government.

October   The Annan agreement with Iraq collapses. Iraq announces it will no longer allow any UN inspections.

November   The *New Yorker* publishes an article by Philip Gourevitch quoting from a 1994 cable sent by Annan's office to General Dallaire in Rwanda. The article criticizes Annan for failing to raise the alarm. But Annan insists that raising the alarm would not have accomplished anything.

December 16   American and British planes bomb Iraqi military installations.

1999

January   The UN Secretariat investigates news reports that Kojo Annan, son of the secretary-general, worked for the Swiss firm Cotecna when it received a contract in the oil for food program. The investigation is perfunctory; Kojo says he severed ties with the company earlier. Staff concludes there was nothing wrong.

March 24   NATO begins bombing of Serbia to halt repression of Albanians in the Serbian province of Kosovo. Annan says that NATO should have sought Security Council approval. But his statement is regarded by NATO as tacit approval. The bombings last eighty-three days before Serbia gives in to NATO demands.

August 30   East Timor votes for independence from Indonesia. After the referendum, militias of young toughs, allied with the Indonesian military, kill several hundred East Timorese.

September 12   President Habibie of Indonesia agrees to Annan request that he allow UN peacekeepers to land in East Timor and restore order.

November 15   Annan issues a report on Srebrenica, laying bare the details of the massacre and assigning blame to both the UN Secretariat and members of the UN Security Council.

December 15   An independent commission issues a report on killings in Rwanda, blaming both the UN Secretariat and members of the UN Security Council.

2000

August   Lakhdar Brahimi, a UN official and former Algerian foreign minister, issues a report on UN peacekeeping. He calls for better-equipped forces with authority to intervene and prevent killings when necessary.

September   World leaders attend UN Millennium Summit in New York and adopt Millennium Development Goals, an extensive program to reduce poverty and hunger in the world and accelerate economic and social development.

2001

June   The Security Council unanimously agrees to select Annan for a second five-year term as secretary-general.

September 11   Al-Qaeda terrorists hijack four commercial airlines. They fly two into the World Trade Center in New York, destroying both of the twin towers. A third plane crashes into the Pentagon, near Washington, D.C., damaging a section. In all, more than three thousand die.

September 12   The Security Council passes a resolution condemning violence and confirming the U.S. right to attack al-Qaeda in self-defense.

October 12   The Norwegian Nobel Committee announces that Kofi Annan and the UN will share the 2001 Nobel Peace Prize.

December 10   Annan receives the Nobel Peace Prize in Oslo, Norway.

2002

May   With secretary-general Annan looking on, East Timor becomes an independent and sovereign state.

September 12   Both Annan and President George W. Bush address the UN General Assembly. Bush insists that the UN will become irrelevant if it allows Iraq to continue defying resolutions that prohibit weapons of mass destruction.

November 8   Security Council unanimously passes Resolution 1441, demanding that Iraq readmit inspectors and that it rid itself of all weapons of mass destruction. Annan persuades Iraqis to allow inspections headed by Hans Blix and Mohamed ElBaradei.

2003

February 5   In a televised briefing of the Security Council, Secretary of State Colin Powell lays out the American evidence that Iraq still maintains a program of weapons of mass destruction. The evidence is later proven incorrect.

March 17   After the United States fails to persuade the Security Council to pass a resolution authorizing an invasion of Iraq and despite pleas by others to allow more time for inspections, President Bush addresses the nation and threatens war if Saddam Hussein does not flee Iraq within forty-eight hours.

March 19   American bombing of Iraq begins, followed by an American-led invasion.

April   As war unfolds, both President Bush and British prime minister Tony Blair promise that the UN will have a vital role in the rehabilitation of Iraq. Having failed to prevent the war, Annan suffers from a bout of melancholia. He loses his voice and appears listless at some meetings.

May   The Security Council passes a resolution accepting U.S.-British occupation of Iraq and laying a role for UN in the reconstruction. Annan sends a mission, headed by Sérgio Vieira de Mello of Brazil to Iraq. Meanwhile, American officials report that they are unable to find any weapons of mass destruction.

June   Iraqi politician Ahmad Chalabi warns Edward Mortimer, Annan's chief speechwriter, that he is going to start a campaign against the UN because it allowed Saddam Hussein to accumulate profits in the oil for food program.

July 23   With UN help, Americans select twenty-five Iraqis to form the Governing Council.

August 19   A suicide car bomber attacks UN headquarters in Baghdad, killing de Mello and twenty-one others.

September 22   A second bombing of headquarters kills one UN guard and two Iraqi police. Annan still keeps a reduced mission in Baghdad.

October 20   A panel led by former Finnish president Martti Ahtisaari issues a report on UN security in Baghdad. The report cites UN failure to provide enough security for its staff. Annan pulls out all UN staff.

2004

January 19   Ambassador L. Paul Bremer III, the head of the Coalition Provisional Authority in Iraq, comes to New York and pleads with Secretary-General Annan to send a UN team to Iraq to persuade Grand Ayatollah Ali el-Sistani that there is no time to hold elections in July for a provisional government. El-Sistani, who has refused to meet with Bremer, says he will only accept a UN decision on this.

February Annan sends Brahimi to Iraq. Brahimi meets with the grand ayatollah. Brahimi agrees with the Americans that there is not enough time for elections but sides with el-Sistani's rejection of an American plan for caucuses. Brahimi promises to help select a provisional government after consultations with numerous Iraqis. The UN official makes three trips to Iraq for consultations.

April American marines begin an assault on Fallujah, an insurgent stronghold in a Sunni area of Iraq. Fearing great loss of civilian life, Brahimi warns he will abandon his mission if the attack continues. The Americans halt the attack.

June Brahimi announces the makeup of the interim Iraqi cabinet. The prime minister is Dr. Ayad Allawi, who was championed by the Americans.

September Annan tells a BBC interviewer that he regards the American-led invasion of Iraq as "illegal." The remark angers the Bush administration. Republicans accuse Annan of trying to influence the American presidential election.

October 31 Annan sends letters to leaders of the United States, Britain, and Iraq, asking that they call off another assault on Fallujah. The letter angers the Bush administration. Republicans again accuse Annan of trying to influence the election. No leader replies to the letter.

November 2 Bush is reelected U.S. president.

November 25 Annan cuts short his visit to a conference in Ouagadougou as a mood of melancholia overtakes him once more. He loses his voice occasionally as well. Senior staff meets with Annan at the apartment of Deputy Secretary-General Frechette in hopes of reviving his spirits. A few days later, Annan meets with outside foreign policy specialists at the home of former UN ambassador Richard Holbrooke. Annan makes several personnel changes; the most important is the appointment of Mark Malloch Brown of Britain as chief of staff.

December 1   Senator Norman Coleman, Republican of Minnesota, writes an article in the *Wall Street Journal* calling for Annan's resignation because of the oil for food scandal.

December 21   Annan tells news conference, "I am relieved this annus horribilis is coming to an end."

December 26   A catastrophic tsunami strikes Southeast Asia. The death toll will reach more than two hundred thousand.

2005

March 3   Annan sends his report "In Larger Freedom: Towards Development, Security, and Human Rights for All" to the General Assembly. In the report, he calls for creation of a new Human Rights Council and for a one-billion-dollar fund for use in relief of victims in sudden disasters like the tsunami that racked Southeast Asia. He also calls for expansion of the Security Council to make it "more broadly representative of the international community as a whole, as well as of the geopolitical realities of today," but he does not recommend any specific new alignment.

March 29   In an interim report, the Volcker commission says that Kojo Annan, the son of the secretary-general, hid his relationship with Cotecna, a Swiss company that won a contract in the oil for food program in 1998. The commission found no evidence that the secretary-general used his influence to help Cotecna win the contract.

August   John R. Bolton assumes his position as U.S. ambassador to the UN. After opposition mounted in the Senate to his nomination, President Bush circumvented the Senate and appointed Bolton while Congress was out of session.

September 7   In its final report, the Volcker commission accuses Annan of a substandard performance in monitoring the oil for food program. But the commission also states that most of Saddam Hussein's illicit profits came from oil smuggling, much of it condoned by the United States, and not from the oil for food program.

December 21   Annan loses his temper at a British reporter's persistent questions about Kojo.

2006

March 3   Annan appoints Mark Malloch Brown of Britain as deputy secretary-general.

March 7   Annan asks the General Assembly to approve an extensive reform program that would shake up personnel practices at the UN. He calls for increased pay for overseas staffers, buyouts of a thousand staff people, and the outsourcing of translations and other activities.

March 15   The General Assembly approves establishment of a new Human Rights Council by a vote of 170 to 4. Only the United States, Israel, the Marshall Islands, and Palau vote against.

May   After a fragile peace agreement is signed, the Security Council votes for UN peacekeepers to take over policing of the Darfur area in Sudan from African Union troops in a few months.

June 6   In a speech, Deputy Secretary-General Malloch Brown accuses the Bush administration of undermining the United Nations by tolerating "too much unchecked UN-bashing and stereotyping." U.S. ambassador John R. Bolton phones Annan and tells him, "I've known you since 1989, and I'm telling you this is the worst mistake by a senior UN official that I have seen in that entire time." But the secretary-general supports the views of his deputy.

July 17   After almost a week of increasing violence in the Middle East, Annan joins British prime minister Tony Blair in proposing an international "stabilization force" in southern Lebanon to prevent the extremist Shia militia Hezbollah from raiding and rocketing Israel. Hezbollah's capture of two soldiers and killing of three others in a raid into Israel triggered wave after wave of Israeli retaliatory air raids in Lebanon; these, in turn, triggered Hezbollah rocket counterattacks on Israeli cities. The Annan-Blair proposal receives a tepid reception from President Bush because the force would arrive after negotiation of a cease-fire. Showing annoyance at Annan for trying to persuade Israel and Hezbollah to agree to a cease-fire, Bush says that Annan should instead put pressure on Syria, a patron of Hezbollah. "What they need to do is get Syria to get Hezbollah to stop doing this shit, and it's over," he tells Blair at a luncheon at the Group of Eight summit in St. Petersburg, Russia. The president did not realize the microphone was on while he spoke to Blair.

August 11   The Security Council unanimously passes a resolution that calls for a cease-fire in the Israeli-Lebanon conflict and authorizes a force of up to fifteen thousand UN peacekeepers to join the Lebanon Army in patrolling southern Lebanon. Lebanon and Israel accept the cease-fire, and Israel promises to withdraw from southern Lebanon when peacekeepers arrive.

December 31   The second term of Annan, now sixty-eight, ends.

1. Ghana and America

Any quotations from Kofi Annan in this book that are not found in the cited sources come from my interviews and conversations with him on various occasions from the early 1990s onward. Quotations from other persons that are not found in the cited sources come from my interviews, phone conversations, or e-mail and fax exchanges with them.

Brief biographical sketches of the secretary-general can be found on the Web sites of the UN (www.un.org), the Global Policy Forum (www.globalpolicy.org), and the Public Broadcasting Service (www.pbs.org); I have depended on them throughout the book for basic facts such as dates, schooling, and positions. More specific details have come from the office of the spokesman of the secretary-general.

The quotation from *Time* magazine comes from "Sunrise on the Gold Coast"— the *Time* cover story for February 9, 1953. The Peace Corps incident comes from Elizabeth Cobbs Hoffman, *All You Need Is Love: The Peace Corps and the Spirit of the 1960s* (Cambridge, Mass.: Harvard University Press, 1998), pp. 157–158.

The quote about being atribal was cited in James Traub, "Kofi Annan's Next Test," *New York Times Magazine*, March 29, 1998. The Annan family photograph is among the illustrations in this book. The family proverb about not hitting a man on the head comes from a Q & A session with Ponchitta Pierce in *AARP* magazine, January–February 2003. The incidents about his father's mock trials and about the underling putting a cigarette in his pocket come from Joseph Cooper Ramo, "The Five Virtues of Kofi Annan," *Time*, September 4, 2000. Annan discusses his early life in Ghana in Thomas G. Weiss, Tatiana Carayannis, Louis Emmerij, and Richard Jolly, *UN Voices: The Struggle for Development and Social Justice* (Bloomington: Indiana University Press, UN Intellectual History Project Series, 2005).

For background on Kwame Nkrumah's Ghana I have consulted David Apter, *The Gold Coast in Transition* (Princeton, N.J.: Princeton University Press, 1959) and Irving Lee Markovitz, "Ghana without Nkrumah: The Winter of Discontent," in Markovitz, ed., *African Politics and Society* (New York: Free Press, 1970). The articles on Ghana and Nkrumah in John Middleton, ed., *Encyclopedia of Africa South of the Sahara* (New York: Scribner's, 1997) were useful. I also spent several days in Nkrumah's Ghana in 1962 and reported on it for the *Atlantic*, November 1962.

Kofi Annan recounted the black-dot story in his foreword to *The Persistence of Paradox: Memoirs of F. L. Bartels* (Accra: Ghana Universities Press, 2003). There is a different version of the black-dot story on www.mfantsipim.com. Bartels's quote about Nkrumah as Hitler is on p. 186 of his memoirs.

The earmuffs story has been recounted many times in profiles. I used it in my profile "Man in the Middle: Travels with Kofi Annan" in the January 2003 issue of the *Smithsonian* magazine. The tape recording of his speech at the college convocation can be heard on the Macalester Web site, www.macalester.edu. A December 9, 2001, article in the *Minneapolis Star Tribune*, "From Macalester to U.N. to Nobel Prize," by Donna Halvorsen, provided details about the car trip through the United States.

For this chapter I also consulted Philip Gourevitch, "The Optimist," a profile in the *New Yorker*, March 3, 2003.

2. Through the UN System

Friederike Bauer describes and quotes Titi Alakija in *Kofi Annan: Ein Leben* (Frankfurt: S. Fischer, 2005).

Annan's 1997 MIT commencement address can be found on www.mit.edu.

There are two useful profiles of Nane Annan, one by Evelyn Leopold distributed by Reuters, January 7, 1997, and the other by James Bone, published in the *Times* of London, February 28, 1998. Thora Klinckowström's account of meeting Modigliani can be found in William Fifield's biography *Modigliani* (New York: William Morrow, 1976). Nane's use of the word "thunderbolt" to describe her meeting with Annan is in Joseph Cooper Ramo, "The Five Virtues of Kofi Annan," *Time*, September 4, 2000. Annan's quotes about punctuality come from Barbara Crossette, "How UN Chief Discovered US, and Earmuffs," *New York Times*, January 7, 1997.

The no-wave quote about Pérez de Cuéllar can be found in Rosemary Righter, *Utopia Lost: The United Nations and World Order* (New York: Twentieth Century Fund, 1995).

I also consulted Giandomenico Picco, *Man without a Gun* (New York: Times Books, 1999); the article on Ghana in John Middleton, ed., *Encyclopedia of Africa South of the Sahara* (New York: Scribner's, 1997); Meryl Gordon, "No Peace for Kofi: A Father's Burden," *New York* magazine, May 2, 2005; Philip Gourevitch, "The Optimist," a profile in the *New Yorker*, March 3, 2003, and the Fred Eckhard interview in the Yale-UN Oral History Project.

I visited and studied Ethiopia often as a Peace Corps official in the 1960s and as the Africa correspondent of the *Los Angeles Times* in the late 1960s and early 1970s.

3. The Grand Illusion of the First Persian Gulf War

For the Iraqi hostage crisis I have depended on Joseph Wilson, *The Politics of Truth* (New York: Carroll & Graf, 2005); *The United Nations and the Iraq-Kuwait Conflict 1990–1996* (United Nations, 1996), part of the UN Blue Book series; Phyllis Bennis, *Calling the Shots: How Washington Dominates Today's UN* (New York: Olive Branch Press, 1996); Michael R. Gordon and Bernard E. Trainor, *The Generals' War: The Inside Story of the Conflict in the Gulf* (Boston: Little, Brown, 1995); *U.S. News & World Report* staff, *Triumph without Victory: The History of the Persian Gulf War* (New York: Times Books, 1993); and James Traub, "Kofi Annan's Next Test," *New York Times* Magazine, March 29, 1998.

I discuss the Persian Gulf War in greater detail in my history *United Nations: The First Fifty Years* (New York: Atlantic Monthly Press, 1995).

4. In the Footsteps of Ralph Bunche

Marrack Goulding set down his account of his administration of peace-keeping in his memoir *Peacemonger* (Baltimore: Johns Hopkins University Press, 2003). Brian Urquhart discusses his resignation in his memoir *A Life in Peace and War* (New York: W. W. Norton, 1991). Boutros Boutros-Ghali discusses the Somali crisis and his appointment of Kofi Annan as chief of peacekeeping in *Unvanquished: A U.S.-UN Saga* (New York: Random House, 1999).

I also consulted John L. Hirsch and Robert B. Oakley, *Somalia and Operation Restore Hope* (Washington, D.C.: U.S. Institute of Peace, 1995); *The Blue Helmets: A Review of United Nations Peacekeeping* (United Nations, 1990); CIA, "Putting Noncombatants at Risk: Saddam's Use of 'Human Shields,'" January 2003; Madeleine Albright, *Madame Secretary* (New York: Miramax Books, 2003); and William J. Durch, "Introduction to Anarchy: Humanitarian Intervention and 'State-Building' in Somalia" in Durch, ed., *UN Peacekeeping, American Politics, and the Uncivil Wars of the 1990s* (New York: St. Martin's Press, 1996).

I discuss the Somalia crisis in greater detail in my history *United Nations: The First Fifty Years* (New York: Atlantic Monthly Press, 1995).

5. Peacekeeping

Boutros Boutros-Ghali discusses the Somali crisis in *Unvanquished: A U.S.-UN Saga* (New York: Random House, 1999). Madeleine Albright offers her account in her memoir *Madame Secretary* (New York: Miramax Books, 2003). The issue is covered in great detail by William J. Durch in "Introduction to Anarchy: Humanitarian Intervention and 'State-Building' in Somalia" in Durch, ed., *UN Peacekeeping, American Politics, and the Uncivil Wars of the 1990s* (New York: St. Martin's Press, 1996). The Tharoor quote about peacekeeping as a fire brigade appeared in his article "The Challenge to UN Peacekeeping" in the *Brown Journal of World Affairs*, Winter/Spring 1996. Ahmad Fawzi's account of his conversation with Boutros-Ghali comes from the DVD video, "A Spokesman's Round-table: The United Nations and the Media 1945–2005," produced by the office of the spokesman, 2005.

Annan's remarks to the Princeton conference were covered in my article "UN Relief Hopes Turn to Despair" in the *Los Angeles Times*, October 25, 1993. His remarks in *Le Monde* ran in a story, "Rwanda: '*Comme si nous étions devenus insensibles,'"* in May 25, 1994. The *Los Angeles Times* Q&A interview ran as "Kofi Annan: The Soft-Spoken Economist Who Runs UN Peacekeeping Forces," June 21, 1994. Fred Eckhard's comments on Annan's relationship with reporters are from his interview in the Yale-UN Oral History Project.

I also consulted Linda Fasulo, *An Insider's Guide to the UN* (New Haven, Conn.: Yale University Press, 2004); and John L. Hirsch and Robert B. Oakley, *Somalia and Operation Restore Hope* (Washington, D.C.: U.S. Institute of Peace, 1995).

I covered Somalia for the *Los Angeles Times* in the late 1960s and early 1970s, followed the Somali discussions at the UN as a *Times* correspondent in the 1990s, and traveled to Mogadishu with Secretary-General Boutros Boutros-Ghali in 1993. The Somali crisis is discussed at some length in my book *United Nations: The First Fifty Years* (New York: Atlantic Monthly Press, 1995).

6. The Stain of Rwanda

My sources for this chapter included *Report of the Independent Inquiry into the Actions of the United Nations during the 1994 Genocide in Rwanda,* December 15, 1999 (published by the UN as Security Council Document S/1999/1257); *The United Nations and Rwanda 1993–1996,* UN Blue Book Series, volume X (New York: UN Department of Public Information, 1996); Madeleine Albright, *Madame Secretary* (New York: Miramax Books, 2003); Roméo Dallaire, *Shake Hands with the Devil: The Failure of Humanity in Rwanda* (New York: Carroll & Graf, 2003); René Lemarchand's article on Rwanda in John Middleton, ed., *Encyclopedia of Africa South of the Sahara* (New York: Scribner's, 1997); Philip Gourevitch, "The Genocide Fax," *New Yorker,* May 11, 1998; Gourevitch, "The Congo Test," *New Yorker,* June 2, 2003; Gourevitch, "The Optimist," a profile in the *New Yorker,* March 3, 2003; and Howard French, *A Continent for the Taking: The Tragedy and Hope of Africa* (New York: Alfred A. Knopf, 2004).

Kofi Annan's news conference in Nairobi in 1998 is quoted in William Shawcross, *Deliver Us from Evil: Peacekeepers, Warlords, and a World of Endless Conflict* (New York: Simon & Schuster, 2000) and in an article, "UN Chief Denies New Rwanda Charges," in the *New York Times,* May 5, 1998. The *Frontline* quotes of Annan and Madeleine Albright can be found on the Web site www.pbs.org. The PBS Web site also reproduces the

two key cables between General Dallaire and the Peacekeeping department in New York. Annan's quotes about his inability to persuade governments to offer peacekeepers can be found in Bassir Pour Afsane, "Rwanda:
'*Comme si nous étions devenus insensibles,*'" *Le Monde*, May 25, 1994.

The Nat Hentoff quotes came from "Time for Kofi Annan to Go,"
Washington Times, April 30, 2001. The letter from Rwandan survivors
blaming Annan was reported by Reuters, May 8, 1988, and reproduced on
the Global Policy Forum Web site, www.globalpolicy.org.

As a *Los Angeles Times* correspondent, I covered the massacre of Hutus
in Burundi in 1972 and the UN deliberations on Rwanda in 1994. I summarized my conclusions on the Burundi massacres in "Holocaust in
Burundi, 1972" in Willem A. Veenhoven, ed., *Case Studies on Human Rights
and Fundamental Freedoms* (The Hague: Martinus Nijhoff, 1976) and in
my report on "Rwanda and Burundi" in the *Atlantic*, September 1973.

7. Charade over Bosnia

My main sources for the chapter are William Shawcross, *Deliver Us from
Evil: Peacekeepers, Warlords, and a World of Endless Conflict* (New York:
Simon & Schuster, 2000), Richard Holbrooke, *To End a War* (New York:
Modern Library, 1999), and Kofi Annan, *Report of the Secretary-General
Pursuant to General Assembly Resolution 53/35: The Fall of Srebrenica* (UN
General Assembly, 1999).

Other sources include Boutros Boutros-Ghali, *Unvanquished: A
U.S.-UN Saga* (New York: Random House, 1999); Madeleine Albright,
Madame Secretary (New York: Miramax Books, 2003); William J. Durch
and James A. Schear, "Faultlines: UN Operations in the Former
Yugoslavia," in Durch, ed., *UN Peacekeeping, American Politics and the
Uncivil Wars of the 1990s* (New York: St. Martin's Press, 1996); David Rieff,
Slaughterhouse: Bosnia and the Failure of the West (New York: Touchstone,
1996); Paul Lewis, "UN Visitors Say Srebrenica Is 'an Open Jail,'" *New York
Times*, April 26, 1993; and Barbara Crossette, "A Salesman for Unity: Kofi
Annan," *New York Times*, December 14, 1996.

Jamie Rubin's quote about Annan replacing Akashi can be found in
Christopher S. Wren, "UN Chief Recalls His Envoy in the Balkans as U.S.
Applauds," *New York Times*, October 11, 1995.

I covered the Security Council debates over Bosnia and accompanied
Secretary-General Boutros Boutros-Ghali on his ill-fated New Year's Eve

visit to Sarajevo. There is a summary of UN policy toward Bosnia in my book *United Nations: The First Fifty Years* (New York: Atlantic Monthly Press, 1995).

8. Supplanting Boutros-Ghali

Their own versions of their troubles can be found in Boutros Boutros-Ghali, *Unvanquished: A U.S.-UN Saga* (New York: Random House, 1999) and Madeleine Albright, *Madame Secretary* (New York: Miramax Books, 2003).

My main published sources for the campaign to block Boutros-Ghali and elect Kofi Annan are Linda Fasulo, *An Insider's Guide to the UN* (New Haven, Conn.: Yale University Press, 2004); Hervé Cassan, "*La Vie Quotidienne à L'O.N.U. au Temps de Boutros Boutros-Ghali,*" in *Boutros Boutros-Ghali Amicorum Discipulorumque Liber,* vol. 1 (Brussels: Bruylant, 1998); Richard A. Clarke, *Against All Enemies* (New York: Free Press, 2004); Barbara Crossette's dispatches in the *New York Times* from June 17 through December 14, 1996; Steven Erlanger, "U.S. Will Oppose Move to Reelect Top UN Official," *New York Times,* June 20, 1996; and the dispatches of Afsane Bassir Pour in *Le Monde,* December 12, 1996, through January 4, 1997.

Josh Friedman's quote about Boutros-Ghali and Annan comes from Fred Eckhard, *Speaking for the Secretary-General: A History of the UN Spokesman's Office* (United Nations: Office of the Spokesman, 2005).

The anecdote about Nane Annan hearing the news of her husband's election comes from Evelyn Leopold, "Wife of UN Chief Seeks Her Own Space in New York," Reuters, January 7, 1997, and from the PBS documentary "Kofi Annan: Center of the Storm."

I profiled Boutros Boutros-Ghali in "Dateline UN: A New Hammarskjöld" in *Foreign Policy,* Spring 1955, and discussed the tension between him and Madeleine Albright in "The United States and the United Nations: A Troubled and Dangerous Relationship," in Han Sung-Joo, ed., *The United Nations: The Next Fifty Years* (Seoul: Korea University International Relations Institute, 1996).

9. The New Secretary-General

Sources on the Congo crisis included Howard French, *A Continent for the Taking: The Tragedy and Hope of Africa* (New York: Alfred A. Knopf, 2004) and Sadako Ogata, *The Turbulent Decade: Confronting the Refugee Crises of the 1990s* (New York: W. W. Norton, 2005). Kofi Annan's report to the General Assembly, "The Causes of Conflict and the Promotion of Durable Peace and Sustainable Development in Africa," was issued April 13, 1998, as UN Document A/52/871-S/1998/318. His 1997 speech to the OAU can be found in UN Press Release SG/SM/6245/Rev. 1.

The secretary-general revealed a good deal about his conversations with Saddam Hussein when he was interviewed by William Shawcross and by the Yale-UN Oral History Project. That material can be found in Shawcross, *Deliver Us from Evil: Peacekeepers, Warlords, and a World of Endless Conflict* (New York: Simon & Schuster, 2000), and in Jean E. Krasno and James S. Sutterlin, *The United Nations and Iraq: Defanging the Viper* (Westport, Conn.: Praeger, 2003). Richard Butler gives his views about UN inspections in Iraq in his book *The Greatest Threat: Iraq, Weapons of Mass Destruction, and the Growing Crisis of Global Security* (New York: Public Affairs Press, 2001). The Annan quote about doing business with Saddam can be found in the transcript of the February 24, 1998, news conference, UN Press Release SG/SM/6470.

Other sources on the Iraq crisis included Madeleine Albright, *Madame Secretary* (New York: Miramax Books, 2003); James Traub, "Kofi Annan's Next Test," *New York Times* magazine, March 29, 1998; Michael R. Gordon and Elaine Sciolino, "Fingerprints on Iraqi Accord Belong to Albright," *New York Times*, February 25, 1998; Elaine Sciolino, "Standoff with Iraq: The Diplomacy; Push for Peace Shows Split over Inspections," *New York Times*, February 6, 1998; Elaine Sciolino, "Standoff with Iraq: The UN; For UN Chief, Scarcely Room for Negotiating," *New York Times*, February 19, 1998; Barbara Crossette, "Standoff with Iraq: The Overview; Iraqi Agrees to Inspections in a Deal with UN Leader; Washington Awaits Details," *New York Times*, February 23, 1998; Eric Schmitt, "The Deal on Iraq: The Overview; Top GOP Senator Opposes UN Deal on Iraq Inspection," *New York Times*, February 26, 1998; and Fred Eckhard's interview in the Yale-UN Oral History Project.

10. Intervention: Kosovo and East Timor

Annan's speech to the Rwanda parliament can be found in UN Press Release SG/SM/6552, May 6, 1998. His reception in Rwanda is described in two articles by James C. McKinley Jr. in the *New York Times*, "Annan

Given Cold Shoulder by Officials in Rwanda," May 8, 1998, and "Ugly Reality in Rwanda," May 10, 1998.

The Ditchley lecture can be found in UN Press Release SG/SM/6613, June 26, 1998.

Barbara Crossette's description of Annan's throne as a hollow box comes from "The World: The Power Stops Here; Annan Makes His Bid to Make His Job Count," *New York Times*, March 8, 1998.

The Kosovo crisis is covered at length in William Shawcross, *Deliver Us from Evil: Peacekeepers, Warlords, and a World of Endless Conflict* (New York: Simon & Schuster, 2000) and Madeleine Albright, *Madame Secretary* (New York: Miramax Books, 2003). There is useful material as well in Thomas W. Lippman, *Madeleine Albright and the New American Diplomacy* (Boulder, Colo.: Westview Press, 2000); Judith Miller, "Conflict in the Balkans: The UN; The Secretary General Offers Implicit Endorsement of Raids," *New York Times*, March 26, 1999; Elaine Sciolino and Ethan Bronner, "Crisis in the Balkans: The Road to War—a Special Report: How a President, Distracted by Scandal, Entered Balkan War," *New York Times*, June 16, 1999; Kofi Annan speech to the International Peace Conference, UN Press Release, SG/SM/6997, May 18, 1999; Blaine Harden, "Crisis in the Balkans: Doing the Deal—a special report; A Long Struggle That Led Serb Leader to Back Down," *New York Times*, June 6, 1999.

In the East Timor crisis, Shawcross details some of the phone conversations between President Habibie and Kofi Annan. Other useful sources on East Timor included "East Timor Revisited" on George Washington University's National Security Archive, www.gwu.edu/nsarchiv; "East Timor" in the CIA *World Factbook*, www.cia.gov/cia/publications; "The Talk of the Town," *New Yorker*, December 9, 1991; Seth Mydans, "Fearful of Militias, East Timor to Vote on Its Future," August 29, 1999; "Secretary-General Informs Security Council People of East Timor Rejected Special Autonomy Proposed by Indonesia," UN Press Release SC/6721, September 3, 1999; Kofi Annan press conference, September 3, 1999, UN Press Release SG/SM/7120; Barbara Crossette, "A Push to Intervene in East Timor Is Gathering Backers at the UN," *New York Times*, September 7, 1999; Barbara Crossette, "Annan Warns Indonesians That Inaction May Lead to Criminal Charges," *New York Times*, September 11, 1999; Seth Mydans, "Indonesia Invites a UN Force to Timor," *New York Times*,

September 13, 1999; and Kofi Annan press conference, December 14, 1999, UN Press Release SG/SM/7259.

11. The Nobel Peace Prize

Judith Miller's quote about the marginalized Security Council can be found in "Security Council Relegated to Sidelines," *New York Times*, March 14, 1999.

The Brahimi report is UN document A/55/305-S/2000/809.

Annan's World Series pitch description can be found in "The Yankees Win," a *New York Times* editorial, October 28, 1999. Richardson's praise comes from Barbara Crossette, "Richardson Reflects on His UN Days," *New York Times*, September 8, 1998; Holbrooke's praise is in Christopher S. Wren, "Era Waning, Holbrooke Takes Stock," *New York Times*, January 14, 2001.

Bolton's comments on Annan can be found in Barbara Crossette, "Kofi Unsettles People, As He Believes UN Should Do," *New York Times*, December 31, 1999.

The reelection of Annan is described in UN Press Release GA/9889.

Annan's September 11, 2001, statement is on Press Release SG/SM/7948. His statement to the Security Council the next day is on Press Release SG/SM/7949. The Council reaction and resolution is on Press Release SC/7143. Annan's speech to the General Assembly on September 24, 2001, can be found in UN Press Release SG/SM/7965. His quote about the civilians of Afghanistan comes from Christopher S. Wren, "U.S. Advises UN Council More Strikes Could Come," *New York Times*, October 9, 2001.

Accounts of the award of the Nobel Prize to Annan include Colum Lynch, "Nobel Peace Prize Goes to Annan, UN," *Washington Post*, October 13, 2001, and Serge Schmemann, "Nobel Peace Prize Is Awarded to Annan and UN," *New York Times*, October 13, 2001. Annan's popularity is discussed in Shashi Tharoor, "A Wonderful Wake-up Call," *Hindu*, October 28, 2001.

Fred Eckhard's remarks on speechwriting come from his interview for the Yale-UN Oral History Project, May 10 and June 7, 2005.

The transcript of Annan's Oslo news conference on December 9, 2001, his encounter with the press outside the residence on October 12, 2001, and his remarks to the staff the same day were released by the spokesman's office as off-the-cuff remarks on the secretary-general's Web site, www.un.org/apps/sg.

The *Sesame Street* show and the encounter in the Oslo synagogue are depicted in the PBS documentary "Kofi Annan: Center of the Storm." Re Israel and the UN, some useful sources include Warren Hoge, "UN Is Gradually Becoming More Hospitable to Israel," *New York Times*, October 11, 2005; the Citizens United Foundation documentary film "*Broken Promises;*" Philippe Bolopion, "*L'offensive de charme d'Israël à l'ONU rencontre un certain succès,*" *Le Monde*, November 4, 2005; and Annan's speech on Holocaust Remembrance Day, UN Press Release SG/SM/10326.

12. Interlude in Vienna and Africa

Portions of this chapter appeared in my article "Man in the Middle: Travels with Kofi Annan" in *Smithsonian* magazine, January 2003.

13. Facing the American Juggernaut

Sources on the White House and UN jockeying before the war include Hans Blix, *Disarming Iraq* (New York: Pantheon Books, 2004), Todd S. Purdum, *A Time of Our Choosing: America's War in Iraq* (New York: Times Books, 2003), and Bob Woodward, *Plan of Attack* (New York: Simon & Schuster, 2004).

There are good analyses of the UN events during the crisis in Julia Preston and Todd S. Purdum, "From Full Steam to Stalled: March to Iraq Turns at UN," *New York Times*, September 22, 2002, and Tyler Marshall, Maggie Farley, and Doyle McManus, "A War of Words Led to Unanimous Iraq Vote," *Los Angeles Times*, November 10, 2002.

Kofi Annan's public statements about the war can be found in the release by the office of his spokesman of his General Assembly speech on September 12, 2002 (www.un.org/apps/sg), the spokesman's release of the transcript of his press encounter on September 16, 2002 (www.un.org/apps/sg), the spokesman's transcript of his comments to the press after meeting with President Bush on November 13, 2002 (www.un.org/apps/sg), the transcript of his press conference at UN headquarters on January 14, 2003 (UN Press Release SG/SM/8581), the UN News Service transcript of his March 10, 2003, news conference in The Hague (www.un.org/apps/news), and the statement issued by the office of his spokesman on March 20, 2003 (www.un.org/apps/sg).

Bush's September 12, 2002, address to the General Assembly can be found on www.whitehouse.gov/news. His speech launching the war was printed in the *New York Times*, March 18, 2003. The *New York Times* published Iraqi foreign minister Naji Sabri's letter to Kofi Annan on September 17, 2002. The *Los Angeles Times* published the Churchill and Chamberlain cartoon on September 15, 2002.

The text of Colin Powell's presentation to the Security Council can be found on www.globalsecurity.org. Dominique de Villepin's response can be found in my March 2, 2003, news commentary on www .stanleymeisler.com.

Another useful source: Patrick E. Tyler, "Ex-Aide to Blair Says the British Spied on Annan," *New York Times*, February 27, 2004.

14. Relevance and Melancholia

An important source for the chapter was L. Paul Bremer's revealing memoir *My Year in Iraq* (New York: Simon & Schuster, 2006).

Richard Perle's article "Thank God for the Death of the UN" appeared in *Guardian*, March 21, 2003. Claire Tréan's article "*L'ONU pourrait sortir renforcée de la crise irakienne*" appeared in *Le Monde*, March 18, 2003.

Sources for the account of the Vieira de Mello mission include George Packer, *The Assassins' Gate: America in Iraq* (New York: Farrar, Straus, & Giroux, 2005); "Excerpts from Remarks by Bush and Blair: 'Iraq Will Soon Be Liberated,'" *New York Times*, April 9, 2003; transcript of Annan/Vieira de Mello press conference, May 27, 2003, UN document SG/SM/8720; Steven Erlanger, "'I Should Always Believe Journalists,' He Said, Adding: 'Please Pray for Me,'" *New York Times*, August 24, 2003; Annan's message to the staff after the August 19 bombing on UN document SG/SM/8826; the UN Staff union's remarks on UN document ORG/1389; *Report of the Independent Panel on the Safety and Security of the UN Personnel in Iraq* (UN publication, October 20, 2003); Colum Lynch, "UN Pullback May Reflect Staff's Willingness to Defy Council," *Washington Post*, November 2, 2003.

Sources for the account of the Brahimi mission include Robin Wright and Colum Lynch, "Wary Annan Set to Discuss a Possible UN Role in Iraq," *Washington Post*, January 19, 2004; Jim Hoagland, "A UN Surprise," *Washington Post*, February 18, 2004; Brahimi's February 23, April 27, and June 7, 2004, reports to the Security Council available on www.un.org/apps/news; Dexter Filkins, "A Worn Road for UN Aide," *New York Times*, May 31, 2004; Warren Hoge and Steven R. Weisman, "Surprising Choice Reflects U.S. Influence," *New York Times*, May 29, 2004; Rajiv Chandrasekaran, "Envoy Bowed to Pressure in Choosing Leaders," *Washington Post*, June 3, 2004; Brahimi's news briefing in Baghdad, June 4, 2004, available on www.un.org/apps/news;

Sources for the account of the "illegal" comment include "Iraq War Illegal, Says Annan" and "Excerpts: Annan Interview" on *BBC News*, September 16, 2004, on www.newsvote.bbc.co.uk.

Sources for the account of the Fallujah letter include Maggie Farley, "UN's Annan Seeks to Prevent an Assault on Fallouja," *Los Angeles Times*, November 5, 2004, Dafna Linzer, "Annan's Warning on Fallujah Dismissed," *Washington Post*, November 6, 2004; and Warren Hoge, "US and UN Renew Quarrel Over Iraq," *New York Times*, November 14, 2004.

15. Oil for Food and Kojo

All the reports of the Independent Inquiry Committee into the United Nations Oil-for-Food Programme—as the Volcker commission was known officially—and the press releases summarizing the reports are on the Volcker commission Web site, www.iic-offp.org. The key reports discussed in this chapter are *The Management of the United Nations Oil-for-Food Programme, vol. III—Report of Investigation, United Nations Administration,* part 1, released on September 7, 2005, and *Second Interim Report: The 1998 Procurement of the Humanitarian Goods Inspection Contract; Other Conduct of United Nations Officials,* released on March 29, 2005.

A thorough and incisive analysis of the reports can be found in Brian Urquhart, "The UN Oil-for-Food Program: Who Is Guilty," *New York Review of Books*, February 9, 2006.

Annan's bouts of melancholia are discussed in Philippe Bolopion, "*La voix perdue de Kofi Annan,*" *Le Journal du Dimanche*, May 15, 2005, and Meryl Gordon, "No Peace for Kofi: A Father's Burden," *New York* magazine, May 2, 2005.

The campaign against Annan is analyzed in Ian Williams, "The Right's Assault on Kofi Annan," *Nation*, January 10, 2005, and in Barbara Crossette's letter to Romenesko, October 17, 2005 (www.poynter.org.). Annan denounces the campaign on the *Charlie Rose Show*, March 7, 2006.

Attacks on Annan included Claudia Rosett, "Oil, Food, and a Whole Lot of Questions," *New York Times*, April 18, 2003; Claudia Rosett, "Kojo & Kofi," *National Review* Online, March 10, 2004 (www .nationalreview.com); Claudia Rosset, "The Oil-for-Food Scam: What Did Kofi Annan Know, and When Did He Know It?" *Commentary* magazine, May 2004; "Annan Past His Time," *Sun* editorial, November 18, 2004; William Safire, "My Son, My Son," *New York Times*, November 29, 2004; Norm Coleman, "Kofi Annan Must Go," *Wall Street Journal*, December 1, 2004; House Committee on International Relations, "The Oil for Food Program: The Systematic Failure of the United Nations," December 7, 2005; and "Kofi's Accountability," *Wall Street Journal* editorial, March 30, 2005.

Useful news accounts include Warren Hoge and Judith Miller, "Annan's Post at the UN May Be at Risk, Officials Fear," *New York Times*, December 4, 2004; Colum Lynch, "U.S. Opposes Annan Leaving UN Position," *Washington Post*, December 10, 2004; Nora Boustany, "Annan's New Top Aide Defines His Ambitions," *Washington Post*, February 16, 2005; James Bone, "Schoolboy Star Who Grew Up to Be a Player," *Times* of London, March 10, 2005; Warren Hoge, "Annan Remark on Oil Sales Draws Nods of Agreement," *New York Times*, April 24, 2005; Warren Hoge, "Annan Failed to Curb Corruption in Iraq's Oil-for-Food Program, Investigators Report," *New York Times*, September 7, 2005; Maggie Farley, "UN Oil-for-Food Inquiry Findings Surprised Volcker," *Los Angeles Times*, October 28, 2005; AP, "Smuggling Seen as Major Source of Illegal Revenue for Hussein," *New York Times*, December 28, 2005; and Warren Hoge, "Annan's Son Will Repay Ghana for Fees on Car," *New York Times*, January 24, 2006.

United Nations documents, available on www.un.org/apps, include the secretary-general's press encounter, June 17, 2004; UN News Service, "Annan Cuts Short Africa Trip to Focus on Iraq at UN Headquarters in New York," November 25, 2004; secretary-general's press encounter, November 29, 2004; Secretary-General's press conference, March 29, 2005; secretary-general's press encounter at the Security Council stakeout, September 7, 2005; and the secretary-general's year-end press conference, December 21, 2005.

Annan's morale-boosting meetings are discussed by Johanna McGeary, "The Fight of His Life," *Time*, December 17, 2004; Warren

Hoge, "Secret Meeting, Clear Mission: 'Rescue' UN," *New York Times*, January 3, 2005; and Richard Holbrooke on the *Charlie Rose Show*, January 2, 2005.

Shashi Tharoor's sketch of Kofi Annan appeared in the *Hindu* as "A Wonderful Wake-up Call," October 28, 2001. Bone's encounters with the spokesman's office were recounted in "Knock, Knock, Who's There? It's the Mercedes," on the UN Forum Web site, www.unforum.com, December 15, 2005.

16. The Year of Summing Up

Annan discussed his legacy on the Charlie Rose Show on PBS, March 7, 2006.

Darfur background can be found in Security Council press release SC/8721, May 16, 2006, which includes the text of Resolution 1679 on steps toward a UN operation; and in International Crisis Group, *To Save Darfur*, Africa Report 105, March 17, 2006.

I summarized the issue of reform in a *Los Angeles Times* article, "It Works Well. Tweak It," November 6, 2005. Reform is discussed in Colum Lynch, "Bolton Plans to Restart Stalled Efforts to Restructure UN," *Washington Post*, January 2, 2006; Warren Hoge, "Annan and Bolton Disagree on Draft for New Rights Group," *New York Times*, February 24, 2006; Warren Hoge, "U.S. Isolated in Opposing for a New UN Rights Council," *New York Times*, March 4, 2006; Jimmy Carter, Óscar Arias, Kim Dae Jung, Shirin Ebadi, and Desmond Tutu, "Principles Defeat Politics at the UN," *New York Times*, March 5, 2006; the secretary-general's statement to the General Assembly on March 7, 2006, available on www.un.org/apps; "Investing in the United Nations: For a Stronger Organization Worldwide," the secretary-general's report to the General Assembly, March 7, 2006, A/60/693; Warren Hoge, "As U.S. Dissents, UN Approves a New Council on Rights Abuse," *New York Times*, March 16, 2006; and Colum Lynch, "UN Votes to Replace Rights Panel," *Washington Post*, March 15, 2006.

Annan's problems with staff are discussed in Warren Hoge, "UN Refugee Chief Resigns, Denying Charges of Harassment," *New York Times*, February 21, 2005; Edith M. Lederer, "Blog behind the Scenes at the UN," Associated Press, March 7, 2006; and Edith M. Lederer, "UN Union: 'No Confidence' in Annan," Associated Press, March 10, 2006.

Background on the Bolton appointment includes Elisabeth Bumiller and Sheryl Gay Stolberg, "President Sends Bolton to UN; Bypasses Senate," *New York Times*, August 2, 2005; "Bolton: U.S. Will Fix UN or Find an Alternative," Associated Press dispatch, November 19, 2005, reprinted on www.newsmax.com; Warren Hoge, "Dispute over Division of Authority at the UN Grows," *New York Times*, November 20, 2005; and Maggie Farley, "UN Hit by a Bolt from the Right," *Los Angeles Times*, December 23, 2005. I discussed the appointment of Bolton in a March 24, 2005, news commentary, "Bolton and History," on my Web site, www.stanleymeisler.com.

The text of Resolution 1701 calling for a cease-fire in the Hezbollah-Israel conflict can be found in UN document SC/8808.

INDEX